Hayekian Systems

The central theme in the work of F.A. Hayek was the problem of order in society, and his focus was epistemological: he was concerned with the constraints on knowledge, the problems associated with its distribution, the structures in which it inheres, and the implications of these issues for the understanding of social phenomena generally. But while his work has greatly improved our understanding of market processes, application to more complex social arrangements was not an unambiguous success.

In seeking to progress beyond Hayek's difficulties in formulating a more general theory of spontaneous order, this book fleshes out an analogy between social orders and the biological order detailed in Hayek's *The Sensory Order* into a theory of adaptive systems. It focuses first on those aspects of the systems which enable them to learn about their environments, and then on the entrepreneurial processes which implement their anticipatory capabilities. The inclusion of anticipatory elements, inspired by the work of Robert Rosen, results in a theory of social orders which integrates many of the disparate findings of Austrian economists into a self-consistent conceptual framework and has applicability to other social arrangements such as firms and governments. Of particular interest is the interaction between the systems of science and government, an issue of significant current concern which is comprehensively explored here both theoretically and empirically.

This book is essential reading for anyone interested in Hayek, Austrian economics, social theory, and the history of economic thought more broadly.

William N. Butos is Professor Emeritus in economics at Trinity College, Hartford, CT, and deputy editor of the journal *Cosmos + Taxis*. His research interests include the economics of science and the interaction of government and science, monetary economics, the history of economic thought, and the social science implications of the work of F.A. Hayek.

Thomas J. McQuade is an independent scholar. He is a former software entrepreneur and has taught economics at Trinity College in Hartford and as a visiting scholar at New York University. His research interests include the economics, philosophy, and history of science, and the development of the concept of "anticipatory systems" as an approach to social theory that encompasses arrangements such as market, science, government, and firm.

Routledge Foundations of the Market Economy

Edited by Mario J. Rizzo, New York University and Lawrence H. White, George Mason University

A central theme in this series is the importance of understanding and assessing the market economy from a perspective broader than the static economics of perfect competition and Pareto optimality. Such a perspective sees markets as causal processes generated by the preferences, expectations and beliefs of economic agents. The creative acts of entrepreneurship that uncover new information about preferences, prices and technology are central to these processes with respect to their ability to promote the discovery and use of knowledge in society.

The market economy consists of a set of institutions that facilitate voluntary cooperation and exchange among individuals. These institutions include the legal and ethical framework as well as more narrowly "economic" patterns of social interaction. Thus the law, legal institutions and cultural and ethical norms, as well as ordinary business practices and monetary phenomena, fall within the analytical domain of the economist.

Economic and Political Change after Crisis
Prospects for government, liberty, and the rule of law
Edited by Stephen H. Balch and Benjamin Powell

Competition and Free Trade
Pascal Salin

Economic Freedom and Prosperity
The Origins and Maintenance of Liberalization
Edited by Benjamin Powell

Capitalism and Inequality
The Role of State and Market
Edited by G.P. Manish and Stephen C. Miller

Hayekian Systems
Research into the Structure of Social Interaction
William N. Butos and Thomas J. McQuade

For more information about this series, please visit www.routledge.com/series/SE0104

Hayekian Systems

Research into the Structure of Social Interaction

William N. Butos and Thomas J. McQuade

Routledge
Taylor & Francis Group
LONDON AND NEW YORK

First published 2023
by Routledge
4 Park Square, Milton Park, Abingdon, Oxon OX14 4RN

and by Routledge
605 Third Avenue, New York, NY 10158

Routledge is an imprint of the Taylor & Francis Group, an informa business

British Library Cataloguing-in-Publication Data
A catalogue record for this book is available from the British Library

Library of Congress Cataloging-in-Publication Data
Names: Butos, William N., author. | McQuade, Thomas J., author.
Title: Hayekian systems : research into the structure of social interaction / William N. Butos and Thomas J. McQuade.
Description: Abingdon, Oxon ; New York, NY : Routledge, 2023. | Series: Foundations of the market economy | Includes bibliographical references and index. |
Identifiers: LCCN 2022043875 (print) | LCCN 2022043876 (ebook) | ISBN 9781032372730 (hardback) | ISBN 9781032372747 (paperback) | ISBN 9781003336150 (ebook)
Subjects: LCSH: Hayek, Friedrich A. von (Friedrich August), 1899-1992. | Economics--Philosophy. | System theory. | Economics--Sociological aspects.
Classification: LCC HB101.H39 B88 2023 (print) | LCC HB101.H39 (ebook) | DDC 330.092--dc23/eng/20221103
LC record available at https://lccn.loc.gov/2022043875
LC ebook record available at https://lccn.loc.gov/2022043876

ISBN: 978-1-032-37273-0 (hbk)
ISBN: 978-1-032-37274-7 (pbk)
ISBN: 978-1-003-33615-0 (ebk)

DOI: 10.4324/9781003336150

Typeset in Bembo
by SPi Technologies India Pvt Ltd (Straive)

For Cindy, John, and Donna

It would be no exaggeration to say that social theory begins with – and has an object only because of – the discovery that there exist orderly structures which are the product of the action of many men but are not the result of human design.

(F.A. Hayek 1973, p. 37)

It was … the great contributions of Bernard Mandeville and David Hume, of Adam Ferguson and Adam Smith, which have opened the way for an understanding, both in biological and social theory, of that interaction between the regularity of the conduct of the elements and the regularity of the resulting structure.

(1967, p. 77)

[Social theories] are not *about* the social wholes as wholes; they do not pretend to discover by empirical observation laws of behavior or change of these wholes. Their task is rather … to *constitute* these wholes, to provide schemes of structural relationships …

(1948, p. 72)

The economic problem of society … is a problem of the utilization of knowledge not given to anyone in its totality.

(1945, pp. 519–520)

I have said on another occasion, and it seems to me important enough to repeat it here, that he who is only an economist cannot be a good economist. Much more than in the natural sciences, it is true in the social sciences that there is hardly a concrete problem which can be adequately answered on the basis of a single special discipline.

(1967, p. 267)

Contents

Figures

Preface

The genesis of the research project documented herein was a series of discussions which took place at Trinity College, Hartford, Connecticut in the late 1990s and over drinks in various Manhattan cafés in the early 2000s. Butos had been sensitized to the importance of the work of F.A. Hayek when participating in graduate seminars conducted by Walter Weimer at The Penn State University. He wrote his dissertation (1983) on monetary theory with an emphasis on Hayek's work in that field, with Weimer as a member of his committee. Weimer had drawn attention to Hayek's work in cognitive psychology as set out in *The Sensory Order* (1952) – in fact, he was the first to pay serious attention to the relevance of Hayek's theory of the mind for economics and social theory. Butos continued working on Hayekian themes, writing (1985) on Hayek's recognition of the limitations of equilibrium theorizing, and he published a series of papers with Roger Koppl (1993; 1997; 1999; 2001) which applied Hayek's sensory order theory to the problem of economic expectations. They proposed that expectations are neither mechanically rational in the way portrayed in typical macroeconomic models nor unanchored and unexplainable thoughts, and certainly cannot be dismissed as "animal spirits", as Keynes had done. Rather, they characterized them as coherent, forward-looking, endogenous, and adaptive, and based on an internal model of the experienced environment – and they emphasized that a large part of any person's environment consists of the rules, conventions, and presuppositions operative in the surrounding society. In short, they showed that the nature of expectations is conditioned by experience of the relevant environment. The conclusion was that such assumptions as "rational expectations", to the extent that they are valid at all, are valid only when behavior is strongly constrained by the environment.[1]

McQuade, whose dissertation (2000) at Auburn University under Roger Garrison, Leland Yeager, and Mark Thornton – all Hayek scholars – focused on Hayek's work on spontaneous orders and with "institutions" as behavioral procedures that are the components of such orders, realized the importance of the Butos–Koppl work[2] and saw that it opened the door to further, more far-reaching, applications of the Hayekian theory of mind. Obviously, the two were thinking along similar lines, and so, when Butos was in the process of developing a paper which was to document Hayek's struggles to justify a (classically) liberal order of society, he asked McQuade to collaborate. The result was "Mind, market, and institutions: the knowledge problem in Hayek's thought" (2002), which not only set out a critique of Hayek's social theory but also proposed how Hayek's work could be developed toward a positive theory of social order – and set the stage for a collaboration extending over the next 20 years.

We have, with permission from the publishers, taken text from a number of our own publications. For this, we thank De Gruyter, Elsevier, Emerald, Informa, Oxford University Press, Springer, The Independent Institute, and The Ludwig von Mises Institute. We are also grateful to the American Association for the Advancement of Science for permission to reproduce some of their graphs and to Informa and The University of Chicago Press for permission to copy the Hayek quotes used as epigraphs. And we particularly thank Leslie Marsh for creating a journal, *Cosmos + Taxis*, which allows full copyright to be retained by authors. We have indicated in a note in each chapter where text has been reused, and any requests for further reproduction of these passages should be directed to the appropriate copyright holder.

For expertly shepherding us through the publication process, we are grateful to Mario Rizzo (the series editor, whose initial support was crucial) and to the Taylor & Francis employees and contractors Andy Humphries, Emma Morley, Harriet Cunningham, Holly Martin, Nick Brock, and Yassar Arafat. We also appreciate the suggestion of a reviewer which has greatly improved the book's Introduction.

Over the years we have had the benefit of the good sense, intellectual companionship, willing support, and helpful criticism of many colleagues and friends, particularly Stephan Böhm, Peter Boettke, Young Back Choi, Roger Garrison, Brian Gladish, Larry Gould, David Harper, Steve Horwitz, Sandy Ikeda, Israel Kirzner, Roger Koppl, Chidem Kurdas, Leslie Marsh, Hu McCulloch, Mario Rizzo, Joseph Salerno, Scott Scheall, Mark Thornton, Allan Walstad, Glenn Whitman, and the members of the NYU Colloquium on Market Institutions and Economic Processes. We are particularly lucky to have had the unfailing tolerance and encouragement of Cindy Butos and Donna McQuade, and the presentation of our work has benefited greatly from Donna's peerless editing skills.

Notes

1 Rational expectations models are premised on statistical data in terms of probability distributions of prices in which the subjective probability distributions must match the relevant economic model. Accordingly, they describe well-behaved "statistical expectations" from mathematically specifiable algorithms rather than cognitively based expectations. See Butos (1997).

2 For a short discussion of the importance of the Butos & Koppl papers on expectations, see McQuade (2019).

Bibliography

Butos, W.N. 1983. Subjectivism in the development of monetary theory: implications of Austrian themes. PhD dissertation, University of Pennsylvania.

———1985. Hayek and general equilibrium analysis. *Southern Economic Journal* 52 #2, pp. 332–343. Reprinted in J.C. Wood & R.N. Woods (eds.), Friedrich A. Hayek: critical assessments, pp. 102–117. Routledge, 1991.

——— 1997. Hayek and rational expectations. In W. Keizer, B. Tieben, & R. van Zijp (eds.), *Austrian economics in debate*, pp. 220–242. Routledge.

Butos, W.N. & R.G. Koppl 1993. Hayekian expectations: theory and empirical applications. *Constitutional Political Economy* 4 #3, pp. 303–329.

——— 1997. The varieties of subjectivism: Keynes and Hayek on expectations. *History of Political Economy* 29 #2, pp. 327–359.

——— 1999. Hayek and Keynes at the Keynesian beauty contest. *Journal des Economistes et des Etudes Humaines* 9 #2&3, pp. 257–275.

——— 2001. Confidence in Keynes and Hayek: reply to Burczak. *Review of Political Economy* 13 #1, pp. 81–86. Reprinted in J.C. Wood & R.N. Woods (eds.), Hayek: critical assessments 4, pp. 213–219. Routledge, 2004.

Butos, W.N. & T.J. McQuade 2002. Mind, market, and institutions: the knowledge problem in Hayek's thought. In J. Birner, P. Garrouste, & T. Aimar (eds.), *F.A. Hayek as a political economist*, pp. 113–133. Routledge.

Hayek, F.A. 1945. The use of knowledge in society. American Economic Review 35 #4, pp. 519–530.

——— 1948. *Individualism and economic order.* University of Chicago Press

——— 1952. *The sensory order.* University of Chicago Press.

——— 1967. *Studies in philosophy, politics, and economics.* University of Chicago Press.

——— 1973. *Law, legislation, and liberty 1: Rules and order.* University of Chicago Press.

McQuade, T.J. 2000. Orders and institutions as objects of investigation. PhD dissertation, Auburn University.

——— 2019. Hayekian expectations, unexpectedly generalized. In J. Alcorn (ed.), *Markets & liberty: a festschrift for William Butos*, pp. 39–50. Shelby Cullom Davis Endowment.

1 Introduction[1]

We present here a new approach to the understanding of market (and other) systems of social interaction. Although, perhaps inevitably, we may appear critical or dismissive of existing methods used by economists, sociologists, and philosophers to model such systems, it is not our intention to represent this new approach as the royal road toward understanding – social systems are complex arrangements, and as such they admit of many perspectives that can be useful in their investigation. What is "new" about our approach, and why it can be complementary to other approaches, is that it is based on the idea that the organization of the processes active within a social system, their dependencies and how they interact, is at least as deserving of attention as are the states of the system characterized in terms of the actors and the material components.

To put that idea in context, consider how the market economy is modeled in mainstream economics. Macroeconomics, the study of the economy as a whole, has developed over many years from the general equilibrium equations of Walras through the marriage with some of Keynes's ideas in the neoclassical synthesis, to the modern dynamic stochastic general equilibrium models, simplified versions of which are employed by central bankers and other government functionaries for policy analysis.[2] Walras self-consciously took his system of equations from classical mechanics, which, not unexpectedly, raised questions of applicability to systems of human interaction, but, in the long process of assimilation and development of Walras's system, where mathematical consistency conflicted with realism of assumptions, it was the former that won out.[3] In particular, the problem of interactions between agents has been avoided by the device of the representative agent, and the problem of agent expectations has been sidestepped by the assumption that the single agent's expectations are never systematically different from the equilibrium of the model.[4] The modern models may be significantly more sophisticated than Walras's original, but they have in common with it that they represent the market economy as a mathematical machine.

The purpose of these models is to compute snapshots of equilibrium states of the economy (in terms of aggregate quantities such as GDP, unemployment level, and inflation rate) resulting from given initial conditions, and this focus on end states does not, and is not intended to, provide understanding of the ways in which the interactions between the individual participants in the economy might (or

DOI: 10.4324/9781003336150-1

might not) move the system as a whole toward an equilibrium state. So, criticism for lack of realism in this regard rather begs the question. But the lack of consideration of the processes of interaction, of the constraints faced by the interacting parties, and of the fact that disequilibrium, rather than equilibrium, would appear to be the more realistic characterization of the normal state of affairs in a market economy, has left a huge gap.

Market process economics, which covers a diverse range of inquiry ranging from evolutionary economics to the theory of the entrepreneur (both Schumpeterian and Austrian), is a recognition of the need to fill this gap, but although much useful work has been done in understanding difficult phenomena such as expectations, entrepreneurship, learning, confidence, and the consequences of regime uncertainty, little or none of this can be readily integrated into the mainstream models.[5]

By focusing on processes of interpersonal interaction and the constraints, incentives, and possibilities for knowledge transmission that they embody, rather than on equilibrium end states, the various strands of market process theories are able to provide understanding of economic activity involved in internal state transitions and of the constraints which impinge on this activity, and which are in turn molded by it. But they do not add up to a theory of the economy as a whole. While we learn a great deal about the nature and operation of particular economic processes, we learn very little as to how these processes are organized, how they are interlinked, how they depend on each other, and how they work together to produce and maintain the complex system that is the economy. The obvious suggestion that follows is that it would be helpful to have, as a complement to theories of process operation, a theory of process organization. That is the thrust of what follows in our treatment of market systems: we describe, admittedly in general terms, the interactions and co-dependencies of the most basic processes operative in a market economy. The exclusive concentration on organization means that normal economic data referring to the movements and magnitudes of quantities of goods, services, and money, and the prices of such things, play no part; it is the structure of the interplay of processes that is in focus.

A number of interesting results follow from a myopic concentration on process organization. First, it becomes plausible that the form of organization in a market economy is conducive to the adaptation of the system as a whole to its environment. Second, one of the organizational elements can be characterized as functioning as an internal model of the system's environment – that is to say, the system is not merely adaptive, but capable of a form of anticipation. Third, the system is a complete self-maintaining whole in the sense that, under the assumed constraints, the conditions for the operation of each of its processes are provided by at least one other process in the system. While the system is materially and energetically open, there is process closure in the limited sense that the processes form a causal cycle. Apart from the maintenance of some fundamental constraints, the system requires no outside process for ensuring that its operation can continue.

Markets are but one of many distinct systems of human interaction in society, and it seems plausible that other interactive arrangements can be usefully described in similar organizational terms, and not, as many economists have done,[6] simply as inherently flawed market-like systems lacking the efficiency of price feedback. We show detailed examples of how, in social arrangements as diverse as science communities, government legislatures and bureaucracies, and market firms and banking arrangements, the characteristic basic processes operative in these interactive contexts can be understood also as being organized into adaptive, anticipatory systems with process closure. As a corollary, one general point stands out clearly: if social science is going to progress in understanding the various social arrangements that pervade modern societies, then a first step is to include in the analysis that government itself is indeed a complex system with its own characteristic structure, internal transaction types, and emergent effects. It is not good enough to point to a possible defect in one system and assume that another system can be deployed at will to fix that defect – with government in the fixing role this is just the implicit invocation of the benevolent dictator model.

Finally, if we may leave the domain of system analysis and advocate for general methodological principles, we think, first, that an important and often-overlooked requirement for the execution of studies of social phenomena is to approach them from a positive standpoint and to refrain, as best as one can, from introducing normative elements. There is no doubt that positive analysis of social phenomena will often carry normative implications; however, we believe the default position should always be to push the positive analysis forward at every opportunity. And second, while it is abundantly clear, as Wagner (2016) explains in detail, that in the real world we are confronted with social systems that are deeply "entangled", we believe that it is necessary as a prelude to understanding the nature of the entanglements and their ramifications that we develop workable theoretical models of the operations of the systems in isolation so that there is a basis on which to introduce, in a manageable fashion, the inter-system interactions that constitute the entanglements. Abstraction of this sort is our best hope for coping with the complexity of the social world.

To summarize, our work is aimed at furthering the understanding of the structure and functioning of prominent social arrangements such as markets, firms, money and banking systems, science communities, and governments. The approach we have taken is to conceive of these arrangements as systems of social interaction, to characterize the modes of interaction between the members in each different arrangement, and to seek to understand how these interactions could support the emergence of the system's capability of adapting to its environment. The various social systems considered vary greatly in the incentives offered to their members, in the constraints imposed on those individuals, in the opportunities for the exercise of entrepreneurship, and in the aspects of the environment to which the system as a whole is sensitive. But we think it has proven possible – and useful – to see them all as specific instances of a more general structure (a "Hayekian system") in which the capability for adaptation is generated through the operation of a functionally closed set of processes of interaction. Understanding the general structure of these social systems has allowed us some insight into what is crucial for their continued operation and how they are likely to react to environmental effects (which include effects emanating from other social systems) which affect, and sometimes impede, their internal processes.

Notes

1 This chapter contains text previously published in McQuade (2019).

2 However, the actual track record of macro models in anticipating economic trends is singularly unimpressive. The US Federal Reserve's policies, informed by such models, have, according to empirical evidence cited by Selgin *et al.* (2012), tended to heighten rather than reduce macroeconomic instability. DeVroey (2016, p. 380) observes that "the rise of DSGE macroeconomics amounted to giving prominence to internal consistency over realism. I find this line defensible yet it bears a heavy price, namely that macroeconomists must refrain from claiming that the policy conclusions of their models have a direct policymaking bearing." For other critical assessments of modern macroeconomics, see Buchanan & Wagner (1977), Timberlake (1993), Reinhart & Rogoff (2009), White (2012), Romer (2016), and Glasner (2018).

3 For a short summary of the influences on Walras in the development of his system, see Jaffé (1983). For an assessment of the influence of Walras on the development of macroeconomics, see Kirman (2011). For a detailed and highly critical assessment of the mathematization of economics, see Mirowski (1989). For histories of the development of modern mainstream macroeconomics from Keynes to the present day, see Garrison (2001, pp. 18–23) and DeVroey (2016).

4 The manifestly *ad hoc* nature of these concessions to mathematical tractability has been one inspiration for the development of agent-based models which, through simulation, allow for repeated individual interactions between heterogenous agents. For an introduction to the large literature which has developed in this vein, see Tesfatsion (2002, 2006); for an early example of the modelling technique, see Epstein & Axtell (1996). Of relevance to the current work is that such models demonstrate the possibility for self-organization in markets and other social and biological systems, a line of thought which has been developed extensively by Kauffman (1993). Related to, and generally compatible with, these new approaches is complex systems theory. See Foster (2005) for a useful taxonomy of types of complex systems and for a discussion of some of the implications of replacing standard macroeconomics with network theory.

5 For an historical treatment of market process theories, see Boettke & Prychitko (1998). For a treatise on evolutionary economics, see Dopfer & Potts (2007) and, for a history of the subject, Hodgson (1995). For an overview of process theory in the Austrian tradition, particularly the seminal contributions of Mises and especially Hayek, see Kirzner (1997). For a discussion of both Schumpeterian and Kirznerian approaches to entrepreneurship and an application and extension of Kirzner's theory of entrepreneurship, see Harper (2003), and for a summary of recent developments in the economics of entrepreneurship, see Parker (2004) and Klein (2008). For a treatment of expectations based on Hayek's work, see Butos & Koppl (1993). For a game-theoretic treatment of learning from feedback see Teck, Lim, & Camerer (2006, pp. 323–325), and for a discussion of the applicability of cognitive science to consumer choice, see Bartels & Johnson (2015). For an analysis of the role of confidence in the context of the Great Recession, see Koppl (2014). For an explanation of regime uncertainty and its role in the Great Depression, see Higgs (1997).

6 See, for example, Nelson (1959), Arrow (1962), Dasgupta & David (1994), Walstad (2002), and Wittman (1989).

Bibliography

Arrow, K.J. 1962. Economic welfare and the allocation of resources for inventions. In R.R. Nelson (ed.), *The rate and direction of inventive activity: economic and social factors*, pp. 609–625. Princeton University Press.

Bartels, D.M. & E.J. Johnson 2015. Connecting cognition and consumer choice. *Cognition* 135, pp. 47–51.

Boettke, P.J. & D.L. Prychitko (eds.) 1998. *Market process theories*. Edward Elgar.

Buchanan, J.M. & R.E. Wagner 1977. *Democracy in deficit: the political legacy of Lord Keynes*. Academic Press.

Butos, W.N. & R.G. Koppl 1993. Hayekian expectations: theory and empirical applications. *Constitutional Political Economy* 4 #3, pp. 303–329.

Dasgupta, P. & P.A. David 1994. Toward a new economics of science. *Research Policy* 23, pp. 487–521.

DeVroey, M. 2016. *A history of macroeconomics from Keynes to Lucas and beyond*. Cambridge University Press.

Dopfer, K. & J. Potts 2007. *The general theory of economic evolution*. Routledge.

Epstein, J.M. & R. Axtell 1996. *Growing artificial societies: social science from the bottom up*. Brookings Institution Press.

Foster, J. 2005. From simplistic to complex systems in economics. *Cambridge Journal of Economics* 29, pp. 873–892.

Garrison, R.W. 2001. *Time and money: the macroeconomics of capital structure*. Routledge.

Glasner, D. 2018. Hayek, Hicks, Radner and three equilibrium concepts: sequential, temporary, and rational expectations. https://ssrn.com/abstract=3210893.

Harper, D.A. 2003. *Foundations of entrepreneurship and economic development*. Routledge.

Higgs, R. 1997. Regime uncertainty: why the Great Depression lasted so long and why prosperity resumed after the war. *The Independent Review* 1 #4, pp. 561–590.

Hodgson, G. 1995. The evolution of evolutionary economics. *Scottish Journal of Political Economy*, 42 #4, pp. 153–172.

Jaffé, W. 1983. Leon Walras. In D.A. Walker (ed.), *William Jaffé's essays on Walras*, pp. 131–138. Cambridge University Press.

Kauffman, S.A. 1993. *The origins of order: self-organization and selection in evolution*. Oxford University Press.

Kirman, A. 2011. Walras' unfortunate legacy. In P. Bridel (ed.), *General equilibrium analysis: a century after Walras*, pp. 109–133. Routledge.

Kirzner, I.M. 1997. Entrepreneurial discovery and the competitive market process: an Austrian approach. *Journal of Economic Literature* 35, pp. 60–85.

Klein, P.G. 2008. Opportunity discovery, entrepreneurial action, and economic organization. *Strategic Entrepreneurship Journal* 2, pp. 175–190.

Koppl, R.G. 2014. *From crisis to confidence: macroeconomics after the crash*. Institute for Economic Affairs.

McQuade, T.J. 2019. Organization, anticipation, and closure in markets and science. *Cosmos + Taxis* 6 #6&7, pp. 1–18.

Mirowski, P. 1989. *More heat than light: economics as social physics, physics as nature's economics*. Cambridge University Press.

Nelson, R.R. 1959. The simple economics of basic scientific research. *Journal of Political Economy* 67, pp. 297–306.

Parker, S.C. 2004. *The economics of self-employment and entrepreneurship*. Cambridge University Press.

Reinhart, C.M. & K.S. Rogoff 2009. *This time is different: eight centuries of financial folly*. Princeton University Press.

Romer, P. 2016. The trouble with macroeconomics. *Commons Memorial Lecture of the Omicron Delta*, January 5, 2016. https://paulromer.net/wp-content/uploads/2016/09/WP-Trouble.pdf.

Selgin, G., W.D. Lastrapes, & L.H. White 2012. Has the Fed been a failure? *Journal of Macroeconomics* 34 #3, pp. 569–596.

Teck, H., N. Lim, & C.F. Camerer 2006. Modeling the psychology of consumer and firm behavior with behavioral economics. *Journal of Marketing Research* 43, pp. 307–331.

Tesfatsion, L.S. 2002. Agent-based computational economics: growing economies from the bottom up. *Artificial Life* 8 #1, pp. 55–82.

——— 2006. Agent-based computational economics: a constructive approach to economic theory. In L. Tesfatsion & K.L. Judd (eds.), *Handbook of computational economics 2: agent-based computational economics*. Elsevier.

Timberlake, R.H. 1993. *Monetary policy in the United States: an intellectual and institutional history*. University of Chicago Press.

Wagner, R.E. 2016. *Politics as a peculiar business: insights from a theory of entangled political economy*. Edward Elgar.

Walstad, A. 2002. Science as a market process. *Independent Review* 7 #1, pp. 5–45.

White, L.H. 2012. *The clash of economic ideas*. Cambridge University Press.

Wittman, D. 1989. Why democracies produce efficient results. *Journal of Political Economy* 97 #6, pp. 1395–1424.

2 Background

The work we describe here was consciously initiated and pursued with the intention of developing the insights of F.A. Hayek in social theory. Hayek, with a lifetime of scientific productivity lasting from the early 1920s to the late 1980s, has left the scientific world with an immense body of work to build on, for which there are a growing contingent of interpreters. The development of Hayek's thought has been traced out in some detail[1] and, as is only to be expected, these accounts show a researcher whose research program undergoes changes in emphasis, direction, and subject matter as a result of his experience dealing with problems encountered and analyzed. It is perhaps possible to look back on the opus and see, with Hutchison (1981), "two Hayeks" – Misesian Hayek and Popperian Hayek – with "Economics and Knowledge" (1937) representing a definitive "turn". However, it is rather more believable to follow Caldwell (1988) in seeing merely a transition taking place in the late 1930s and early 1940s as Hayek's attention shifted from problems in equilibrium analysis to a broader, more process-oriented, consideration of problems of social organization, without any distinctive break. In fact, once pointed out, it is almost impossible not to see, with Weimer (1982) and Gray (1984), an underlying, fundamental continuity in Hayek's work deriving from his ongoing concern with what are as much problems in epistemology as problems in economics or social science. Even in his theoretical economics, for example *Prices and Production* (1931) and *Monetary Theory and the Trade Cycle* (1933a), there was lurking in the background the awareness of the significance of "knowledge problems". Weimer (1982, p. 263) goes so far as to claim that "Hayek is at all times an epistemologist, especially when doing technical economics, and even in his historical and popular writings".

Hayek's (1933b) publication of "The Trend of Economic Thinking" coincided with his editing the *Collected Works of Carl Menger*.[2] That essay may be seen as a watershed in Hayek's understanding of spontaneous order – it was Hayek's "rediscovery" of Menger, especially his *Problems of Economics and Sociology* (1883), with its characterization of the market and other social structures as spontaneous orders. Menger's (1871, pp. 257–262) chapter on "The Nature and Origin of Money" in his *Principles* had provided a classic spontaneous order analysis of the emergence of monetary exchange, and in the later book he extended his treatment of spontaneous orders, observing that many social institutions, including "language, religion, law, even the state itself, and … the phenomena of markets, of competition, of

DOI: 10.4324/9781003336150-2

money, and numerous other social structures" are relevant examples. And he emphasized (1883, p. 146, emphasis in original) "a noteworthy, perhaps the most noteworthy, problem of the social sciences: *How can it be that institutions which serve the common welfare and are extremely significant for its development come into being without a* **common will** *directed toward establishing them*?" Menger's influence can clearly be seen in Hayek (1933b, p. 130)[3]:

> In the natural sciences, we have gradually ... learned that the interaction of different tendencies may produce what we call an order, without any mind of our own kind regulating it. But we still refuse to recognize that the spontaneous interplay of the actions of individuals may produce something which is not the deliberate object of their actions but an organism in which every part performs a necessary function for the continuance of the whole, without any human mind having devised it. In the words of an Austrian economist, we refuse to recognize that society is an organism and not an organization.

Hayek, sensitized to the importance of spontaneous order theorizing for the understanding of social phenomena, continued this line of thought in his "knowledge papers" beginning with "Economics and Knowledge" (1937), then "The Use of Knowledge in Society" (1945), and also "The Meaning of Competition" (1946) – all of which describe the functional attributes of a market as characteristic of a spontaneous order.

A second line of Hayekian thought stems from an essay in cognitive psychology which Hayek wrote as a student paper. In "Contributions to a Theory of How Consciousness Develops" (1920), Hayek argued as his central thesis that cognitive phenomena, including consciousness, are not "elementary psychic elements" but rather byproducts of physiological processes. In opposing the then-current Machian orthodoxy, Hayek (2017, p. 321) stated that his aim was "to base his explanation exclusively on the physiological processes that underlie association processes" and "to limit the explanation to a single physiological law compatible with the perspective of the natural sciences". He claimed (p. 332), with respect to impulses in the brain resulting from stimuli, that the "psychic content of an impulse depends not on the impulse as such but how it resonates with other impulses" within a complex of neurons whose connections were in part conditioned by the passage of past impulses. This was (although he could not have articulated it at the time) a characterization of the mind as a spontaneous order – a system whose operational capability is distributed, without the necessity for any centralized control. But it was not until the 1940s that Hayek turned his attention back to the manuscript of 1920, first within a long essay "Scientism and the Study of Society" (1942; 1943; 1944b), and then, having realized that the field of cognitive psychology had not progressed a great deal since 1920 (and certainly not along the lines he thought it should), with a concerted effort to restate and further develop the ideas in his early paper. The result was *The Sensory Order* (1952).

Hayek's cognitive theory as set out in *The Sensory Order* provides an explanation for the relationship between two quite distinct orders – the subjective order produced by the mind of the individual and the objective order external to, but sensed by, the individual. Mental processes produce a classification of flows of impulses from sensory inputs against the backdrop of a preexisting classification that partly has been learned and partly has been made possible by the evolved genetic makeup of the species. For Hayek, classification is the primary activity of cognitive functioning – any sensory input is meaningful to the individual only through its classifications. He describes the cognitive structures involved in an individual's cognitive processes in terms of "map" and "model", with the map being the mutable matrix of neural connections that have been built up over time in reaction to past stimuli and which is the basis for sensory classifications, and the model being the current complex of impulses circulating within the map and serving as a "model" of the currently experienced environment. Recurring positive stimuli fortify the connection paths that the impulses they generate travel, and paths that are rarely traveled weaken, so that the map changes as learning takes place. The brain is also capable of generating hypothetical stimuli within the map, and in this case the resulting model enables anticipation of possible future events and the results of possible future actions, i.e., expectations.

It is obvious that Hayek saw the connection between these two lines of thought. Indeed, he was very clear about how much his work in social theory owed to his theory of mind, commenting (1979, p. 199, n. 26) that, although his colleagues found *The Sensory Order* "uninteresting or undigestible",[4] he knew that

> the work on it has helped me greatly to clear my mind on much that is very relevant to social theory. My conception of evolution, of a spontaneous order and of the methods and limits of our endeavors to explain complex phenomena have been formed largely in the course of the work on that book.

Looking back through his various works on social theory, it is easy to see that this is the case. In his exposition of the theory of complex phenomena, he noted (1967, p. 34) that it

> should not be difficult now the similar limitations applying to theoretical explanations of the phenomena of mind and society … that here individual events regularly depend on so many concrete circumstances that we shall never in fact be in a position to ascertain them all; and that in consequence … the ideal of prediction and control must largely remain beyond our reach.

Even more pointedly, in "Notes on the Evolution of Systems of Rules of Conduct" he went as far as to say (1967, p. 74) that there is

> no reason why a polycentric order [like a social order] in which each element is guided only by rules and receives no orders from a centre should not be capable of bringing about as complex and apparently as 'purposive' an adaptation to circumstances as could be produced in a system [like an organism with a brain] where a part is set aside to perform such an order on an analogue or model before it is put into execution by the larger structure.

But here is the point where he becomes cautious and warns against pressing the connection too far – that although "the brain may be organized on principles similar to those on which a society is organized, society is not a brain and must not be represented as a sort of super-brain". We suspect that this unwillingness to pursue the potential analogy farther was because first, he was recoiling from any conception of society as a purposeful entity commanding allegiance from individuals, and second, having actually posed the analogy as being between society and an organism (with a brain) rather than between society and a brain (with sensory and motor capabilities), he, understandably, did not want to be perceived as endorsing a picture of society as a mute body of people controlled by a decision-making elite.

Despite noting Hayek's hesitation, we have proceeded to develop the analogy between the operation of the brain as an adaptive system (as set out in *The Sensory Order*) and the operation of various spontaneous orders identifiable within society, including particularly markets and scientific communities. We find no reason to ascribe to these decentralized, dynamic arrangements any division into controller and controlled or any purposefulness other than what is implied in their ability to adapt and grow within the constraints of their environment. The social systems obviously differ from the brain in the nature of their component elements and they differ from the brain and each other in the nature of their internal interactions (their "rules of conduct") and in the sorts of emergent effects (or classifications of inputs) these interactions produce but, at a high level of abstraction, they have strong similarities in the way their internal processes are organized to facilitate adaptation.[5] And the recognition of this similarity opens the door to a better understanding of how they work and, crucially, how they can be compromised. Hayek's classificatory theory, by providing a base on which to develop a unified theory of social spontaneous orders, has been indispensable in this regard.

Hayek was clear about the difficulties facing any theory of social phenomena. In "Economics and Knowledge" (1937, p. 35) he observed that

> the methods which we employ in pure analysis have a clear meaning only when confined to the analysis of the action of a single person and that we are really passing into a different character when we apply it to the explanation of interactions of a number of different individuals.

He was able to overcome this fundamental barrier to a considerable extent in the context of markets, where his theorizing in terms of the systemic solution of the problem of dispersed knowledge in the context of a self-adjusting spontaneous order was a stunning advance in the understanding of a social arrangement. When he turned his attention to broader social issues, Hayek attempted to breathe new life into what he termed (1944a) "the abandoned road" of classical liberalism. His aim was to correct the rationalist-constructivist intellectual mistake of assuming that central planning and interventionist policies would better serve society than the decentralized operations of an order based on general underlying rules of law and property. In *The Constitution of Liberty* (1960) he suggested various reforms to the existing political arrangements which he hoped would better promote the operation of a liberal society, but later, in *Law, Legislation, and Liberty* (1973; 1976; 1979) he despaired of the ability of traditional democratic liberal constitutionalism to secure liberty given the widespread lack of appreciation for the superior epistemic properties of spontaneous orders. But here is where his argument faltered – he could show clearly in the context of markets good reasons for these "superior epistemic properties" – albeit quite plausibly, given his understanding of "knowledge problems" – but could only assert them in the context of the less-understood complex of arrangements comprising society at large. It is here that we see the need to pick up where he left off and proceed to bolster the positive understanding of societal arrangements before claiming superior properties for one arrangement over another.

The following chapters expand on the summary given here of Hayek's work and the reservations we have about the way Hayek applied insights from his market theory to the problems of society at large. In seeking to avoid Hayek's difficulties, we flesh out the analogy we have drawn between social orders and the biological order detailed in *The Sensory Order* into a theory of adaptive systems, focusing first on those aspects of the systems which enable them to learn about their environments, and then on the entrepreneurial processes which implement their anticipatory capabilities. The inclusion of anticipatory elements into the theory, inspired by the work of Robert Rosen (1985), results in a general theory of social orders which integrates many of the disparate findings of Austrian economists into a self-consistent conceptual framework and has applicability to other social arrangements such as firms and governments.

One particular line of investigation characterizes the types of reactions in social systems resulting from interactions with other social systems. These fall into three general classes: (1) those which do not change the characteristic transaction types and the associated incentives and constraints but simply induce an adaptive response which results in a change in the affected system's output (a change in "direction") from what it otherwise would have been; (2) those which also leave transaction types unaffected but result in unsustainable bursts of activity ("destabilization" or "boom and bust") which, when they have run their course, necessitate retrenchments which negatively affect the participants; and (3) those which alter the characteristic transaction types or introduce new incentives or constraints ("distortion") which result in adaptations that fundamentally alter the character of the system's output. We have described these phenomena in detail, documenting specific examples, in the case of government interactions with science, through centralization of funding, through funding driven by fleeting political enthusiasms, and through funding and reputational enhancement conditional on supporting one theory over another.

Another line of investigation has been to characterize, in terms of the relationships and dependencies between a social system's internal processes, the conditions for the system to be self-maintaining – i.e., requiring for its continuing operation material input from the environment but not the assistance of any outside process.[6] An unexpected result of this work has been a new explanation of why the scientific revolution of the 17th century has, in contrast to previous scientific revolutions, been characterized by continuous growth in results, in scope, in participation, and in social acceptance. Related to this is comparative analysis of different social systems in terms of those aspects of the environment to which the system is sensitive – the system's "anchor" – which has implications for understanding why governments might not act "in the public interest", why the reorganization of firms to enhance both communication and competition between employees may result in better adaptation to customer responses, and why some academic disciplines appear to be more directionally progressive than others.

We hope to have shown that, taken in a particular direction, Hayek's insights linking economics and knowledge form the basis of a social science investigation of significant scope and, we think, of promising fertility. It is to be emphasized that we are not claiming to explain "what Hayek really said" or "what he must have meant", or even "what he should have meant if he were to make consistent sense". This book is not an exercise in the interpretation of scripture but is the articulation of an interesting and viable research program begun by Hayek, founded on Hayek's work, but following a direction not clearly anticipated by Hayek himself.

Notes

1 Especially by Hutchison (1981), Weimer (1982), Gray (1984), and Caldwell (1988, 2004).
2 Menger's *Collected Works* was published in German; however, Hayek's (1934) introduction is in English (available as an article in *Economica* and, as a part of volume 1, at https://cdn.mises.org/Collected%20Works%20of%20Carl%20Menger%20(in%20German)%20Volume%20I_5.pdf)
3 In this quote, Hayek's nod to "an Austrian economist" was a reference to Mises's *Gemeinwirtschaft* of 1922 – published in English as Mises (1936) – in which Mises asserted that "society is an organism and not an organization".
4 It was only in the 1980s that *The Sensory Order* caught the attention of psychologists and economists. Walt Weimer's work (1979) provided the impetus for its rediscovery. See Butos (2010, pp. 2–5).
5 We can differentiate orders through the kinds of classification and outputs that they generate. The market process, for example, generates a mutable spectrum of market prices and reputations for usefulness or desirability to various goods and services – a classification which cannot be duplicated by any non-market process. In science, the emergent classification is knowledge of natural phenomena. Both market and science are spontaneous orders each with its unique rules or informal norms of interaction whose operations result in classifications of inputs specific to the order. By analogy with the order instantiated in the brain, these classifications by market and science systems are the system's knowledge, and it is in this sense that orders can be characterized as "knowledge-generating".
6 None, that is, beyond the lower-level implementation of fundamental constraints, such as property, contract, and monetary institutions in markets.

Bibliography

Butos, W.N. 2010 (ed.). *Advances in Austrian Economics* 13: *The social science of Hayek's The Sensory Order*. Emerald.

Caldwell, B. 1988. Hayek's transformation. *History of Political Economy* 20 #4, pp. 513–542.

——— 2004. *Hayek's challenge: an intellectual biography of F.A. Hayek*. University of Chicago Press.

Gray, J. 1984. *Hayek on liberty*. Routledge.

Hayek, F.A. 1920. Contributions to a theory of how consciousness develops. G. Heinz (tr.). *Hoover Institution, Hayek Papers* box 93 folder 1. Reprinted in Hayek (2017, pp. 321–347).

——— 1931. *Prices and production*. Routledge.

——— 1933a. *Monetary theory and the trade cycle*. Jonathan Cape.

——— 1933b. The trend of economic thinking. *Economica* 13, pp. 121–137. Reprinted in Hayek (1991, pp. 17–34).

——— 1934. Carl Menger. *Economica* 1 #4, pp. 393–420. Reprinted in Hayek (1992, pp. 61–107).

——— 1937. Economics and knowledge. *Economica* 4 (n.s.), pp. 33–54. Reprinted in Hayek (1948a, pp. 33–56).

——— 1942. Scientism and the study of society, part 1. *Economica* 9 #35, pp. 267–291.

——— 1943. Scientism and the study of society, part 2. *Economica* 10 #37, pp. 34–63.

——— 1944a. *The road to serfdom*. University of Chicago Press.

——— 1944b. Scientism and the study of society, part 3. *Economica* 11 #41, pp. 27–39.

——— 1945. The use of knowledge in society. *American Economic Review* 35 #4, pp. 519–530. Reprinted in Hayek (1948a, pp. 77–91).

——— 1946. The meaning of competition. Reprinted in Hayek (1948a).

——— 1952. *The sensory order*. University of Chicago Press. Reprinted in Hayek (2017, pp. 113–316).

——— 1960. *The constitution of liberty*. University of Chicago Press.

——— 1967. *Studies in philosophy, politics, and economics*. University of Chicago Press.

——— 1973. *Law, legislation, and liberty* 1: *Rules and order*. University of Chicago Press.

——— 1976. *Law, legislation, and liberty* 2: *The mirage of social justice*. University of Chicago Press.

——— 1979. *Law, legislation, and liberty* 3: *The political order of a free people*. University of Chicago Press.

——— 2017. *The collected works of F.A. Hayek* 14: The Sensory Order *and other writings on the foundations of theoretical psychology*. V.J. Vanberg (ed.). University of Chicago Press.

Hutchison, T.W. 1981. *The politics and philosophy of economics*. Blackwell.

Menger, C. 1871. *Principles of economics*. J. Dingwall & B.F. Hoselitz (trs.). The Free Press, 1950.

——— 1883. *Problems of economics and sociology*. F.J. Nock (tr.). University of Illinois Press, 1963.

Mises, L. 1936. *Socialism*. Jonathan Cape. Retranslated and reprinted by Yale University Press, 1951.

Rosen, R. 1985. *Anticipatory systems: philosophical, mathematical & methodological foundations*. Pergamon Press.

Weimer, W.B. 1979. *Notes on the methodology of scientific research*. Lawrence Erlbaum.

——— 1982. Hayek's approach to the problems of complex phenomena: an introduction to the theoretical psychology of *The Sensory Order*. In W.B. Weimer & D.S. Palermo (eds.), *Cognition and the symbolic processes* II, pp. 241–285. Lawrence Erlbaum.

3 Spontaneous order and its discontents[1]

The concept of "spontaneous order" – the idea that complex but orderly systems can arise from the interactions of component entities whose actions are directed toward more local concerns and not at all toward the creation and maintenance of the overall systemic order – has found applicability in the study of many diverse phenomena in the physical, biological, and social sciences. The self-organization of chemical oscillators, the coherence of living cells, the activity of ant colonies, and the social arrangements of market and science are all examples of spontaneous order. In the cases of physical and lower-level biological phenomena, the interacting components obviously exhibit no purpose at all, let alone an intention to create the ordered system; in the cases where the components are purposeful their local activity betrays no obvious direct concern for the maintenance of the system as a whole. But in each case the components interact according to particular rules – physical laws in the simpler systems and behavioral regularities which, by and large, restrict interactions to certain forms in the social systems. A critical feature of such systems is that, although they are open to their environment and depend on it for energy and material for system maintenance, they are able, up to a point, to retain their integrity in the face of environmental changes, and to achieve this adaptation without direction from some centralized locus of control.

The subjects of this book are social orders – markets and science, particularly – and it has been with reference to these that the theory of spontaneous order and its implications has been developed most fully. But despite the seeming promise of the theory for understanding both the origins and the operations of a wide range of social phenomena, it has received relatively little attention in both economics and sociology, where mechanistic equilibrium-based theorizing and data mining in search of empirical regularities are the preferred approaches. There are, however, good reasons why it has not conquered the world of social theory. It is true that the concepts of "spontaneous" and "order" are surprisingly difficult to pin down, and can be construed so widely as to lose explanatory force. If spontaneity has to do with unintended results of interaction, then one can wonder if there are any interactions that do not have unintended consequences. And some element of orderliness can be found even in quite disorderly situations – such as a riot, for example, in which spontaneous self-reinforcing interactions can be present. But such problems arise from attempts to make the theory of spontaneous order a "theory of everything" in the social domain. Where the theory has seen its most

DOI: 10.4324/9781003336150-3

mature development has been in the efforts of Friedrich Hayek and Michael Polanyi – Hayek in focusing on market phenomena and Polanyi on the community of scientists – efforts which restrict their attention to specific, large-scale, long-lasting systems of interaction.

Polanyi and Hayek in context

The idea of "spontaneous order" was in the air in the 1920s. The term itself was not yet in use – that came later in the work of first Wilhelm Röpke, then Michael Polanyi, and, finally and decisively, Friedrich Hayek[2] – but the concept was there.[3] The setting was not in the context of economics, despite obvious earlier foreshadowing in the writings of Mandeville, Ferguson, Hume, and Smith in the 1700s and Menger in the 1800s,[4] but in biology and psychology, where theorists of both were seeking to establish their fields as positive sciences distinct from physics and chemistry. In the 1920s the biologists Joseph Woodger at the University of London and Paul Weiss and Ludwig von Bertalanffy in Vienna argued against the vitalist account of the biological world for its apparent introduction of a non-material animating force and against materialism for its reductionist neglect of the importance of the relations between the constituent parts of a biological system.[5] Their crucial innovation was the emphasis on "system thinking" – the taking account of the interrelations and interactions between the ordered components of biological systems which resulted in the emergence of phenomena at the system level which could not be described except in terms of the system context, thereby justifying a distinctive subject matter for biology.

A similar argument was taking place at the same time among psychologists, and doubtless the ideas of biologists and psychologists cross-fertilized each other. In opposition to the associationist's reduction of mental phenomena to elementary sensations and to the behaviorist's mechanistic concentration on elementary stimulus and response and denial of higher-level mental phenomena, and also in opposition to any suggestion of a "thinking substance" separate from physical matter, Max Wertheimer, Kurt Koffka, and Wolfgang Köhler, working at the Psychological Institute in Frankfurt-am-Main and building on earlier work of Wilhelm Wundt, developed the theory of the "Gestalt". The basic thrust of Gestalt psychology is the insistence that perceptions are not the sum of elementary sensations but result from the capacity of the nervous system to organize and mold those sensations into a perceived whole.[6] Again, we see the idea of the emergence of system-level phenomena from the ordered interactions of the constituents of the system. In both biology and psychology, "system thinking" was on the rise.

This, then, was the intellectual environment in which Polanyi and Hayek, early in their careers, moved. Although Polanyi established himself as a distinguished physical chemist at the world-class Kaiser Wilhem Institute in Berlin in the 1920s and then from 1933 at the University of Manchester, he became immersed in social theory and the sociology of science as a result of his alarm at the growing pressure for state planning of science in the UK. From 1935 on he dedicated much of his academic activity to this field. Hayek emigrated from Austria to England in 1931, joining the faculty of the London School of Economics. Already well versed in philosophy, law, and psychology, and familiar with the work of Menger, Hayek began to question the equilibrium focus of economics, and increasingly incorporated into his work the sort of system thinking described above.[7] The concept of spontaneous order had been discovered many times before, but after Polanyi and Hayek it didn't need discovering again.[8]

Polanyi and the order of science

Polanyi (1945, p. 142) conceived of science as a process of mutual adjustment among scientists. If a scientist has free rein over his research, including the selection of problems to pursue, "his task is to discover the opportunities in the given state of science for the most successful applications of his own talents and to devote himself to the exploitation of these openings". These choices, Polanyi told us, are essentially driven by educated guesses about useful ways to proceed based on scientists "constantly collecting, developing, and revising a set of half-conscious surmises" and "an assortment of private clues". Yet (1962, p. 54) scientists are "in fact cooperating as members of a closely knit organization" by virtue of "the adjustment of the efforts of each to the hitherto achieved results of the others". This "mutual adjustment of independent initiatives" represents a dynamic coordinating principle among scientists whereby the growth of knowledge is seen as a byproduct of the separate actions of individual scientists that "leads to a joint result which is unpremeditated by any of those who bring it about" (1962, p. 55). This adjustment and the cooperation among scientists that it reflects can only proceed, Polanyi (1966, p. 55) explained, in a stepwise fashion as advances are made on the basis of previous results in the "discovery of a hidden system of things". Whatever advances are forthcoming are derived from the considered judgments made by scientists as to which problems to pursue. Thus, the discovery of knowledge will take on contours that are determined by the process itself as it moves toward an unending and unknown end result. The growth of knowledge, according to Polanyi, is a byproduct of the mutual adjustments that scientists make that could not have been predicted or been made to follow a blueprint.[9] That is, scientific knowledge is advanced by the process itself of scientists adjusting their research efforts to previous results and that the discovery of such knowledge cannot be divorced from that process.[10]

The freedom of scientists to freely choose and pursue questions and problems is central to Polanyi's vision of science. It is precisely this freedom that gives teeth to science as a dynamic order and which makes possible the growth of knowledge by means, as he put it, of the "mutual adjustment of initiatives" within the community of scientists. Polanyi claimed that without this freedom the advancement of science would come to a standstill because the predetermination of lines of inquiry by directives from a central planning board is incompatible with scientific research that seeks to discover knowledge. For Polanyi, science is a process of discovery and scientists adapt their research efforts to the ongoing discovery of new knowledge and the attendant questions and directions that discovery puts into motion.

Polanyi, however, noted that the freedom of scientists to pursue research in the absence of constraints is not strictly absolute. Consider the governing role played by scientific communities in establishing standards and conferring legitimacy on what individual scientists do. Within any community, we would expect internally generated constraints to emerge if the order is to be sustained and to remain viable. Such provisions are not arbitrary or optional but ordinarily have been accepted through trial and error, or as marginal adjustments to the order, and have demonstrated a compatibility with the system's success and in satisfying the aims of its participants. As such, the evolved internal constraints of the order which contribute to its success are not problematic per se. If they become so, Polanyi argues that the community's participants would have the option to follow a different path and attract others to join in.[11]

Beyond such internally generated standards, Polanyi argued that the ideal of science is made possible by the framework of values provided by a conception of conservative liberalism closely aligned, for example, to Edmund Burke. Polanyi's conception of liberalism is based on a nexus of shared values among individuals who practice certain traditions. Liberty for Polanyi means adhering and submitting to these shared traditions by self-dedication and in the practice of transcendent moral ideals that are ends in and of themselves and not a means to anything else. Within this broader social context, he saw the emergence of spontaneously generated orders, such as science, made possible by generations of scientists committing themselves to transcendent ideals, such as truth-seeking,[12] that supersede the values that motivate activities for personal gain and profit. According to Polanyi, transcendent ideals are necessarily contained and transmitted in the evolved traditions of science, serving as the bedrock upon which science must function. The "origin of the spontaneous coherence amongst scientists", he said (1946, p. 38), "arises because they are informed by the same tradition". Absent these traditions, he argued (1946, p. 36), the ongoing viability and success of a dynamic scientific order is not possible:

> It seems clear enough then that the self-governing institutions of science are effective in safeguarding the organized practice of science … [but] their functions are mainly protective and regulative and are themselves based … on the preexistence of a general harmony of views among scientists …

And (1946, p. 40):

> Only if scientists remain loyal to scientific ideals rather than try to achieve success … can they form a community which will uphold these ideals. … The discipline required to regulate the activities of scientists cannot be maintained by mere conformity to the demands of scientific opinion, but requires the support of moral conviction … Scientists must feel under obligation, both in exercising authority and in submitting to that of their fellows, otherwise science must die. … It would then appear that when the premises of science are held in common by the scientific community each must subscribe to them as by act of devotion. … These premises … are not merely indicative, but also normative. The tradition of science, it would seem, must be upheld as an unconditional demand if it is to be upheld at all.

Polanyi called the kind of freedom required for science "public liberty" and argued that it ought to be "upheld as an aim in itself". But this kind of liberty, which he differentiated from "private liberty", is not meant to insulate individuals from arbitrary incursions or to establish a protected domain within which each may freely function.[13] Rather, Polanyi (1941, p. 438) saw public liberty in a "positive" sense, as a "kind of liberty that goes far beyond personal freedom" in that it calls for a "judgment of a higher order" and on that account warrants one's freedom "to act according to his own convictions". Importantly, however, he claimed such privileges come with considerable duties and responsibilities necessitated by the devotion to practicing the ideals of science. These transcendent ideals are principally embodied in and secured by practiced traditions – traditions that are held tacitly by all members.

Hayek and the order of market

In 1933 Hayek delivered "The Trend of Economic Thinking" (TET) at the London School of Economics. Although he reaffirmed economics as a theoretical science and chided the German Historical School, especially the second generation led by Gustav Schmoller, the more important theme may have been his discussion of spontaneous order and unintended effects, themes he saw as arising out of the Scottish Enlightenment in the work of Hume, Smith, and others. It was in this context that Hayek (1933, p. 131) cited Mises' *Socialism* in referring to society as an "organism and not an organization". His discussion of spontaneous order, however, was perhaps aligned most closely with Carl Menger's (1883) extended remarks on the subject in *Problems of Economics and Sociology*.[14] But while TET and Hayek's ideas on spontaneous order are sometimes linked to his rediscovery of Menger's work, there is evidence that ideas and questions relevant to spontaneous order had been lurking in the shadows since Hayek's student days and would continue to surface throughout his life. Such questions clearly emerge as an important part of his research agenda as he matured and as his interests turned increasingly toward issues in broader social theory and the various domains of social life we understand as spontaneous orders.

Although Hayek directed his efforts in the 1930s and 1940s largely to economics, his remarks in TET seem to signal a deepening interest in broader questions – an interest which would bear fruit in the appearance of his "knowledge papers" beginning with "Economics and Knowledge" (1937), then "The Use of Knowledge in Society" (1945), and also "The Meaning of Competition" (1946) – all of which address the functional attributes of a catallaxy as a spontaneous order.[15] But it was not until *The Constitution of Liberty* (*CL*) in 1960 that Hayek explicitly couched his restatement of the principles of the liberal order in terms of spontaneous order and evolution. At this time, Hayek (1960, p. 1) was resigned to the fact of liberalism as an "abandoned road"[16] but still believed that, by systematically restating the "ideal of freedom" and expounding fundamental insights of liberal thought, the existing institutional framework could undergo reform to produce an environment conducive to the reemergence of liberal society. By 1973, when volume 1 of *Law, Legislation, and Liberty* (*LLL*) was published, Hayek (1973, p. 2) believed that the "traditional doctrine of liberal constitutionalism" had not secured liberty and that liberal democratic institutions were the cause for the erosion of freedom. *CL* approaches its task by working within a set of rules, as Buchanan might have said, whereas *LLL* is concerned about changing the rules or, in Hayek's (1973, p. 4) words, a "problem of constitutional design".

Despite these rather different agendas, Hayek, in both *CL* and *LLL*, prominently featured the constraints imposed by "the knowledge problem" within an evolutionary context. In *LLL*, the evolutionary argument was couched in terms of the implications of contending philosophical positions – evolutionary rationalism and constructivist rationalism – for understanding the emergence, nature, and evolution of social orders. Hayek claimed that constructivist rationalism is demonstrably erroneous on scientific grounds because it is based on the untenable assumption that a planning board has the capacity to "assemble as a surveyable whole all the data which enter into the social order". He emphasized in both *CL* and *LLL* (1973, p. 13) that the "fact of irremediable ignorance of most of the particular facts which determine the processes of society is, however, the reason why most social institutions have taken the form they actually have". Spontaneous orders, such as the catallaxy or grown law, he argued, are superior because they confer epistemic advantages to individuals in adjusting to new and unforeseen circumstances. Such advantages are closed to central planners because they must direct the actions of individuals toward specific ends solely on the knowledge available to a single voice. In a spontaneous order, on the other hand (1973, p. 49), individuals are free to use "knowledge which nobody possesses as a whole".[17]

Hayek argued that achieving the benefits of spontaneous orders required rules of conduct regarding social interactions (e.g., rules of property and contract) and rules governing the relationship between individuals and government. Rules of conduct for Hayek are themselves often undesigned and, like traditions and conventions, are byproducts of an evolutionary process. Yet (1960, p. 63), "it is this submission to undesigned rules and conventions whose significance and importance we largely do not understand, this reverence for the traditional, that ... is indispensable for the working of the free society". The transmission of rules of conduct, including the nexus of traditions and habits, is driven according to Hayek by a selection and retention process via imitation and the weeding out of rules, habits, and traditions that yield poor results in terms of the advantages they confer. The selection mechanism functions at the societal level among groups with competing systems of rules; Hayek (1960, p. 63) claimed that "better rules of conduct" will prevail by displacing inferior sets of rules and by sustaining larger populations.[18]

In this way, Hayek identified a dynamic, evolutionary process of adaptation based on the epistemic consequences of alternative social arrangements and institutions, a viewpoint central to his broader social theory. But Hayek, like Polanyi, also sought to go beyond this scientific approach and defend the liberal order as a normative ideal. And these two perspectives are joined in his broader social theory in the claim that adherence to liberal principles tends to generate better outcomes.[19] Hayek, to his credit, attempted to defend his normative claims on scientific grounds centering on the superior epistemic properties of spontaneous orders. The liberal goal of freedom and the corresponding limitations placed on government, the rule of law, and a domain of individual autonomy protected from arbitrary incursions, were seen by Hayek as essential for the emergence of spontaneous orders and, hence, the generation of the epistemic advantages necessary for progress. Hayek grounded this argument on his work in economics with regard to the constraints implied by the division of knowledge and in so doing thereby elevated it to a generalizable social principle. But compared to the analytics of catallactic theory, Hayek's broader social theory is less definitive in establishing exactly how arrangements promoting spontaneous orders are fully consistent with the liberal order.

Prescriptivism and interventionism in Polanyi and Hayek

Both Polanyi and Hayek, in defending the autonomy of market and science, found it necessary to cast their analyses in the context of broader social theory.[20] In so doing, issues concerning the justification of unhampered market and science were couched by them in terms of their conceptions of liberalism. While their scientific arguments against central planning are cogent, locating their analyses within a broader social theory required reliance on increasingly more normative claims and criteria that supervene on particular spontaneous orders.[21]

Polanyi (1946, ch. II; 1962) argued that maintaining a well-functioning spontaneous order, such as science, requires communities in which authority is vested in various institutional structures. These include journal editors and scientists who have secured sway among colleagues and peers. Polanyi is keenly aware that these provide the essential feedback for self-corrective science; yet he sees these also as necessary disciplinary mechanisms serving a higher good: the preservation of transcendent scientific ideals.[22] In this way, Polanyi's approach to science as a spontaneous order – an approach crucially based on the primacy of and requirement for transcendent and tacitly held ideals – introduces unnecessary normative criteria which mar his analysis.

We see this in Polanyi's distinction between "private" and "public" liberty, a notion reflecting no doubt the culture of pure science as he experienced it, but one which adds a complicating layer of normative claims to the analysis. Importantly, Polanyi believed "public liberty" required – in a prescriptive sense – that scientists adhere to certain duties in implementing transcendent ideals, such as a commitment to truth, and in accepting the evolved standards and traditions of science embedded in existing institutions. Such ideals for Polanyi function much like a "Constitution of Science" in prescribing certain values and practices scientists must hold and submit to, even if that means intrusive constraints on an individual's otherwise noncoercive actions.

Polanyi claimed that scientists' commitment to the pursuit of truth is among the enabling transcendent values required for science. While this motive, indeed, may apply to scientists, we dispute whether it is a necessary condition for the growth of knowledge on the grounds that it is the procedures of science that are determinative in establishing scientific knowledge and that such knowledge is an emergent *system-level* property of the scientific order. The psychological motives of scientists, including their understandings of what truth is and their sincerity in pursuing truth, are independent of the growth of knowledge because, as Harper (2016) puts it, it is the "inter-subjective error-correcting network" of scientists that "subjects theories to empirical testing and potential refutation".[23] What matters are the critical procedures[24] deployed by the community of scientists that ignore, reject, or tentatively accept knowledge claims, and not the noble psychological intentions of scientists.

Polanyi is led to favor a proactive stance to preserve the ideals and traditions by which they are transmitted. But this represents a failure to appreciate fully the ordering capabilities of the spontaneous orders he himself has done so much to elucidate. Polanyi emphasized the role of tutoring, textbooks, training, working in labs, and the role of editors in publishing research, and these transactions, executed repeatedly under the feedback from previous transactions, would be expected to produce (and have in fact produced) internally not only an emergent "ordering" of scientists based on their scientific accomplishments and reputations but also various enforcement mechanisms. Contra Polanyi, science's "constitution" can be seen as an emergent byproduct of the functioning of the scientific order; rigidly specifying these institutions as normative preconditions of science is a typical constructivist mistake.

Hayek also populates his positive analysis of spontaneous order with normative criteria. He claimed (1960, p. 63) on the one hand that "it is this submission to undesigned rules and conventions whose significance and importance we largely do not understand, this reverence for the traditional, that … is indispensable for the working of the free society", but on the other hand (perhaps more tellingly) he also raised the problem of spontaneous order "dead ends" – outcomes that he deemed to be inconsistent with normative criteria endemic to liberalism. In the context of a discussion of the common law and its spontaneous origin in the customary law of England, Hayek (1973, ch. 4) contended (p. 88) that "the spontaneous process of growth may lead into an impasse from which it cannot extricate itself by its own forces or which it will at least not correct itself quickly enough", which "therefore does not mean that we can altogether dispense with legislation". His particular reason (pp. 88–89) for this conclusion was his concern that the application of the doctrine of *stare decisis* binds a judge to uphold precedent "although he may clearly recognize that another rule would be better, or more just". But Hayek is confusing modern common law, where the judge is the central actor in interpreting precedent while being cognizant of the downstream societal consequences of his ruling, with pre-19th-century common law and the customary law which preceded it. As Hasnas (2005) points out, the spontaneously evolved "law of liberty" which Hayek was trying to describe was in fact a system in which the case decisions of juries[25] were not strongly constrained by precedent, would tend to depart from it in the interest of present justice, and were concerned only with the justice of the decision at hand and not its presumed future social impact. Modern common law, on the other hand, is the older customary and common law blanketed with constructivist arrangements which have produced the "dead ends" that Hayek was rightly concerned about. If Hayek had had a clearer grasp of the history of the common law he could not have applied his critique to the actual "grown law" and, by implication, to spontaneous orders in general.

Hayek's reservations about fully spontaneous orders are also found in explicit discussions that attempt to describe the relevant boundaries between legislative design and the market order consistent with liberal principles, particularly that of the rule of law and its three criteria for legislation (1960 pp. 208–209): "true laws" must be "general, abstract rules", "must be known and certain", and must be enforced equally to all. These criteria in Hayek's hands clear a large swath for possible government actions. Hayek's resolution of the boundary lines was to evaluate government actions based on his conception of the liberal order, and that allowed him to deflect his attention away from the analysis of spontaneous order and toward policy issues. Our criticism is not with that direction nor the policy positions that Hayek endorses; our concern is that to secure his normative ends directly he cuts short the budding analysis of spontaneous orders.[26]

That predisposition can be seen in his Introduction to *Collectivist Economic Planning* (1935, pp. 1–40) and continuing with remarks in *The Road to Serfdom* (1944, p. 81) claiming that *laissez faire* "is a highly ambiguous and misleading description of the principles upon which a liberal policy is based".[27] Hayek would later develop this theme in greater detail in *CL* and *LLL* in claiming (1960, p. 231):

> The range and variety of government action that is, in principle, reconcilable with a free system is thus considerable. The old formulae of laissez-faire ... do not provide us with an adequate criterion for distinguishing between what is and is not admissible in a free system. There is ample scope for experimentation and improvement within that permanent legal framework to operate most efficiently. ... But the continuous growth of wealth and technological knowledge which such a system makes possible will constantly suggest new ways in which government might render services to its citizens and bring such possibilities within the range of the practicable.

Hayek (1960, p. 223) sanctions several kinds of particular measures of government that refer to the provision of collective goods that are "clearly desirable but which will not be provided by competitive enterprise".[28] Such services rendered by government must also be evaluated, Hayek emphasizes, on the basis of expedience and net benefits, and, just as importantly, he rejects artificial barriers being erected to maintain the government monopoly. So, while the scope for government activity is large in principle for Hayek, he also includes provisos that as a practical matter clearly constrain such activities. But the result is that, in the hope of coming to closure on the relation between the spontaneous order of the market and deliberate legislative design, we are swept into an ambiguous and muddied realm anchored in normative beliefs and lacking an analysis of the extent to which past interventions have contributed to the perceived need for current government activity – in short, an approach which prematurely closes the path toward a fuller understanding of spontaneous orders.

Both Polanyi and Hayek, in their different ways, allowed certain normative claims to inform their analyses of spontaneous orders and in doing so both came to advocate inroads by which spontaneous orders should be subject to government intervention and remediation. It is our contention that, in both cases, the introduction of normative considerations was not only unnecessary but also undercut the theory of spontaneous order, leaving it open to misunderstanding and confusion.

The way forward in spontaneous order theory

While both Polanyi and Hayek employed the concept of spontaneous order to expose the unintended consequences of government control, neither put forward a fully internally consistent theory of the sorts of social arrangements implied by the characterization of spontaneous order. Polanyi not only favored prescriptive rules for science but also, in arguing that government funding would be helpful in enabling scientific research to proceed unhampered, seemed oblivious to the unintended effects that could arise from such funding. Hayek, influenced by both Polanyi and the "general systems" ideas of Bertalanffy, later tried to generalize the spontaneous order concept from markets to other social orders, but his use of the idea in the defense of classical liberalism introduced normative elements that betrayed the basic scientific thrust of his approach. Notwithstanding these problems, we believe that there can be a fully positive and robust approach to the study of social order which advances the understanding of spontaneous order in general, allows for comparative systems analysis, and is grounded in generalizations from observable structures and characteristics of actual social systems.

In his social theory, Hayek seems to cast his problem in terms of understanding the nature of social order in general, as opposed to understanding, as at least conceptually separate things, the various orders that have formed or could be formed in a social context. His orientation comes through fairly clearly in his specific definition of order (1973, p. 36, emphasis omitted):

> By 'order' we shall throughout describe a state of affairs in which a multiplicity of elements of various kinds are so related to each other that we may learn from our acquaintance with some spatial or temporal part of the whole to form correct expectations concerning the rest, or at least expectations which have a good chance of being correct.

This is a concept of "order" in a very general sense, encompassing as it does simple physical orders such as inorganic crystals. It is also a surprisingly passive view of orders – especially of social orders – in that it abstracts completely away from any idea of orders as active, adapting systems. Bianchi (1994) has perceptively taken issue with the characterization of "order" as simply an orderly state – in particular, with the fact that it abstracts away from the procedures of discovery going on within social orders. She points out (p. 245) that order "is not a state of affairs, but a process; not a correct state, but a corrigible one". We suggest that Bianchi's insight can be captured by conceptualizing social orders as knowledge-generating systems, as complex and dynamic objects in a state of continual adaptation to their environment, capable of generating classifications of events in that environment. Spontaneous orders can be characterized in terms of the forms of knowledge specific to them, dependent on the particular structure of the order and on the properties of its elements and the processes through which they interact. The processes within the systems of science and market both generate knowledge, but it is very different knowledge. The challenge is to elucidate, in each case, how the processes operative within the system generate their characteristic form of knowledge, and how this knowledge feeds back to maintain the operation of the component processes in the face of an uncertain and changing environment.

The fundamental continuity in Hayek's work derives from his ongoing concern with what are as much problems in epistemology as problems in economics or social science. In following the idea that there may well be some explanatory potential in pushing forward the notion of orders as systems within which particular forms of knowledge are generated, it is possible to characterize Hayek's project as the scientific study of various aspects of such objects. These are structures, with both tangible and intangible components, that have the effect of generating the attribute we call "knowledge" in that they form abstract representations of phenomena external to them by a process of classification. Such an inquiry would be a science in the same way that biology is the study of various aspects of living objects – it would be epistemology treated as a natural science, not as a branch of philosophy. In this sense, it quite literally follows that the Hayekian research program should be viewed as a scientific project about knowledge.

Notes

1 This chapter contains text previously published in Butos & McQuade (2017).

2 Polanyi used the term "dynamic order" to refer to arrangements observed in physical, biological, psychological, and social realms that spontaneously emerged from mutual adjustment between the relevant elements stemming from free interactions, contrasting this form of ordering with deliberately "planned order". See Polanyi (1941, pp. 431 *et seq.*). Hayek (1937, 1945) employed a very similar idea in an economic context in contrasting central planning with the localized planning that involves the "spontaneous interaction" of people possessing only "divided knowledge", i.e., "the knowledge of the particular circumstances of time and place". Hayek (1960, pp. 159–161), quoting Polanyi, is even more explicit, and there he deploys the term "spontaneous order".

3 The investigation of the background of the term "spontaneous order" is an area of some controversy. For documentation of Röpke's terminological priority, see Bladel (2005), who quotes Röpke (1937, pp. 4–5). Earlier, Jacobs (1998, 1999) had argued for the priority of Polanyi (1948), and before that Hamowy (1987) gave Hayek (1960) the credit. But see Hayek (1955, p. 30) in which he credits Polanyi (1951, pp. 114 *et seq.* & 154 *et seq.*) for employing the phrase "spontaneous formation of a polycentric order". For a comprehensive treatment of the issue, see D'Amico (2015).

4 See Mandeville (1714, pp. 68–69), Ferguson (1767, p. 187), Hume (1740, pp. 490, 529, & 579), Smith (1776, pp. 24–32 & 484–485), and Menger (1871, pp. 257–285; 1883, pp. 139–159 & 223–234). See Barry (1982), Hamowy (1987), and Ames (1989) for detailed histories.

5 See Woodger (1929), Weiss (1925), and Bertalanffy (1928). For short biographies and a detailed exposition of the intellectual connections between these biologists and their contemporaries and predecessors, see Drack *et al.* (2007). For Gestalt psychology's influence on Hayek, see De Vecchi (2003) and Lewis (2016a). See also Bertalanffy (1950), Weiss (1977), Weckowicz (2000), and Lewis (2016a, 2016b).

6 See Köhler (1930) for a full exposition of Gestalt theory. For a discussion of Wundt's influence on Hayek as early as 1920, see Lewis (2016a). For Kohler's influence on Polanyi, see Mullins (2010). See also Drack *et al.* (2007) for documentation of the

exchange of ideas between the Gestalt psychologists and the organicist biologists, particularly Bertalanffy.

7 Although Polanyi and Hayek did not meet until 1938 when both attended Walter Lippmann's *Le Colloque* in Paris, their intellectual positions were not in full agreement but were compatible in broad-brush terms. Both were consciously incorporating the idea of spontaneous order into their theorizing, both employed it in their opposition to the calls for central planning (whether of science or the economy), both read and commented on each other's work, and both incorporated elements of the other's work into their own. For an extended discussion of their interactions and intellectual cross-fertilization, see Howard (2008).

8 Since our focus here is at the level of complex social systems (in line with Hayek and Polanyi) we see "spontaneous orders" as self-organizing social systems displaying properties emergent from the interactions of the people composing them and distinct from the properties of their components. We make no distinction between spontaneous order and emergent order, a distinction, as Harper and Endres (2012) show, is necessary at lower levels of organization.

9 Polanyi's discussion is simultaneously also a critique of the attempt to centrally plan science since scientists (and, of course, the central planners) cannot know *a priori* what adjustments they should make in their research as new advances are discovered.

10 For an exposition of the same idea in a market context, see Buchanan (1982).

11 In this way, the success of modern science has solidified around widely accepted standards as to what it means to do science. This, of course, only circumscribes the activity in terms of scientific procedures but does not predetermine outcomes those procedures uncover.

12 While adherence to truth-seeking is the primary ideal, Polanyi (1945, p. 142) also cites the secondary norms of admiration for scientific "courage and reliability" and scorn for the "commonplace and fanciful". Such informal moral norms underlie science practice in much the same way as the norms of trust and promise-keeping underlie market practice. (We thank Paul Lewis for this insight.) But these secondary norms are distinct from those ideals that are *required* (1941, p. 438) to maintain science as a "dynamic order". Polanyi's scientist functions in the world of public liberty – freedom to do research but only by practicing the traditions of liberalism, a tradition that is learned tacitly by practicing it. Polanyi, however, is quite vague on what exactly is "liberalism", as he sees it as revealing itself as is practiced. It is not a "protected domain" libertarianism nor even rule-utilitarianism, but it does bear an affinity to Hayek's conception of liberty in its stress on the importance of tradition.

13 "Private liberty" is seen by Polanyi as "personal freedoms" that enable individuals to autonomously operate within a defined and protected sphere of activity in pursuit of private interests. In *The Logic of Liberty* (1951, p. 157) he refers to private freedom as a "class of individualistic manifestations which do not contribute to any system of spontaneous order in society". He goes on (p. 158) to note that "A free society is characterized by the range of public liberties through which individualism performs a social function, and not by the scope of socially ineffective personal liberties". These "public liberties" lift and justify personal freedom and are preeminent by virtue of the underlying transcendent ideals these traditions support.

14 Hayek does not cite Menger in "The Trend of Economic Thinking", although he was certainly familiar with Menger's 1883 monograph – see Menger (1883, bk. 3, chs. 1 & 2, pp. 127–159). Hayek published an essay on "Carl Menger" in *Economica* in 1934 that served as the "Introduction" to the four-volume *Collected Works of Carl Menger* edited by Hayek and published (in German) in 1934. His discussion (1992, p. 79) of Menger's 1883 book in the 1934 essay is revealing: "Probably it did more than any other single work to make clear the peculiar character of the scientific method in the social sciences". Hayek then goes on to say, "But to me … its main interest to the economist in our days seems to lie in the extraordinary insight into the nature of social phenomena. … Discussions of somewhat obsolete views, as that of the organic … interpretation of

social phenomena, give him an opportunity for an elucidation of the origin and character of social institutions which might, with advantage, be read by present-day economists and sociologists."

15 For summaries of the trend of Hayek's thinking beginning with the "knowledge papers", see Caldwell (2014) and Lewis & Lewin (2015).

16 "The abandoned road" is the title of ch. 1 of Hayek (1944), *The Road to Serfdom*.

17 Also see, for example, Hayek (1960, p. 30) where he says that "all institutions of freedom are adaptations to this fundamental fact of ignorance".

18 In *The Fatal Conceit* (1988, pp. 120–121), Hayek contended that "the close connection between population size and the presence of, and benefits of, certain evolved practices, institutions, and forms of human interaction" implied "that socialism constitutes a threat to the present and future welfare of the human race, in the sense that neither socialism nor any other known substitute for the market order could sustain the current population of the world".

19 On Hayekian grounds, in the catallaxy the absence of particular ends governing the overall order and the impossibility of interpersonal utility comparisons render standard welfare economics irrelevant. Hayek's (1978, p. 184) own normative criterion turns on a coordination norm regarding the probability of a randomly selected individual achieving his ends. Later, Hayek (1988, p. 132) explicates this criterion in terms of sustaining population growth and emphasizes the process by which rules are selected that are compatible with that criterion: "Yet if the market economy did indeed prevail over other types of order because it enabled those groups that adopted its basic rules the better to multiply, then the calculation in market values is a calculation in terms of lives: individuals guided by this calculation did what most helped to increase their numbers, although this could hardly have been their intention."

20 Particular social structures and orders function within broader contexts and do not exist independently of those contexts. The catallactic theory of the market is nested in a set of institutions pertaining, for example, to the existence and enforcement of property rights and contracts, but these conditions can and should be taken as given if we wish to understand the role of price formation. Although exogenous conditions will certainly affect how the catallaxy functions, viewing the catallaxy in positive terms as a complex adaptive order is the lens by which such outside conditions can be analyzed.

21 This issue is broached in some detail in Butos & McQuade (2002).

22 Also see Polanyi (1945, pp. 143–144).

23 Also see Popper (1972, ch. 3), Musgrave (1974), Weimer (1979, ch. 5), Bartley (1962, ch. 5), and Harper (1996, pp. 58–60).

24 By "critical procedures" we mean the transactions of publication and citation, whose effects constitute feedback, both positive and negative, due to their effect on scientific reputation. Repeated iteration of these transactions in the context of feedback produced by earlier transactions results is the major stabilizing mechanism for the system of science and the source of the emergent product we call "scientific knowledge".

25 It was not "judge-made" law – judges were necessary elements in ensuring that proper procedure was adhered to, but it was the jury who were expected to decide the case in a manner that was fair given the particular circumstances and expectations involved. See Hasnas (2005, pp. 89–92).

26 Our criticism of Hayek's treatment of legal institutions echoes that of the more extended discussions in Stringham (2015, ch. 13) and Zywicki & Stringham (2012). As Stringham (2015, p. 218) points out, "Hayek [in his discussion of legal institutions] treats as normative concepts what are fundamentally questions of positive analysis and institutional design".

27 Hayek (1935, pp. 21–22): "To say that partial planning [in a capitalistic society] of the kind we are alluding to is irrational is, however, not equivalent to saying that the only form of capitalism which can be rationally advocated is that of complete laissez-faire in the old sense. There is no reason to assume that the historically given legal institutions are necessarily the most 'natural' in any sense." In "Planning, Science, and Freedom"

(1941, p. 583) he says: "The alternative [to central planning] is, of course, not laissez-faire, as this misleading and vague term is usually understood. Much needs to be done to ensure the effectiveness of competition; and a great deal can be done outside the market to supplement the results."

28 Examples mentioned by Hayek include a sound monetary system, a system of weights and measures, the dissemination of statistics and other information, supporting and organizing education, sanitary and health services, safety regulations, roads, and public works, which he says (1960, pp. 222–226 & 257–260) should be financed by taxes. Support of the indigent, the unemployed and sick (p. 285) "has long been accepted as a duty of the community", yet Hayek argues (p. 286) that an obvious corollary would be "to compel them to insure ... against those common hazards of life". Also see Hayek's extensive discussion of government financing, though not necessarily the provision, of collective goods (1979, ch. 14) and his insistence (p. 47) that such services should not "be reserved to government if other means can be found for providing them".

Bibliography

Ames, B. 1989. *Science and spontaneous order.* Social Philosophy and Policy Center.

Barry, N.P. 1982. The tradition of spontaneous order. *Literature of Liberty* 5 #2, pp. 7–58. http://www.econlib.org/library/Essays/LtrLbrty/bryTSOCover.html.

Bartley III, W.W. 1962. *The retreat to commitment.* Open Court, 2/e, 1984.

Bertalanffy, L. 1928. *Modern theories of development: an introduction to theoretical biology.* J.H. Woodger (tr.). Oxford University Press, 1933.

——— 1950. An outline of general system theory. *British Journal for the Philosophy of Science* 1, pp. 134–165.

Bianchi, M. 1994. Hayek's spontaneous order: the 'correct' versus the 'corrigible' society. In J. Birner & R. van Zijp (eds.), *Hayek, co-ordination, and evolution*, pp. 232–251. Routledge.

Bladel, J.P. 2005. Against Polanyi-centrism: Hayek and the re-emergence of "spontaneous order". *Quarterly Journal of Austrian Economics* 8 #4, pp. 15–30.

Buchanan, J.M. 1982. Order defined in the process of its emergence. *Literature of Liberty* 5 #4, p. 5. http://oll.libertyfund.org/pages/reader-s-forum-on-norman-barry-s-the-tradition-of-spontaneous-order.

Butos, W.N. & T.J. McQuade 2002. Mind, market, and institutions: the knowledge problem in Hayek's thought. In J. Birner, P. Garrouste, & T. Aimar (eds.), *F.A. Hayek as a political economist*, pp. 113–133. Routledge.

——— 2017. Polanyi, Hayek, and Adaptive systems theory. *Cosmos + Taxis* 4 #1, pp. 1–22.

Caldwell, B. 2014. Introduction. In B. Caldwell (ed.), *The collected works of F.A. Hayek, v. 15: The market and other orders*. University of Chicago Press.

D'Amico, D.J. 2015. Spontaneous order. In P.J. Boettke & C.J. Coyne (eds.), *The Oxford handbook of Austrian economics*, pp. 115–142. Oxford University Press.

De Vecchi, N. 2003. The place of Gestalt psychology in the making of Hayek's thought. *History of Political Economy*, 35, pp. 135–162.

Drack, M., W. Apfalter, & D. Pouvreau 2007. On the making of a system theory of life: Paul A Weiss and Ludwig von Bertalanffy's conceptual connection. *Quarterly Review of Biology* 82 #4, pp. 349–373. http://www.ncbi.nlm.nih.gov/pmc/articles/PMC2874664.

Ferguson, A. 1767. *An essay on the history of civil society*. Edinburgh University Press, 1966. https://books.google.com/books?id=-04uAAAAYAAJ.

Hamowy, R. 1987. *The Scottish Enlightenment and the theory of spontaneous order.* Southern Illinois University Press.

Harper, D.A. 1996. *Entrepreneurship and the market process: an enquiry into the growth of knowledge*. Routledge.

——— 2016. Popper on commitment. *Personal correspondence.*

Harper, D.A. & A.M. Endres 2012. The anatomy of emergence, with a focus upon capital formation. *Journal of Economic Behavior & Organization* 82, pp. 352–367.

Hasnas, J. 2005. Hayek, the Common Law, and fluid drive. *NYU Journal of Law & Liberty* 1, pp. 79–110.

Hayek, F.A. 1933. The trend of economic thinking. *Economica* 13, pp. 121–137. Reprinted in Hayek (1991, pp. 17–34).

——— (ed.) 1935. *Collectivist economic planning: critical studies on the possibilities of socialism*. Routledge.

——— 1937. Economics and knowledge. *Economica* 4 (n.s.), pp. 33–54. Reprinted in Hayek (1948, pp. 33–56).

——— 1941. Planning, science, and freedom. *Nature* 148, pp. 580–584.

——— 1944. *The road to serfdom*. University of Chicago Press.

——— 1945. The use of knowledge in society. *American Economic Review* 35 #4, pp. 519–530. Reprinted in Hayek (1948, pp. 77–91).

——— 1946. The meaning of competition. Reprinted in Hayek (1948).

——— 1948. *Individualism and economic order*. University of Chicago Press

——— 1955. *The political ideal of the rule of law*. National Bank of Egypt.

——— 1960. *The constitution of liberty*. University of Chicago Press.

——— 1973. *Law, legislation, and liberty* 1: *Rules and order*. University of Chicago Press.

——— 1978. *New studies in economics, politics, philosophy, and the history of ideas*. University of Chicago Press.

——— 1979. *Law, legislation, and liberty* 3: *The political order of a free people*. University of Chicago Press.

——— 1988. *The fatal conceit*. University of Chicago Press. Reprinted in *The collected works of F.A. Hayek* 1: *The fatal conceit*. W.W. Bartley III (ed.). University of Chicago Press.

——— 1992. *The collected works of F.A. Hayek* 4: *The fortunes of liberalism*. P.G. Klein (ed.). University of Chicago Press.

Howard, E.S. 2008. A joint pursuit: the unique epistemic project of Friedrich Hayek and Michael Polanyi. The Polanyi Society Conference *Personal Knowledge at Fifty*, Loyola University, Chicago, June 13–15. https://www.missouriwestern.edu/orgs/polanyi/Loyola08/Loy08Pprs/Howard-ppr-7-10.pdf.

Hume, D. 1740. *A treatise of human nature*. Clarendon Press, 1978.

Jacobs, S. 1998. Michael Polanyi and spontaneous order, 1941–1951. *Tradition and Discovery*, 24 #2, pp. 14–28. http://www.anthonyflood.com/jacobspolanyi.htm.

——— 1999. Michael Polanyi's theory of spontaneous orders. *Review of Austrian Economics*, 11, pp. 111–127. https://www.academia.edu/3203498/Michael_Polanyis_Theory_of_Spontaneous_Orders.

Köhler, W. 1930. *Gestalt psychology*. Bell & Sons.

Lewis, P.A. 2016a. The emergence of "emergence" in the work of F.A. Hayek: an historical analysis. *History of Political Economy* 48, pp. 111–150.

——— 2016b. Systems, levels of organization and structural properties: the influence of Ludwig von Bertalanffy on the development of F.A. Hayek's work on complexity. *Research in the History of Economic Thought and Methodology* 34A, pp. 125–159.

Lewis, P.A. & P. Lewin 2015. Orders, orders, everywhere … on Hayek's *The Market and other Orders*. *Cosmos + Taxis* 2, pp. 1–16.

Mandeville, B. 1714. *The fable of the bees*. P. Harth (ed.). Penguin Classics, 1989.

Menger, C. 1871. *Principles of economics*. J. Dingwall & B.F. Hoselitz (trs.). The Free Press, 1950.

——— 1883. *Problems of economics and sociology*. F.J. Nock (tr.). University of Illinois Press, 1963.

Mullins, P. 2010. Michael Polanyi's use of Gestalt psychology. In T. Margitay (ed.), *Knowing and being: perspectives on the philosophy of Michael Polanyi*, pp. 10–29. Cambridge Scholars Publishing.

Musgrave, A.E. 1974. The objectivism of Popper's epistemology. In P.A. Schlipp (ed.), *The philosophy of Karl Popper*, pp. 560–596.

Polanyi, M. 1941. The growth of thought in society, *Economica* 8, pp. 428–456.

——— 1945. The autonomy of science. *The Scientific Monthly* 60 #2, pp. 141–150.

——— 1946. *Science, faith, and society*. Oxford University Press, 1964.

——— 1948. Planning and spontaneous order. *The Manchester School of Economic and Social Studies* 16, pp. 237–268.

——— 1951. *The logic of liberty*. University of Chicago Press.

——— 1962. The republic of science: its political and economic theory. *Minerva* 1, pp. 54–73. Reprinted in M. Grene (ed.), *Knowing and being: essays by Michael Polanyi*, pp. 49–72. University of Chicago Press, 1969.

——— 1966. *The tacit dimension*. University of Chicago Press.

Popper, K.R. 1972. *Objective knowledge: an evolutionary approach*. Clarendon Press.

Röpke, W. 1937. *Economics of the free society*. P.M. Boarman (tr.). Libertarian Press, 1994.

Smith, A. 1776. An Inquiry into the nature and causes of the wealth of nations. Modern Library, 1994. https://books.google.com/books?id=C5dNAAAAcAAJ.

Stringham, E.P. 2015. *Private governance: creating order in economic and social life*. Oxford University Press.

Weckowicz, T.E. 2000. Ludwig von Bertalanffy (1901–1972): a pioneer of general systems theory. Center for Systems Research, U. Alberta, Working Paper No. 89-2. http://www.richardjung.cz/bert1.pdf.

Weimer, W.B. 1979. *Notes on the methodology of scientific research*. Lawrence Erlbaum.

Weiss, P.A. 1925. Animal behavior as system reaction: orientation toward light and gravity in the resting postures of butterflies. *Yearbook of the Society for General Systems Research* 4, pp. 19–44.

——— 1977. The system of nature and the nature of systems: empirical holism and practical reductionism harmonized. In K.E. Schaefer, H. Hensel, & R. Brady (eds.), *A new image of man in medicine* 1: *towards a man-centered medical science*. Futura.

Woodger, J. 1929. *Biological principles*. Kegan Paul.

Zywicki, T.J. & E.P. Stringham 2012. Common law and economic efficiency. In F. Parisi & R. Posner (eds.), *Encyclopedia of law and economics*, pp. 107–131. Edward Elgar.

4 Inspiration from *The Sensory Order*[1]

In *The Sensory Order* (1952a), Hayek provided a high-level description of the brain as a physical system capable of maintaining an order of sensory qualities by operating as an apparatus of classification. Although Hayek explicitly considered this one of his most important works,[2] it initially received very little attention from Hayekian economists and social theorists. But, with the rise in interest in cognitive issues in social theory during the 1990s, the work has started to find an audience, and capsule presentations of its content can be found in several papers.[3] However, it was the cognitive psychologist Walter B. Weimer who should be chiefly credited with bringing Hayek's theory of mind before a larger audience and making the case for its wider significance for economics and social theory generally.[4] Beginning in the mid-1970s, Weimer (1979) started using and developing the ideas in *The Sensory Order* for his work in cognitive science and the methodology of scientific research. Coming from a background in the philosophy of science, he was especially influenced by the late W.W. Bartley's *The Retreat to Commitment* (1962) and Kuhn's *The Structure of Scientific Revolutions* (1962), and he saw Hayek's work in cognitive science, constraints on knowledge, and spontaneous order, as compatible with Bartley's epistemological stance on "comprehensively critical rationalism" and Kuhn's evolutionary theory of science. In 1981, Weimer organized a cognitive science conference at Penn State University that featured Hayek as the principal speaker, and Weimer's (1982) own address to that conference presented the case for the significance of Hayek's cognitive psychology for the social sciences. This paper became the preeminent, and for several years the only useful, entrée to *The Sensory Order*.

Most Hayek scholars now accept the importance of Hayek's cognitive theory as integral to his oeuvre. Hayek himself tended to highlight the significance of this work for issues in methodology, a direction that has been enthusiastically picked up by contemporary methodologists, especially Caldwell (2004) and Di Iorio (2010). However, he was less clear in making an argument that his work in psychology might be germane to non-methodological questions in social theory. Although various attempts have examined whether his cognitive theory carries in its own right useful applications to economics and social theory,[5] Hayek did not undertake such inquiries directly, except to obliquely note in *The Fatal Conceit* (1988) that his cognitive work was important for the development of his ideas on evolution and spontaneous order. Hayek's hesitancy to claim too much might have been a sensibility induced by the long-standing aversion within the Austrian

DOI: 10.4324/9781003336150-4

School to psychological explanations for the praxeological science of economics, as articulated by Mises (1949, pp. 11–12 and 1957, ch. 12). In *The Counter-Revolution of Science*, Hayek (1952b, p. 39) argued that "it is a mistake" for social scientists "to believe that their aim is to *explain* conscious behavior", which he saw as "the task of psychology".[6] It may be that once we move beyond methodological issues, an unmistakable tension arises from within Hayek himself as to the value of his cognitive theories for economic and social theory.

In finding inspiration in *The Sensory Order* for furthering the understanding of social spontaneous orders, conflating economics with psychology is *not* what we have in mind. Rather, by drawing out the ramifications both from Hayek's work on epistemology and psychology, we hope to point to the possibility of a coherent new view of economic and other social systems in which individuals have realistic capabilities, where emergent effects are recognized as macro phenomena which supervene on micro activity rather than being simply reducible to it, and where systemic characteristics such as adaptation and knowledge generation are given their due.

Hayek's theory of the sensory order

Hayek describes the basic structure of the brain as a network of components, physically connected, that interact via the transmission of electrical impulses. The components are neurons, cells capable of generating outgoing impulses ("firing") if stimulated sufficiently by incoming impulses, but limited in their ability to continuously fire by the requirement for a relaxation period between firings and because of the onset of fatigue. Each neuron is connected to many others (but nowhere near to all of the others in the network) by means of extensions called axons, and new connections can be established, or existing ones eliminated, depending on ongoing activity, so that pathways with impulses often occurring concurrently will tend to become connected. The strengths of established connections (their ability to induce follow-on firing) can change depending on the activity they experience. The connections can form complex patterns in the network that involve groupings of neurons in which all neurons in a group connect mostly with the same downstream groups – but not exclusively, allowing for the possibility of re-entrant patterns that support the operation of feedback loops.

The system is open to its environment and interacts with it in both sensory and motor modes. Events in the environment (including those in the body of the organism containing the brain) impact on sensory organs that transmit impulses to the brain, and some neuronal pathways within the brain connect to motor neurons that can induce actions affecting the environment. The firings and subsequent refirings of interconnected neurons within the brain, induced by the flux of incoming stimuli, results in the system as a whole maintaining a continuous, fluctuating level of activity which forms a background over which reverberations due to newly incident stimuli are superimposed.

The network of connections (of varying strengths) between the component neurons, which changes as a long-term result of the stimulus-induced patterns of activity, effectively functions as a "map" of the environment as experienced in the past in that it enables the emergence, from a given stimulus, of an induced pattern of impulses characteristic of that stimulus and of other potential stimuli which have accompanied the given stimulus in the past. This pattern of impulses generated in the map by the current stimuli is, therefore, a "model" of the environment as currently experienced. The model is anticipatory in that trains of impulses originating from a stimulus induce a "following", i.e., impulses in neuronal pathways that, in the past, have tended to be active at the same time as the pathways excited by the current stimulus (and these followings can in turn induce further followings). The model thus embodies expectations of subsequent stimuli by virtue of the fact that the map enables the inducement of patterns characteristic of associated stimuli even when those stimuli may not be actually present. Since connections exist to motor neurons at many levels and these connections, like all connections in the map, have been developed as a result of experience (phylogenetic or ontogenetic), the model can result in the selection of motor activity consistent with expectations it embodies as to the character of the current situation.

The network of neurons and their axons acts as a system of classification in that the impulses from stimuli produce particular patterns of follow-on impulses within the network. Two stimuli are classified as identical if they produce the same impulse pattern; they are similar to the extent that their patterns overlap. And, since both subject and object of classification are patterns of impulses, further classifications can proceed at higher levels in terms of the effects the (classified) follow-on patterns have on subsequent neuronal groups. This classification is multiple in several senses – any particular stimulus can be a member of multiple classes, an assignment of a particular stimulus to a class may change depending on the presence of concurrent stimuli, and classes (being represented in terms of impulses) can themselves be further classified at subsequent levels.

The map is effectively an apparatus of long-term memory in that its configuration enables the effects of one stimulus to reconstruct the effects of other stimuli with which it has been associated in past experience. (There is also short-term memory in that the effects of stimuli reverberate in the network for some time before being damped out.) The physical changes in neurons and their connections implement a form of learning in which the system adapts to its environment.[7] The reverberation of activity in the network, supplemented by the effects of current stimuli (*i.e.*, the model) generates associations which are in effect predictions of the consequences which are possible in the existing external situation and as such create dispositions to act accordingly. These associations may be of various strengths, and the combined effect of their interaction will be resolved in a selection process in which a path of least resistance determines the action actually taken.

The network adjusts to injury to or loss of a component or connection (or to a localized group of components and connections) simply by continuing operation. The system as a whole will continue to function, but it will have "forgotten" whatever long-term memory was embodied in the lost or degraded connections and its classification of stimuli whose followings are seriously affected by the loss will be changed (probably in unpredictable ways). The learning activity of the system will continue, however, and eventually the injury will tend to be "worked around", with other connections forming or being co-opted to perform classifications similar to those in effect prior to the injury.

The sensory order and social orders

Hayek's theory characterizes the brain[8] as a system interacting with and adapting to its environment by performing a multi-level classification on the stimuli it receives from the environment – an adaptive system with no central locus of control. It has been pointed out by others[9] that there exist a variety of "complex adaptive systems" besides the brain that seem to have some level of capability for adaptation through changes in structure based on system experience, but we propose to follow up that observation in a novel way by abstracting from the particular implementation of the neural order described by Hayek what seem to be the essential attributes of such a system. We are proposing that these basic processes of classification described by Hayek as operating in the brain, including particularly the formation of a mutable map of the brain's environment as experienced in the past and the ability of that map to support a model driven by current experience, have their counterparts in adaptive social orders, implemented differently, of course, but very similar in principle. We are certainly not proposing that social orders are brains but that they are brain-like in certain very specific and circumscribed respects. The interactions between their components implement a classifying process on stimuli, both external and internal, to the system, and this generated "knowledge" of the environment has effects on component behavior that constitute adaptive reactions of the system to changes in its environment.

Despite the obvious differences and qualifications, social orders have many characteristics in common with the neural order. The following are some distinctly brain-like aspects of social systems:

1. The systems have structural integrity while at the same time exhibiting a mutability in response to environmental experience. The pathways of interaction within the system are affected by environmental change in characteristic ways – fundamental, long-used interaction patterns, such as the institutions of property and exchange in markets and publication and citation in science, are very resistant to change, whereas the more peripheral, more recently acquired, less pervasive ones are much more easily modified or discarded. The structural rearrangements are path-dependent and irreversible, with any change altering the context in which the system reacts to subsequent change.
2. One can observe an expansion of number of elements involved in pathways associated with a particular stimulus as that stimulus becomes more frequent or more pressing, and a concomitant reduction in numbers of elements associated with relatively less pressing stimuli. This is the analog of "competitive plasticity" observed in brains. The effect shows up most noticeably as "creative destruction" in markets and "paradigm changes" in science. When a particular type of stimulus has not been experienced for some time, the pathways associated with reactions to it will tend to atrophy, with any permanent resources involved being devoted to other interactions. An obvious example of such "forgetting" is seen in the relatively small part of a modern economy devoted to horse technology.
3. The systems exhibit functional mutability – the foreclosing of interaction pathways (by whatever means, by natural events or by intentional

intervention) does not, in general, permanently cut off the response to the stimuli which activated these pathways. Instead, the system tends to work around the impediment, often co-opting neighboring pathways previously used for servicing other inputs.

4 The systems exhibit anticipation in the sense that their current structure predisposes them to react to future events in ways dictated by their experience of past events. Examples of such anticipatory capability are seen in the futures prices in markets and the predictive aspects of scientific theories. Its conservative side (the assumption that the future will be much like the past) shows up, for example, in the tendency of science to focus on phenomena consistent with an accepted paradigm and to ignore conflicting data.[10]

5 The systems exhibit reactions analogous to addiction – with cash or credit (in markets) or funding (in science) as the analog of neurotransmitters in brains. In markets and science, the ensuing "hangover" of recession and readjustment are predictable features of the recovery process.

6 The classifications performed by these systems are relational, and what are being related in the final analysis are internal states of activation. The classes are the focal interaction patterns that the current configuration of the system's map supports. These particular patterns of activation, learned from past experience, are the "attractors" which form the basis of the system's classifications of future inputs. To give an illustration, if one observes the interaction patterns of Austrian economists – in papers, conference speeches, and conversations – one sees that the notion of capital as a structured entity is deeply embedded in these interactions. One could say that the scientific subsystem of Austrian economists knows that capital is a structure (or is fruitfully modeled as such). Confrontation with empirical phenomena involving capital generates interactions in which structured capital is a feature. Interactions characterized by structured capital tend to get follow-on notice; those with an unstructured, "capital stock" characteristic tend to die out rather quickly. Structured capital is an "attractor" in the interaction space of Austrian economists.

7 There are areas of interaction that are within the boundaries of the system but which are, by and large, confined to a local context and dedicated to specific tasks, analogous to transmissions within the amygdala (concerned with processing and responding to threats) within brains. Examples include production activities in firms within markets, research activities in labs within science, and interactions in families within markets.

8 How a system reacts to a particular stimulus depends not only on the stimulus but also on the current state of the system. For example, in markets, there is no guarantee that small minimum wage increases will cause observable unemployment increases – one needs to look at the available modes of adjustment in the current circumstances whose complications may hide the first-order effects. Simple supply-and-demand analyses abstract from this context and assume no constraints on adjustment.

Suggestions that economies and other social arrangements can be understood as examples of "complex adaptive systems" have been made many times before in complexity theory – see, for example, Kauffman (1993, pp. 395–402) – and sociology – see, for example, Buckley (1998). It is also implicit in Hayek – see, for example, Hayek (1967, pp. 66–81), where he asserts that

> there is no reason why a polycentric order in which each element is guided only by rules and receives no orders from a center should not be capable of bringing about as complex and apparently as 'purposive' an adaptation to circumstances as could be produced [in a more hierarchically organized system].

Kauffman (1993, pp 173–235 and 1995, pp. 71–92), discussing "the twin sources of order", makes the important point that, in biological systems, natural selection is not the only source of order, for the tendency in certain systems to self-organization is, in a sense, "order for free". But systems involving some form of self-organization are members of a very large and diverse set, and so the commonalities are likely to be of such a general nature as to provide very little assistance in understanding particular social systems. So, while endorsing Kauffman's insight, we prefer to considerably narrow the field so that more concrete things can be said about the structure of the particular systems of interest. Our purpose here in what follows is to push beyond such programmatic statements by injecting more explicitness into the idea.

Notes

1 This chapter contains text previously published in McQuade & Butos (2005) with permission from Springer, in Butos & McQuade (2015) with permission from Oxford University Press, and in McQuade & Butos (2009).

2 See Hayek (1948), Hayek (1979, pp. 199–200), and Hayek (1994, pp. 138–139).

3 See, for example, Agonito (1975), Weimer (1979), Miller (1979), Weimer (1982), Yeager (1984), Herrmann-Pillath (1992), Streit (1993), Butos & Koppl (1993, 1997, 2007), Langlois (1997), Smith (1997), Birner (1999), Rizzello & Turvani (2000), Steele (2002), and Vanberg (2017).

4 See Weimer (2011). Agonito (1975) is perhaps the first article-length treatment of *The Sensory Order*.

5 See Butos & Koppl (1993, 1997) and McQuade (2007).

6 The point of Mises' and Hayek's anti-psychologism was to isolate from economics underlying psychological motivations. We do not disagree with this. At the same time, however, we believe that Hayek's work in this area goes well beyond such concerns precisely because it deals with epistemic issues relevant to social theory and a variety of methodological insights that clearly fall within the purview of modern economics. Runde (1988, p. 107), in an otherwise useful overview of the status of psychology in Austrian economics, surprisingly asserts that "Hayek's psychological treatise … has little to do with economics", although he astutely notes that the aversion to psychology exhibited by Mises and Hayek is, in fact, directed at behavioristic psychology. Also see Butos (1997) and Butos & Koppl (2007).

7 Hayek was certainly not the first to emphasize the importance for learning of the formation of connections between concurrently active neural elements – see James (1890, p. 566) and Hull (1943, pp. 68–69).

8 Although Hayek's object of interest was the human brain, we note that this is a system that displays certain emergent attributes (consciousness, for instance) that play no part in our generalization. The attributes of neural orders upon which we base our

generalization do not include such "higher" functions. Although consciousness is obviously an attribute of the brains of the people that populate human social systems, there is no reason to ascribe it (or some analog of it) to such systems as a whole. An adaptive classifying system certainly does not have to be conscious to exhibit adaptiveness and even anticipation. In any case, consciousness probably arises as a result of particular structural arrangements that have evolved in certain types of brain, and there is no reason at all to expect that a similar path of evolution would be followed by other, quite different, orders.

9 See, for example, Kauffman (1993) and Holland (1995).

10 An interesting example of this characteristic of seeing only what is expected is described in Pickering (1984, pp. 301–302) where experimental data reported by some *atomic* physicists inconsistent with electroweak gauge theory was dismissed by *particle* physicists without any specific flaws in experimental technique ever being suggested.

Bibliography

Agonito, R. 1975. Hayek revisited: mind as a process of classification. *Behaviorism* 3, pp. 162–171.

Bartley III, W.W. 1962. *The retreat to commitment.* Open Court, 2/e, 1984.

Birner, J. 1999. The surprising place of psychology in the work of F.A. Hayek. *History of Economic Ideas* 7 #1&2, pp. 43–84.

Buckley, W.F. 1998. *Society – a complex adaptive system.* Gordon & Breach.

Butos, W.N. 1997. Hayek and rational expectations. In W. Keizer, B. Tieben, & R. van Zijp (eds), *Austrian economics in debate*, pp. 220–242. Routledge.

Butos, W.N. & R.G. Koppl 1993. Hayekian expectations: theory and empirical applications. *Constitutional Political Economy* 4 #3, pp. 303–329.

——— 1997. The varieties of subjectivism: Keynes and Hayek on expectations. *History of Political Economy* 29 #2, pp. 327–359.

——— 2007. Does *The Sensory Order* have a useful economic future? In E. Krecké, C. Krecké, & R. Koppl (eds.) *Advances in Austrian Economics* 9: *Cognition and economics*, pp. 19–50. Elsevier.

Butos, W.N. & T.J. McQuade 2015. *The Sensory Order*, neuroeconomics, and Austrian economics. In P.J. Boettke & C.J. Coyne (eds.), *The Oxford handbook of Austrian economics*, pp. 612–639. Oxford University Press.

Caldwell, B. 2004. *Hayek's challenge: an intellectual biography of F.A. Hayek.* University of Chicago Press.

Di Iorio, F. 2010. *The Sensory Order* and the neurophysiological basis of methodological individualism. In W.N. Butos (ed.), *Advances in Austrian Economics* 13: *The social science of Hayek's* The Sensory Order, pp. 179–210. Emerald.

Hayek, F.A. 1948. Letter of 6 Nov. to J. Nef. *Hoover Institution, Hayek Papers*, box 55, folder 1.

——— 1952a. *The sensory order.* University of Chicago Press. Reprinted in Hayek (2017, pp. 113–316).

——— 1952b. *The counter-revolution of science.* The Free Press, 1955.

——— 1967. *Studies in philosophy, politics, and economics.* University of Chicago Press.

——— 1979. *Law, legislation, and liberty* 3: *The political order of a free people.* University of Chicago Press.

——— 1988. *The fatal conceit.* University of Chicago Press. Reprinted in *The collected works of F.A. Hayek* 1: *The fatal conceit.* W.W. Bartley III (ed.). University of Chicago Press.

——— 1994. *Hayek on Hayek: an autobiographical dialogue.* S. Kresge & L. Wenar (eds.). University of Chicago Press.

——— 2017. *The collected works of F.A. Hayek* 14: The Sensory Order *and other writings on the foundations of theoretical psychology.* V.J. Vanberg (ed.). University of Chicago Press.

Herrmann-Pillath, C. 1992. The brain, its sensory order, and the evolutionary concept of mind: on Hayek's contribution to evolutionary epistemology. *Journal of Social and Biological Structures* 15 #2, pp. 147–187.

Holland, J.H. 1995. *Hidden Order*. Addison Wesley.

Hull, C.L. 1943. *Principles of behavior*. Appleton-Century-Crofts.

James, W. 1890. *Principles of psychology*, vol. 1. Dover, 1950.

Kauffman, S.A. 1993. *The origins of order: self-organization and selection in evolution*. Oxford University Press.

——— 1995. *At home in the universe: the search for laws of self-organization and complexity*. Oxford University Press.

Kuhn, T.S. 1962. *The structure of scientific revolutions*. University of Chicago Press, 2/e (enlarged), 1970.

Langlois, R.N. 1997. Cognition and capabilities: opportunities seized and missed in the history of the computer industry. In R. Garud, P. Nayyar, & Z. Shapira (eds.), *Technological entrepreneurship: oversights and foresights*, pp. 71–94. Cambridge University Press.

McQuade, T.J. 2007. Science and market as adaptive classifying systems. In E. Krecké, C. Krecké, & R. Koppl (eds.). *Advances in Austrian Economics* 9: *Cognition and Economics*, pp. 51–86. Elsevier.

McQuade, T.J. & W.N. Butos 2005. The sensory order and other adaptive classifying systems. *Journal of Bioeconomics* 7 #3, pp. 335–358.

McQuade, T.J. 2009. The adaptive systems theory of social orders. *Studies in Emergent Order* 2, pp. 76–108. https://cosmosandtaxis.files.wordpress.com/2014/05/sieo_2_2009_mcquadebutos.pdf.

Miller, E.F. 1979. The cognitive basis of Hayek's political thought. In R.L. Cunningham (ed.), *Liberty and the rule of law*, pp. 243–267. Texas A&M University Press.

Mises, L. 1949. *Human action*. Henry Regnery, 3/e, 1966.

——— 1957. *Theory and history*. Yale University Press, 1967.

Pickering, A. 1984. *Constructing quarks*. University of Chicago Press.

Rizzello, S. & M. Turvani 2000. Institutions meet mind: the way out of an impasse. *Constitutional Political Economy* 11 #2, pp. 165–180.

Runde, J. 1988. Subjectivism, psychology, and the modern Austrians. In P. Earl (ed.), *Psychological economics*, pp. 101–120. Kluwer.

Smith, B. 1997. The connectionist mind: a study of Hayekian psychology. In S.F. Frowen (ed.), *Hayek: economist and social philosopher*, pp. 9–30. Macmillan.

Steele, G.R. 2002. Hayek's sensory order. *Theory and Psychology* 12 #3, pp. 125–147.

Streit, M.E. 1993. Cognition, competition, and catallaxy: in memory of F. A. Hayek. *Constitutional Political Economy* 4 #2, pp. 223–262.

Vanberg, V. 2017. The "knowledge problem" as the integrating theme of F.A. Hayek's oeuvre: an introduction to *The Sensory Order*. In V. Vanberg (ed.), *The Collected Works of F.A. Hayek* 14: The Sensory Order *and other writings on the foundations of theoretical psychology*. University of Chicago Press.

Weimer, W.B. 1979. *Notes on the methodology of scientific research*. Lawrence Erlbaum.

——— 1982. Hayek's approach to the problems of complex phenomena: an introduction to the theoretical psychology of *The Sensory Order*. In W.B. Weimer & D.S. Palermo (eds.), *Cognition and the symbolic processes* II, pp. 241–285. Lawrence Erlbaum.

——— 2011. "Marginal men": Weimer on Hayek. In L. Marsh (ed.), *Advances in Austrian Economics* 15: *Hayek in mind: Hayek's philosophical psychology*, pp. xxv–xxviii. Elsevier.

Yeager, L.B. 1984. Hayek and the psychology of socialism and freedom. *The AEI Economist* 175, pp. 1–5.

5 Inspiration from biological systems theory[1]

By the "structure" of a social order we mean the organization of the processes constituting the system. The basic idea that the organization of system processes is just as important a subject of study as the physical effects of those processes has a long history in biology,[2] dating back at least to Kant but with earlier glimmerings as far back as Aristotle.[3] Kant (1790) described biological organisms as purposeful systems in which the parts "so combine in the unity of a whole that they are reciprocally cause and effect of each other's form". He pointed out that such systems are self-organizing and self-maintaining: the system is formed and maintained by the interaction of the parts of the system, and the parts are formed and maintained by the system's processes.[4] He contrasted such systems with a mechanical arrangement such as clockwork, in which "one part is for the sake of the others, but it does not exist by their means. In this case the producing cause of the parts and of their form is not contained in the nature (of the material), but is external to it." Machines require external maintenance processes; organisms do not.

Although Kant's characterization of biological organization was well appreciated throughout the 19th century, it was not until the 1920s that the idea of "system thinking" gained major traction in the work of biologists, particularly Bertalanffy (1928).[5] In arguing for biology's status as a science independent of physics, he directed attention to the emergence of phenomena at the system level, phenomena that arose only as a result of the interactions of the system components and were not reducible to the characteristics of the components in isolation. It is notable that when Bertalanffy talked about the organization of a biological system he emphasized the organization of the internal processes rather than the organization of the physical matter – in fact, he held that the former determined the latter. In Bertalanffy's (1968, p. 27) own words: "In the last resort, structure (*i.e.*, order of parts) and function (order of processes) may be the very same thing: in the physical world matter dissolves into a play of energies, and in the biological world structures are the expression of a flow of processes." This prescient observation foreshadows recent developments in process metaphysics, which takes the fundamental nature of the world to be organizations of processes.[6] Bertalanffy also elaborated on the thermodynamic openness of such systems, describing organisms as systems in "flux equilibrium", dynamically maintaining themselves through exchange of matter and energy with the environment.[7]

DOI: 10.4324/9781003336150-5

Process closure and systemic anticipation

In the development of his theory of cognitive development in children as a self-organizing complex of processes, Piaget, working from an analogy with biological systems, introduced the concept of closure as the operation in the system of a set of processes which, together, without the aid of any outside process, reconstitute each other and thus maintain the operation of the system. Coupled with Bertalanffy's notion of thermodynamic openness, this conceptual combination characterizes biological systems as materially and energetically open systems with closed, self-maintaining organization.[8] The persistence in such systems is in the functional processes within the system; the physical components are continuously being reconstituted with the help of inputs from the environment.

Rosen (1985, 1991) made two significant contributions to the theory of biological systems: a general treatment of anticipation based on the many examples of anticipatory behavior evident in biological systems, and a reformulation of the twin phenomena of thermodynamic openness and process closure in terms of the Aristotelian categories of causation.[9] These two contributions are closely linked, as will become evident. Rosen's treatments in both cases were highly mathematical – he did, after all, style himself as a "mathematical biologist"[10] – but the essential ideas behind his work can be understood with a minimum of mathematical notation.

A process **F** which transforms inputs A to outputs B can be represented concisely as **F**: A → B, *i.e.*, as a mapping from domain A to range B. To give a specific example used by Rosen, **F** could represent a metabolic process in which food items (elements of the domain set A) were processed to produce items of fuel (elements of the range set B). It is possible for the domain and range set elements to be themselves mappings – for example, the mapping process **F**, realized as an enzyme, could itself be the product of a replacement process replenishing the metabolic enzyme from available inputs. Given the process notation **F**: A → B, Rosen (1991) identified the material cause of (the elements of) B as (the relevant elements of) A, and the efficient cause of B as **F**. Interacting combinations of such processes, represented in terms of such mappings, describe the organizational structure of the system as a whole. The thermodynamic openness of biological systems was, for Rosen, represented by openness to material causation, while process closure was represented by closure to efficient causation, i.e., a network of mappings in which every mapping was an entity in the range set of at least one of its companion mappings within the network.

In addition to material openness and efficient closure, the capacity for adaptation is another characteristic of biological systems. As open systems, they are affected by environmental change and may react to that change in various ways that maintain their structure and coherence, including the adoption of internal changes. Simple biological systems may adapt wholly as feedback homeostats that smooth out randomness in the environment, but in more complex systems there is the phenomenon of anticipation, where adaptation is informed by a prediction of possible future states of the environment. Rosen (1974) defined

> anticipatory modes of behaviour of organisms … [as those] in which an organism's present behaviour is determined by: (a) sensory information about the present state of the environment; and (b) an 'internal model' of the world, which makes predictions about future states on the basis of the present data and the organism's possible reactions to it.

Note that this phenomenon of anticipation allows for a straightforward understanding of final cause as a possible future state which is anticipated in the present.

Rosen's work has been very influential among "organicist" biologists, and while there is ongoing debate surrounding some of his more detailed claims, his status as a prominent contributor to the field seems assured.[11] The general attributes of thermodynamic openness, process closure, and anticipatory adaptation are all recognized as salient characteristics of biological organisms, although work continues to understand how the processes responsible for these characteristics function at a more specific level. But the biological details, however interesting, are not the concern here – what is of present interest is to what extent those characteristics of biological systems have analogues in social systems, and whether such analogies assist in understanding the function of social systems.

Process organization

A system is anticipatory if it contains a predictive model of itself and of its environment which allows it to change state on account of the model's predictions as to a future situation. This ability to develop plans for possible futures, to form expectations of the future based on an internal model, allows for modification of the system's current state in the course of implementing these plans or predictions and may result in output to the environment conditioned by that modification. And the system's input from the environment may be processed within the system to confront, and perhaps modify, the model – for the model to be useful for anticipation, the system must be capable of learning, i.e., adjusting its model to reflect experience of reactions from the environment, especially in situations where prior expectations were not met.

These essential features, in terms of process organization, of a materially open anticipatory system are illustrated in Figure 5.1, where the box represents the conceptual separation of the system from its environment.

Here, the processes of learning, anticipation, and action are shown forming a self-supporting set in which the output of one feeds into the next as input in a closed process loop: the action processes, informed by expectations, produce output to the environment to which the environment reacts; the learning processes sense this reaction (and other environmental phenomena) and update the system's internal model of itself and its environment; and the anticipation processes form expectations for future action based on the internal model. This is a very abstract picture of an anticipatory system, containing only the essentials for anticipatory performance, and it is obvious that one would expect that these processes and their inputs and outputs would be implemented very differently in biological and also – if this sort of arrangement is to have any relevance in the social domain – in social systems.

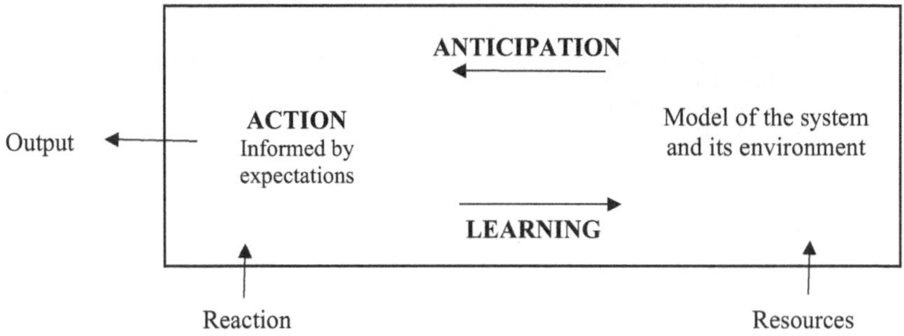

Figure 5.1 An anticipatory system.

Back to *The Sensory Order*

Hayek's description of the structure and operation of the brain and Rosen's description of the organization of the fundamental processes in an adaptive biological system are couched in very different language and emphasize different systemic characteristics. But each describes an anticipatory system, and it is straightforward to show their essential compatibility. Both are process rather than substance theories – they are primarily concerned with the organization of the systemic processes and how they combine to produce the emergent effects characteristic of the system and not with the distribution of material within the system. Hayek's treatment is, of course, closely tied to the physical implementation; Rosen's has the advantage of being rather more abstract, and this will be an advantage in applying it to the understanding of systems that differ widely in physical implementation. Still, Hayek's theory suggests insights into aspects of system operation that are ignored in Rosen's treatment.

Hayek's map – the mutable network of neuronal connections – does double duty: it supports and constrains the activity of classification by which the system learns, and its physical structure implements the model that is the system's knowledge of itself and its environment. Thus, it is both the substrate in support of a process (learning) and the implementation of the effects of that process (knowledge). Hayek's model – the current activity within the map – also serves different roles in different contexts: the execution of the learning process, and the operation of the process (anticipation) which informs action. Hayek's theory does introduce an important element glossed over in the Rosen-inspired schema – a recognition that the anticipation process takes place in two steps: an expectation process which generates dispositions for future action, and a judgment process which selects from the competing dispositions those which will contribute to action in the current environment.

Figure 5.2 is an elaboration of the Rosen-inspired schema, showing the organization of the basic processes of an anticipatory system, including specific listings of their inputs and outputs, without any indication of their physical implementation, but taking account of considerations from the Hayekian picture. Processes (or, more accurately, process classes) are shown in bold within the system boundary; process output classes are indicated by closed-headed arrows and input classes by open-headed ones.

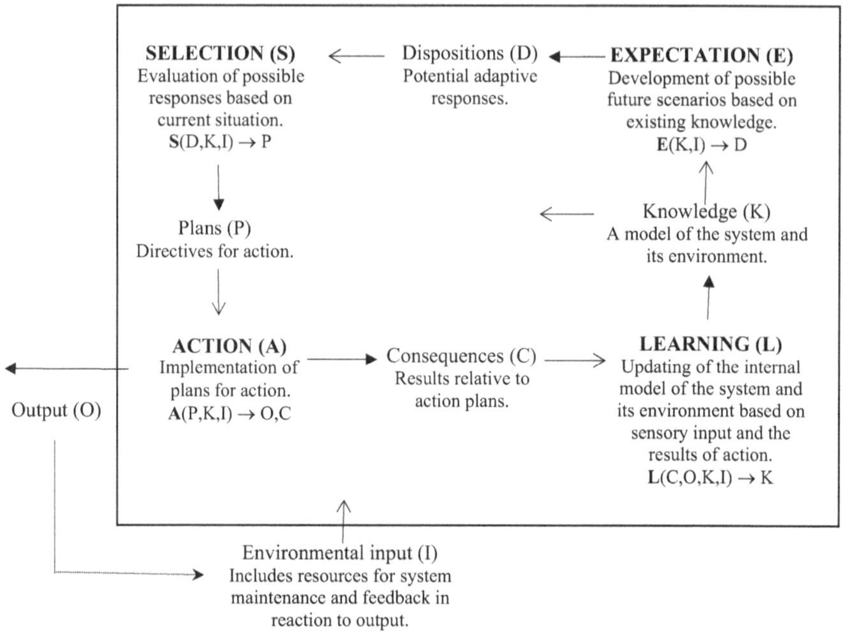

Figure 5.2 Process structure of an anticipatory system.

The arrangement described here can be characterized as an epistemic system, a system capable of building within it some relevant knowledge of its environment, and capable of employing that knowledge within the system (as indicated by the left-pointing arrow from "Knowledge" and the inclusion of K in all of the functional descriptions of the system processes) to anticipate environmental effects and thereby to successfully adapt to them. Echoing Harper (1996, p. 282), it could usefully be described as a self-organizing and self-maintaining Popperian system[12] in that its adaptive apparatus consists of a process for developing conjectures based on existing knowledge, a process for implementing these conjectures so that they may be confronted by the environment, and a "refutation" or "error elimination" process through which failures and successes of this confrontation are learned from and the systemic knowledge updated.

The question which we are now primed to address is whether specific long-lived social arrangements can be usefully modeled as anticipatory systems.

Biological analogies in social theory

The employment of biological analogies to economics and social theory has a long, interesting, and sometimes controversial history.[13] Even as careful an economist as Alfred Marshall was very inclined to countenance the future usefulness of biological analogies. In fact, he is widely quoted as saying (1920, p. 14) that "the Mecca of the economist lies in economic biology rather than in economic dynamics".[14] Less often quoted, however, is the warning that follows this directly:

"But biological conceptions are more complex than those of mechanics ...". And this complexity, though not incompatible with the subject matter, leaves a lot of room for misapplication. Probably the most disturbing critique of biological metaphors in social theory was that of the historian Hofstadter (1944), who successfully attached the epithet "social Darwinism" to free-market economics, and who opined that

> such biological ideas as the 'survival of the fittest', whatever their doubtful value in natural science, are utterly useless in attempting to understand society; that the life of man in society, while it is incidentally a biological fact, has characteristics that are not reducible to biology and must be explained in the distinctive terms of a cultural analysis.[15]

In economics, Penrose (1952), citing Hofstadter favorably, famously addressed the biological analogies employed by the "biological economists" Boulding and Alchian, who, she said, "view firms as organisms and conclude that they grow like organisms", and critiqued them on the grounds that their "variant of the growth approach leaves no room for human motivation and conscious human decision".[16]

The possibility for the application of the characteristics of biological systems such as process closure and anticipation to social contexts has not gone unnoticed. Rosen himself explicitly entertained the idea, discussing at length how understandings of adaptiveness in complex biological systems might be usefully applied to complex economic systems.[17] Leydesdorff & Dubois (2004) incorporate anticipation into a social system of interacting groups modeled by a version of the logistic equation. Louie & Poli (2011) discuss the application, at a very high level of generality, of Louie's extension of Rosen's work on self-referential systems to physiology, ecology, cognitive science, and social science, concluding that many natural systems, including brains and societies, appear to be systems closed to efficient causation. But while suggestive, none of these applications rises to a level much beyond the citing of possibilities and rather vague hints as to how progress might be made.

There certainly are conceptual hurdles to be overcome. The following are fundamental differences between biological systems and social systems:

- In social systems, the efficient causes all have as their basis the purposeful action of the participants in the system. There is not "closure to efficient causation" in the same sense of the biological requirement for closure that the elements that act as efficient causes (the processes themselves) be generated within the system. It is the purposeful agency of the individuals acting within the social system, in the course of acting according to their subjective preferences and motivations ("pursuing happiness") within the constraints on action imposed by the system and employing the modes of transaction available within the system, which provides the motive force animating the system's processes.
- Much of the structure in social systems is abstract. The transaction modes and rules, norms, and conventions which condition all participants' interactions within social arrangements are essential elements of the structure but, in

contrast to their counterparts in biological systems, they are not physical entities; nonetheless, they can be regarded as having causal efficacy.[18] They can also be abstract in the sense that, although carried out in action, and generally observed within the social group, they are not necessarily consciously articulated.[19] Their abstract character may make them difficult to identify and, at the very least, introduces a significant element of theory-dependency to any such identification.[20]

- People are vastly more complex than biological entities such as neurons or enzymes – their brains, after all, are themselves anticipatory systems of a highly specialized kind, capable of supporting purposeful and innovative behavior and accumulating tacit knowledge and therefore exhibiting considerable flexibility in learning and adaptation and pursuing interests. Each is capable of sensing aspects of the environment, so that there is no necessary localization of sensory input to the system. While these attributes can promote the formation of a wide range of cooperative interactions, they also introduce the phenomenon of competition which, as economists have long been aware, is of the utmost importance in accounting for the activity in social systems and necessitates the identification, at least in general terms, of personal motives that rationalize what the competition is about.
- The internal systemic knowledge produced within social systems is, in principle, observable to the component participants, and can serve as useful information to them which, in turn, may cause them to alter their behavior within the system.[21] This feedback effect is important in the maintenance and growth of social systems, for it represents a benefit to participation.

These differences, while significant, are not impediments to deploying the analogy we wish to pursue. The attractiveness of the Hayek- and Rosen-inspired model of biological anticipatory systems for application to social systems is that it is cast at a sufficiently high level of abstraction to accommodate very different systemic implementations. Expressed in terms of abstract process sets and their abstract input and output sets, it specifies only the essential functions for enabling self-maintenance and anticipatory adaptation, leaving the details of the underlying implementation to be addressed when particular social systems are considered.

Notes

1 This chapter contains text previously published in McQuade (2019).
2 For a more extended historical overview of the development of the role of process organization in biology, with references to the historical literature, see Mossio *et al.* (2016).
3 Aristotle (350BCa) emphasized the necessity for studying the parts of an organism with an eye to explaining the organizational interdependence of their parts in achieving their purpose: "Now that with which the ancient writers, who first philosophized about Nature, busied themselves, was the material principle and the material cause. … But if men and animals and their several parts are natural phenomena, then the natural philosopher must take into consideration not merely the ultimate substances of which they are made, but … must examine how each of these comes to be what it is, and in virtue of what force. … For the formal nature is of greater importance than the material nature. … It is plain, then, … that the true method is to state what the definitive

characters are that distinguish the animal as a whole; to explain what it is both in substance and in form".

4 In Kant's (1790) words: "For a body then which is to be judged in itself and its internal possibility as a natural purpose, it is requisite that its parts mutually depend upon each other both as to their form and their combination, and so produce a whole by their own causality; while conversely the concept of the whole may be regarded as its cause according to a principle (in a being possessing a causality according to concepts adequate to such a product). In this case then the connexion of effective causes may be judged as an effect through final causes."

5 For a history of the development of "system thinking" in early 20th-century biology, embryology, and psychology see Drack *et al.* (2007).

6 Bickhard (2000, p. 12), in a discussion of the difficulties of accounting for the causal properties of emergent phenomena within a substance metaphysics, proposes that "organization is not something superimposed on a more basic level of reality; it is a necessary aspect of all reality. So, delegitimating process organization as a potential locus of emergence renders all reality epiphenomenal, because there is no reality that is not constituted as process organization." In particular, according to Campbell & Bickhard (2011, p. 31): "Biological systems – including humans – are not substantial entities ('things' in the thick sense) whose constituents are cells (smaller things), which in turn (after a few more reductions) are constituted out of elementary particles. They are open, organized action systems, in essential interactions with their environments, such that we cannot say what they are without taking those interactive processes into account." "Process philosophy", however, is not a new trend – its roots go back at least to Heraclitus. But it has gained interest in modern times, firstly due to the impact of the theory of evolution, secondly due to the efforts of biologists (including Bertalanffy and Rosen) to study and explain the dynamic phenomena of self-organization, emergence, and adaptation, and thirdly due to recent developments in quantum field theory which point to a process ontology being more fundamental than a substance one. A recent influential treatment of process metaphysics is that of Rescher (2000). For a useful overview of and commentary on process philosophy, see Seibt (2018).

7 See Bertalanffy (1968, pp. 156–160). Georgescu-Roegen (1976, p. 53) has also invoked thermodynamics to emphasize the open nature of economic systems: "The economic process is a partial process that, like all partial processes, is circumscribed by a boundary across which matter and energy are exchanged with the rest of the material universe. ... From the viewpoint of thermodynamics, matter-energy enters the economic process in a state of low entropy and comes out of it in a state of high entropy." For a fine discussion of "openness" and "closedness" particularly with respect to economic systems, see Chick & Dow (2005).

8 According to Piaget (1967): "The central ambiguity is that of the 'open system', for, if system exist, then something like a closure intervenes, which has to be reconciled with the 'opening'. ... The opening then is the system of exchanges with the environment, but this in no way excludes a closure, in the sense of a cyclic rather than a linear order ... [and so] we are confronted by a closed cycle, which expresses the permanent reconstitutions of the [material and dynamic] elements [of the structure], and which is characteristic of the organism; but each interaction ... at the same time represents an opening into the environment as a source of aliment."

9 See Aristotle (350BCb). The following simple example, dealing with the construction of a house, may be helpful in understanding the Aristotelian categories. The material cause of the house is the physical matter out of which the house is built, the formal cause is the architect's plan for the house, and the efficient cause is the builder's construction activity. The final cause is the use of the house as a home, which can be characterized as the purpose of the house. Note that the notion of "purpose", while sounding natural enough when applied to biological entities, does not fit well into the normal Newtonian framework of physical science, where present states are determined by past states only and not future states such as, in the present example, the homey services of the completed house.

10 See Rosen (1973). Rosen expressed his later work in the notations of category theory, a very general branch of mathematics which deals with collections of specific mathematical objects (sets, maps, groups, vector spaces) and the transformations between them. The focus in category theory is on the relationships between the objects rather than the objects themselves. For a formal exposition of category theory in a biological context, heavily dependent on Rosen's work, see Louie (1983).

11 For assessments of Rosen's contributions, see Louie (2006, 2008, 2010), Cornish-Bowden *et al.* (2007), Pattee (2007), and Cárdenas *et al.* (2010). Debates continue about some of Rosen's more controversial claims, such as that closure to efficient causation is a sufficient criterion for life, and that living systems are not machines and are not simulable in finite time – see Wells (2006), Gatherer & Galpin (2013), Zhang *et al.* (2016), and Siekmann (2018). However, Rosen's work is a foundation for ongoing research into biological systems – see Montévil & Mossio (2015) and Mossio *et al.* (2016). For a survey of applications of Rosen's work, see Cárdenas *et al.* (2018).

12 See Popper (1963, p. vii): "The way in which knowledge progresses … is by unjustified (and unjustifiable) anticipations, by guesses, by tentative solutions to our problems, by conjectures. These conjectures are controlled by criticism; that is, by attempted refutations, which include severely critical tests." See also Popper (1972). In Harper's words (1996, pp. 290–291): "The competitive market process is a *spontaneously evolved* set of institutions which facilitates the testing of entrepreneurial conjectures and the generation of new structural knowledge. The fact that the market process is a learning process which is spontaneous in origin means that it has been created from forces within the system (*i.e.*, its structure is endogenous). It has formed itself through a process of selective evolution – it is a self-organising system."

13 For brief history of economists employing biological analogies, citing instances going back to Mandeville, Quesnay, and Adam Smith, see Callejas (2007). See Hodgson (1998) for a comprehensive series of articles on the history of evolutionary economics.

14 That this was a consistent feature of Marshall's thought is evident from other statements of his, for example (1898, p. 314), "in the later stages of economics [*i.e.*, as the subject develops] better analogies are to be got from biology than from physics; and, consequently, that economic reasoning should … gradually become more biological in tone".

15 But see Leonard (2009) for a perceptive study of Hofstadter's inconsistencies and misunderstandings – and his honesty in calling out the eugenicist and racist aspects of progressive era social science.

16 But apparently, according to Levallois (2011), her objection to biological analogies later mellowed, and she cited favorably the work of the evolutionary economists Nelson, Winter, and Hodgson.

17 See Rosen (1975). Also, in his introduction to his major treatise on anticipatory systems, Rosen (1985, pp. 4–5) noted the possibility for biological metaphors to be applied in social theory: "It is plain, on the face of it, that many tantalizing parallels exist between the processes characteristic of biological organisms and those manifested by social structures or societies." One upside he cited for the employment of such parallels was that since "it is hard for us to conceive what an external observer of our society as a whole would be like … [but] by exploiting biological experience, obtained from a standpoint of an external observer, we could … develop entirely new insights into the properties of our social systems".

18 This ontological thrust seems to be compatible with the ontology espoused by Lawson (1997) which goes under the rubric of "critical realism".

19 Hayek (1960, pp. 149–150) carefully distinguishes laws in the sense of abstract general rules from commands (or law in the modern sense of legislation): "But a general rule that everybody obeys, unlike a command proper, does not necessarily presuppose a person who has issued it. It also differs from a command by its generality and abstractness … however … we must recognize that laws shade gradually into commands as their content becomes more specific."

20 Hayek (1973, p. 38) makes the point clearly in the context of explaining why the orderly nature of markets and the benefits flowing therefrom are not readily recognized: "The main reason is that such orders as that of the market do not obtrude themselves on our senses but have to be traced by our intellect. We cannot see, or otherwise intuitively perceive, this order of meaningful actions, but are only able mentally to reconstruct it by tracing the relations that exist between the elements. We shall describe this feature by saying that it is an abstract and not a concrete order."

21 This is the phenomenon highlighted by Hayek (1945) in which he describes (pp. 526–527) the price system as "a mechanism for communicating information … a kind of machinery for registering change … a system of telecommunications which enables individual producers to watch merely the movement of a few pointers, as an engineer might watch the hands of a few dials, in order to adjust their activities to changes of which they may never know more than is reflected in the price movement".

Bibliography

Aristotle 350BCa. On the parts of animals. In J.A. Smith & W.D. Ross (eds.), *The works of Aristotle* 5, Book 1, ch. 1. Clarendon Press, 1912. https://archive.org/details/worksofaristotle05arisuoft.

——— 350BCb. *Physics*. In W.D. Ross (ed.), *The works of Aristotle* 2, Book 2, ch. 3. Clarendon Press, 1930. https://archive.org/details/workstranslatedi02arisuoft.

Bertalanffy, L. 1928. *Modern theories of development: an introduction to theoretical biology*. J.H. Woodger (tr.). Oxford University Press, 1933.

——— 1968. *General system theory: foundations, development, applications*. George Braziller.

Bickhard, M.H. 2000. Emergence. In P.B. Andersen, C. Emmeche, N.O. Finnemann, & P.V. Christiansen (eds.), *Downward Causation*, pp. 322–348. University of Aarhus Press. https://lehigh.edu/~mhb0/Emergence27Jul97.pdf, pp. 1–15.

Callejas, D. 2007. Biology and economics: metaphors that economists usually take from biology. *Ecos de Economía* 24, pp. 153–164.

Campbell, R.J. & M.H. Bickhard 2011. Physicalism, emergence, and downward causation. *Axiomathes* 21 #1, pp. 33–56. https://lehigh.edu/~mhb0/physicalemergence.pdf, pp. 1–33.

Cárdenas, M.L., J. Letelier, C. Gutiérrez, A. Cornish-Bowden, & J. Soto-Andrade 2010. Closure to efficient causation, computability, and artificial life. *Journal of Theoretical Biology* 263 #1, pp. 79–92.

Cárdenas, M.L., S. Benomar, & A. Cornish-Bowden 2018. Rosennean complexity and its relevance to ecology. *Ecological Complexity* 35, pp. 13–24. http://bip.cnrs-mrs.fr/bip10/Complexity.pdf.

Chick, V. & S. Dow 2005. The meaning of open systems. *Journal of Economic Methodology*, 12 #3, pp. 363–381.

Cornish-Bowden, A., M.L. Cárdenas, J. Letelier, & J. Soto-Andrade 2007. Beyond reductionism: metabolic circularity as a guiding vision for a real biology of systems. *Proteomics* 7, pp. 839–845.

Drack, M., W. Apfalter, & D. Pouvreau 2007. On the making of a system theory of life: Paul A Weiss and Ludwig von Bertalanffy's conceptual connection. *Quarterly Review of Biology* 82 #4, pp. 349–373. http://www.ncbi.nlm.nih.gov/pmc/articles/PMC2874664.

Gatherer, D. & V. Galpin 2013. Rosen's (M,R) system in process algebra. *BMC Systems Biology* 7, article 128.

Georgescu-Roegen, N. 1976. The entropy law and the economic problem. In *Energy and economic myths: institutional and analytical economic essays*, pp. 53–60. Pergamon Press.

Harper, D.A. 1996. *Entrepreneurship and the market process: an enquiry into the growth of knowledge*. Routledge.

Hayek, F.A. 1945. The use of knowledge in society. *American Economic Review* 35 #4, pp. 519–530.

——— 1960. *The constitution of liberty*. University of Chicago Press.

——— 1973. *Law, legislation, and liberty* 1: *Rules and order*. University of Chicago Press.

Hodgson, G. (ed.) 1998. *The foundations of evolutionary economics, 1890–1973*. Edward Elgar.

Hofstadter, R. 1944. *Social Darwinism in American thought, 1860–1915*. University of Pennsylvania Press.

Kant, I. 1790. Things considered as natural purposes are organized beings. In J.H. Bernard (tr.), *Critique of Judgment*, Sect. 65. Macmillan, 2/e, 1914. http://oll.libertyfund.org/titles/kant-the-critique-of-judgement.

Lawson, T. 1997. *Economics and reality*. Routledge.

Leonard, T.C. 2009. Origins of the myth of social Darwinism: the ambiguous legacy of Richard Hofstadter's *Social Darwinism in American thought*. *Journal of Economic Behavior & Organization* 71, pp. 37–51.

Levallois, C. 2011. Why were biological analogies in economics "a bad thing"? Edith Penrose's battles against social Darwinism and McCarthyism. *Science in Context* 24 #4, pp. 465–485.

Leydesdorff, L. & D.M. Dubois 2004. Anticipation in social systems: the incursion and communication of meaning. *International Journal of Computing Anticipatory Systems* 15, pp. 203–216.

Louie, A.H. 1983. Categorical system theory. *Bulletin of Mathematical Biology* 45 #6, pp. 1047–1072.

——— 2006. (M,R)-systems and their realizations. *Axiomathes* 16, pp. 35–64.

——— 2008. Functional entailment and immanent causation in relational biology. *Axiomathes* 18, pp. 289–302.

——— 2010. Robert Rosen's anticipatory systems. *Foresight* 12 #3, pp. 18–29.

Louie, A.H. & R. Poli 2011. The spread of hierarchical cycles. *International Journal of General Systems* 40 #3, pp. 237–261.

Marshall, A. 1898. Mechanical and biological analogies in economics. In A.C. Pigou (ed.), *Memorials of Alfred Marshall*, pp. 312–318. Macmillan & Co., 1925.

——— 1920. *Principles of economics*. Macmillan, 8/e.

McQuade, T.J. 2019. Organization, anticipation, and closure in markets and science. *Cosmos + Taxis* 6 #6&7, pp. 1–18.

Montévil, M. & M. Mossio 2015. Biological organisation as closure of constraints. *Journal of Theoretical Biology* 372, pp. 179–191.

Mossio, M., M. Montévil, & G. Longo 2016. Theoretical principles for biology: organization. *Progress in Biophysics and Molecular Biology* 122 #1, pp. 24–35.

Pattee, H.H. 2007. Laws, constraints, and the modeling relation – history and interpretations. *Chemistry and Biodiversity* 4, pp. 2272–2295.

Penrose, E.T. 1952. Biological analogies in the theory of the firm. *American Economic Review* 42 #5, pp. 804–819.

Piaget, J. 1967. *Biology and knowledge: an essay on the relations between organic regulations and cognitive processes*. University of Chicago Press, 1971.

Popper, K.R. 1963. *Conjectures and refutations: the growth of scientific knowledge*. Routledge & Kegan Paul.

——— 1972. *Objective knowledge: an evolutionary approach*. Clarendon Press.

Rescher, N. 2000. *Process philosophy: a survey of basic issues*. University of Pittsburgh Press.

Rosen, R. 1973. Is there a unified mathematical biology? In R. Rosen (ed.), *Foundations of Mathematical Biology* 3, pp. 361–393. Academic Press.

——— 1974. Planning, management, policies, and strategies: four fuzzy concepts. *International Journal of General Systems* 1, pp. 245–252.

——— 1975. Biological systems as paradigms for adaptation. In R.H. Day & T. Groves (eds.), *Adaptive economic models*, pp. 39–72. Academic Press.

——— 1985. *Anticipatory systems: philosophical, mathematical & methodological foundations*. Pergamon Press.

——— 1991. *Life itself: a comprehensive inquiry into the nature, origin, and fabrication of life*. Columbia University Press.

Seibt, J. 2018. Process philosophy. In E.N. Zalta (ed.), *The Stanford Encyclopedia of Philosophy*. https://plato.stanford.edu/archives/win2018/entries/process-philosophy.

Siekmann, I. 2018. An applied mathematician's perspective on Rosennean complexity. *Ecological Complexity* 35, pp. 28–38.

Wells, A.J. 2006. In defense of mechanism. *Ecological psychology* 18 #1, pp. 39–65.

Zhang, L., R.A. Williams, & D. Gatherer 2016. Rosen's (M,R) system in Unified Modelling Language. *BioSystems* 139, 29–36.

6 Economic systems[1]

The conception of the market economy as a "catallaxy" animates the work not only of Austrian economists such as Mises (1949) and Hayek (1975, 1976) but also of many others – Buchanan (1979), for example. A catallaxy is understood to comprise an order of interacting agents who engage in the voluntary exchange of claims to property. Organized markets are a systemic arrangement that allows buyers and sellers, cross-sectionally and through time, to regularly exchange with each other. Such catallactic activity generates a unique kind of output in the form of market prices. The separate activities of many individuals, each motivated by their respective goals and intentions, interact in ways that produce at every moment a constellation of market prices for goods and services – an outcome that, as Böhm (1994) puts it, could not have been generated in any other way. This is because, as Buchanan & Vanberg (1991) remind us, the catallaxy's capacity to produce such prices is an emergent property of the system and such outcomes cannot be defined independently of the process itself.

This conception of a market economy abjures the usage of a formal device such as the Walrasian auctioneer or an idealized central planner as a *deus ex machina* who ensures coordination, and points instead to the coordinating mechanisms, supported by evolved institutions of property, contract, and exchange, endogenous to the system itself. The preeminent characteristic of catallactic functioning is that the personal, often private, knowledge of each individual in the market undergoes a transformation as a consequence of catallactic interactions, producing, as an emergent byproduct of those interactions, marketable goods and market prices that tend to become consistent with the abilities and expressed individual preferences of market participants.

It is often stated that markets work uniquely well to coordinate behavior in a societally beneficial way because markets alone possess a price system and other systems do not.[2] But this doesn't get to the heart of the matter – the price system is indeed crucial in markets in that it is the vehicle through which the feedback effects of prior transactions act on current and contemplated ones. Yet since it is, in turn, an emergent effect of those processes, it depends on the ways in which those processes interact within the market context. At the most general level, what is crucial for adaptation in social systems of all sorts is not the specific ability to form prices but the ability to generate feedback effects which constrain self-interest while at the same time encouraging innovation and growth. In other

DOI: 10.4324/9781003336150-6

long-lasting arrangements – such as science – no prices are generated, and yet there is coordination of behavior in a societally beneficial way because the feedback effects from the characteristic processes of the order both constrain the interactions of the system's members and encourage creativity. It is the structure of the system that matters and the capability of that structure to adapt to changes in external environment and to grow in a stable manner which is sustainable in the long term. Attention to the structural characteristics of systems such as markets provides an understanding of how the effects of the intra-system processes work to generate the observed emergent systemic properties and how these properties enable systemic anticipation and adaptation.

The structure of market systems

A "market system", as defined here in very general terms, is a complex of people in their roles of producers, entrepreneurs, buyers, and sellers engaging in activity mediated by the institutions of property, contract, exchange, and money.[3] Observable as an emergent[4] result of the exchange interactions is the formation of a "price structure" – most obviously, a set of generally recognized "monetary market prices" attached to specific goods and services, including capital goods,[5] each of which, while usually stable in the short run within small limits, can change as circumstances of supply and demand change. The sensitivity of the price structure to changes in external conditions and to changes in the preferences and plans of market participants makes it the obvious candidate for a structure within the system that serves as a model of the system's environment – a model that is continuously updated by environmental feedback transmitted by the agency of repeated exchange transactions.[6] Entrepreneurs within the system rely, at least in part, on price structure data in innovating plans for the production of future products and in exercising judgment (in the face of uncertainty) in assessing the feasibility of these projected production plans, and thus act as an anticipatory process affecting the system's production propensities.[7]

Exchange transactions in both consumer and capital goods (with the latter being the lion's share) are the instrument through which the system's model is continuously updated to register the state of external conditions relevant to the market system. The nature of the exchange transactions is such that their effects are generally stable enough to be useful as information – in the case of prices, for example, attempted deviations from market price tend to encounter negative feedback in that, all other things being equal, a seller asking a price higher than the market price tends to lose business. But if all other things are not equal, if real circumstances of supply and demand change, then market prices change in adaptation to the new environment. Similarly with the structure of capital goods – entrepreneurial success or failure, ultimately shown up in the course of exchange transactions reflecting consumer preferences,[8] will result in changes not only to the prices of capital goods but also to their appraisals as complements and substitutes within the capital structure. The market system is firmly anchored to the environment in that its production processes are sensitive to real changes in resource availabilities, and such changes are reflected in changes to the price structure.[9]

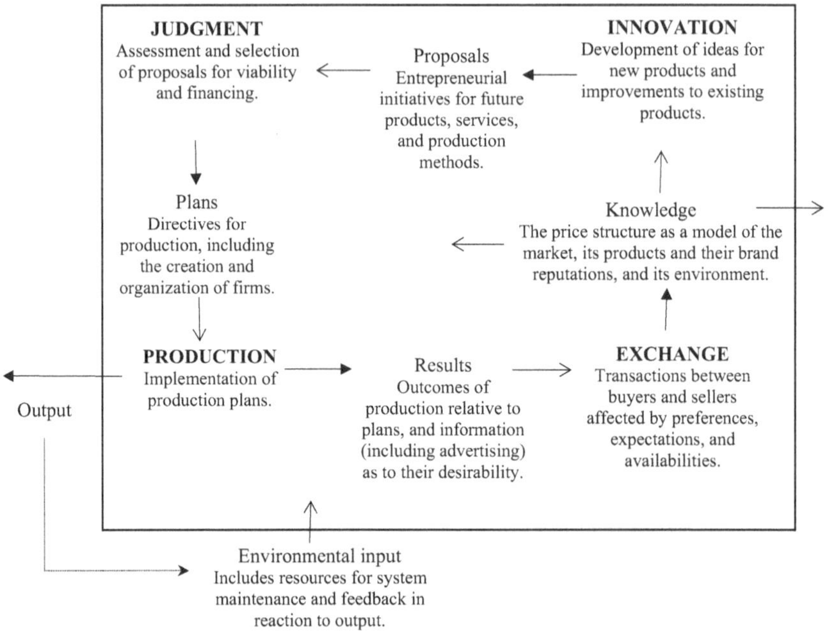

Figure 6.1 Process organization in a market system.

Given these identifications of market process and structure, the overall process organization of the market system can be represented as shown in Figure 6.1 as a functionally closed but materially open anticipatory system.[10]

The goods generated by production processes are the obvious inputs (along with services) to the exchange processes. But the market system's output to the environment includes not only these material goods but also advertising and any material side-effects of production – such as pollution – and this can generate feedback from the environment to which some market participants may be sensitive.

The model of the market as an anticipatory system has a significant virtue – it relates and puts into context some important observations and hypotheses about the functioning of the market system, showing them to be consequences of the fundamental process organization. These involve aspects of economies which appear to be of obvious significance for understanding how markets actually work, but yet have no obvious place in the usual mechanical macroeconomic models featuring quantities in equilibrium.[11] In fact, the history of economic thought is replete with observations, studies, and hypotheses centering on such phenomena as entrepreneurship and the epistemic characteristics of markets, all of which clearly say something important about the functioning of markets, and yet none of this finds its way into mainstream macroeconomic theory. They, as Klein (2008, p. 175) puts it, "are viewed as interesting, but idiosyncratic, insights that do not easily generalize to other contexts and problems" and certainly present difficulties in rendering in mathematical terms. For example, consider the following classics:

- Schumpeter's vision of the entrepreneur as "the pivot on which everything turns".[12] It is the entrepreneur, according to Schumpeter, whose innovations and judgments drive economic development. Entrepreneurship is a process that is both creative, resulting in the emergence of new production possibilities, and destructive, rendering obsolete existing methods and products and the firms which depend on them for profitability.[13] Significantly, it is portrayed as a process internal to the economic system. Although Schumpeter (1954, p. 529) was correct in noting that economists had never "accomplished the impossible feat of overlooking the most colorful figure in the capitalist process", modern macroeconomics comes very close to that accomplishment, rendering entrepreneurial effects as unexplained technological shocks impinging on the economic system from without.
- McCloskey's explanation of the "great enrichment". McCloskey (2010) focuses on what she correctly thinks should be the major phenomenon requiring economic explanation: the increase of real income per head since 1800 by a factor of something between 16 and 100 (but probably closer to the latter), an increase which (together with its timing) is not explainable in terms of either supporting institutions or efficiency increases. After analyzing, and rejecting, a long list of possibilities, her explanation (p. 394) is that "a pair of positive externalities", specifically, "a new dignity for the bourgeoisie in its dealings and a new liberty for the bourgeoisie to innovate in economic affairs" which emerged in Holland and England in the 1700s are the crucial factors at play. The ability for entrepreneurs to be tolerated and accorded sufficient respect and forbearance meant that practically creative people could respectably, and with expectation of profitability, attempt to implement their innovative plans and conjectures. That the economic growth unleashed by this freeing of the entrepreneurial process was unprecedented underlines the essential role of that process in the functioning of the market system.
- Mises' "problem of economic calculation". Mises (1920) explained in detail the indispensability of market prices for the entrepreneurial assessment of possible production plans, a process he called "economic calculation". He pointed out that the ability to "calculate" based on market prices (p. 14) "affords us a guide through the oppressive plenitude of economic potentialities ... Without it, all production involving processes stretching well back in time and all the longer roundabout processes of capitalistic production would be gropings in the dark."[14] In short, without a price structure which is the result of market activity, a rational system of production processes is not possible.
- Hayek's "knowledge problem". Hayek (1945, pp. 519–520) identifies "the economic problem of society" as "a problem of how to secure the best use of resources known to any members of society, for ends whose relative importance only these individuals know", i.e., "a problem of the utilization of knowledge not given to anyone in its totality". He (pp. 526–527) points to the price system, the process of monetary exchange under the norms of property and contract, as ameliorating the problem by providing the function of "communicating information ... which enables individual producers ... to adjust

> their activities to changes of which they may never know more than is reflected in the price movement". The process is one of learning about environmental inputs, generating knowledge about environmental changes, not through analysis by individuals but as the emergent result of continuous exchange transactions.

The picture of market process organization developed here integrates all of these prescient contributions into a single schema. The central importance of the entrepreneurial processes of innovation and judgment described by Schumpeter, the potency of which for productive economic growth and prosperity is pointed to by McCloskey, is linked to, and made possible by, the existence of the price system as explained by Mises, which, in turn, is characterized by Hayek as the result of a process in which the local, idiosyncratic, and dispersed knowledge of individuals of the state of their environment as they assess it is rendered into a useful form that is widely accessible. The closed circle of the processes of innovation, judgment, production, and exchange, informed by an internally generated model of the environment, constitutes the basic organization of the market as an anticipatory system.

Firms and markets

It is a given in modern business literature that, in order to be successful, a firm must have a good working knowledge of both its available capabilities and the environment in which it operates, such knowledge being the basis not only for successful production but also for anticipation of the reception of the products the firm may decide to supply to that market. The question arises, then, of how such knowledge is learned, how it is instantiated within the firm, how it is deployed in product planning, and how it is adapted with ongoing experience. For a firm (usually a small firm) controlled by a dominant individual, there is little mystery – it is this individual who learns by observation and experience, the knowledge is in his head, and his are the expectations and the product decisions and the reactions to market feedback. But when a firm grows beyond the direct control of an individual, the questions become more complicated and in a significant sense it is the firm itself which learns, which anticipates, which decides, and which adapts.[15] Current economic and sociological theories of entrepreneurship and the firm either do not address such epistemological questions or do not fully develop them into a model of the firm as a social arrangement capable of operating, learning, surviving, and maintaining itself within an uncertain environment. What is proposed here is a systemic theory of the firm which neither assumes that a firm is simply a vehicle for enabling the actions of a single entrepreneurial individual nor anthropomorphizes it as a super-individual but treats it as an adaptive system of mutually compatible processes within which learning and anticipation can emerge.

Figure 6.2, following the general model of an anticipatory system, shows the firm and its links to its environment, and portrays the firm in terms of a cycle of processes organized to effect learning, innovation, judgment, and production.

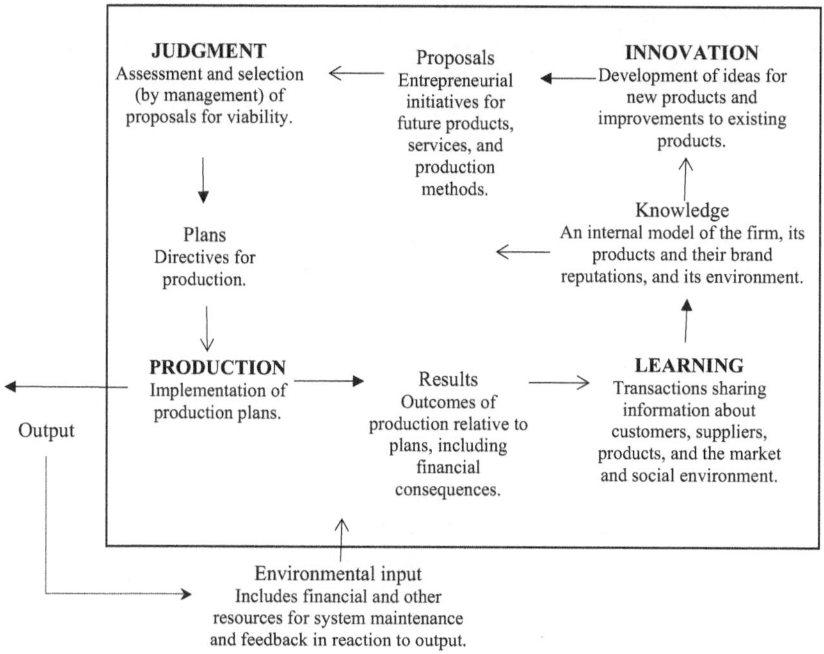

Figure 6.2 Process organization in a firm.

This organization of processes represents a firm as an anticipatory system incorporating and maintaining a working model of itself and its environment, a model which can be accessed internally within the system to project the anticipated effects of future actions taken by the system in the context of possible future environmental states. This model constitutes the firm's knowledge.[16] Reaction from the environment is taken into account in the processes which update the model, and this, in turn, provides an enhanced picture of the environment upon which innovative actors can base proposals which condition the propensities of the system to act on the environment. The processes of interest here are by no means the only processes taking place within the firm – under the heading of "production" are processes involving construction, sales, and the deployment of the firm's current products and services, financial accounting, facility maintenance, and management of and training for such operations; these are examples of activity not under further consideration. The processes of concern are those that have the emergent effect of endowing the firm with adaptability in the face of the changing state of the environment and its reactions to the firm's activity to which, for its own survival, it must be sensitive.

Actual multi-person firms vary greatly in the implementation of these epistemic processes and the internal model of the environment. This seemingly banal observation is actually quite interesting, for in some other forms of human interaction which exhibit the emergence of anticipation, the processes for generating the system's knowledge have become solidly entrenched customs. In modern markets, as we have seen, the exchange of property for money in a competitive environment is the customary transaction, and repeated execution of this transaction, involving many items of property and observable by other market participants, results in the emergence of what is known as "the price structure", which is, from the point of view of the market system, a mutable model of the market's environment of actual and potential resources and buyer and seller preferences. But no analogous customary transaction types have arisen (yet) in the case of firms.

As larger corporations replaced smaller family firms in the 19th and 20th centuries, the major form of business firm organization that emerged was the administrative hierarchy which, particularly (but not exclusively) in its instantiations in government departments, is called "bureaucracy". Max Weber, the preeminent theorist of bureaucracy, characterized it as a pyramidal arrangement of strictly defined levels, with each level managed by the one above it and responsible for executing specialized, well-defined, and documented functions – a rule-based machine-like arrangement with clear chain of management command and standardized division of labor. While Weber stressed bureaucracy's positive potential for technical efficiency and stability,[17] Robert Merton pointed to its darker side in which adherence to strict rules becomes an end rather than a means,[18] and since then there have been extensive discussions on bureaucracy's merits and shortcomings. But the point of interest here has to do with the potential for bureaucratic procedures within corporate hierarchies to generate actionable knowledge of the firm's environment. Any observations, insights, or ideas coming from individuals at any level within the organization can only be communicated to the manager at the level above, from whence the information may or may not filter upwards, actionable only when, probably in attenuated and reinterpreted form, it reaches the manager with permission to act on it.[19] In terms of its ability to anticipate and adapt to change, the bureaucratic organization can be an improvement on an isolated individual, but only to the extent that the filter of level-by-level transmission retains the fidelity of the information. Of course, as is the case in all private firms, the measure of profitability can be an indicator of successful adaptation, but it is a lagging indicator.

In a slowly changing environment, a limited capacity for learning, innovation, and adaptation may not be a big problem. But, especially since the 1970s, the business environment has become one of much more rapid change and increased competition, due especially to the emergence of computers and communication technology, to the trend toward globalization, to advances in transportation, and to increasing pressure from institutional investors.[20] In such an environment, the ability to anticipate and adapt becomes much more important for survival, so that the bureaucratic arrangement's deficiencies in this area have become apparent, and the business management literature is replete with studies of organizational experimentation as companies react to the new environmental realities.[21]

There are recurring themes that have emerged from this organizational experimentation. While these can be characterized as moves to dismantle the strict hierarchy to some extent, reducing the number of levels, enabling the formation of project teams from what were different areas of the firm and thus allowing for direct, sometimes *ad hoc*, interactions between people at various levels, and allowing these smaller units increased authority and responsibility, the significant underlying effects have been to foster increased communication within the firm,[22] especially with regard to understanding the firm's culture and capabilities, its customers, and its environment (market, social, political, and natural), and to inculcate a new tolerance for idiosyncratic ideas and suggestions, some of which may lead to innovations in product, service, and internal procedures.[23]

The model of the anticipatory firm provides a structure within which these developments can be related in a coherent manner. The firm's internal model of its environment and of itself is not a physical thing; it is the result of repeated interactions between people in the firm communicating observations, ideas, and opinions.[24] Like the price structure in a market system, it is neither one person's opinion nor the average of all, but is emergent from transactions in which those opinions are exercised. To be effective for reliable knowledge generation, it is necessary that these transactions involve the possibilities of benefits and costs to the participants – most effectively in the forms of reputation and status, but in general providing a means by which the individuals involved pursue happiness as they see it in the context of the firm. The underlying openness and tolerance may have been policy initiated by the firm's founder and supported by subsequent management and therefore describable as idiosyncratic "company culture", but to stop the description there is to forestall understanding of the necessary transactions and the knowledge-generating possibilities that can emerge from them.

Individuals working within the firm have, depending on their particular roles, day-to-day contact with the firm's customers, its products and their production methods, and the firm's internal procedures. They also have their own experiences and observations from living in the greater society. They can bring to the firm their individual knowledge and ideas derived from their local experience.[25] This input may be idiosyncratic, incomplete, and even contradictory, but if it is communicated and assessed widely within the firm as a result of individuals repeatedly engaging in interactions from which there is a possibility of reputational or other gain (or loss), then what emerges as a common understanding will be the firm's knowledge, its model of itself and its environment.[26] One of management's roles is to enable and encourage transactions which have this emergent property.[27]

Based on this understanding (which, by the nature of its generation, is continually being updated), some entrepreneurial individuals (or teams) within the firm may come up with ideas for product, service, or internal procedure enhancement,[28] and again these may be communicated and analyzed in interactions in which personal gain might be the outcome. Determining which, if any, of the emerging proposals can be implemented, and where and when they should be implemented, calls for judgment, and again there will be interactions (probably among senior individuals) that implement this particular function. It is to be emphasized that these judgments, the end result of the anticipatory series of processes, are not necessarily direct predictions of the future; they will be, more likely, conditional anticipations of what to do depending on what shape the future takes. In this, they are like the anticipations every individual develops – a repertoire of hopefully appropriate responses to possible future situations.

The theory of the anticipatory firm represents these epistemological activities of the firm as a linked cycle of processes implementing learning, innovation, and judgment in which the output from one is a necessary input to the next. The business experiments which are currently underway can be seen (from the vantage point of the theory) as attempts to implement processes of that kind – fostering communication, diffusing responsibility, ensuring contact between what used to be different departments, creating small project teams in which each member's contribution is known and can be assessed and appreciated, providing tools and time for imagining and discussing possible future scenarios, and rewarding innovative thinking. What specific arrangements and modes of interaction eventually emerge from this ongoing experimentation as best serving the purposes of firm survival and stable growth is not yet clear, nor is whether what does emerge will be widely applicable to all firms or will vary depending on firm size or industry type. What the theory of the anticipatory firm does predict, however, is that these arrangements, whatever their specific form, will involve widespread participation within the firm, and will involve cooperative interactions which are sufficiently competitive that there is incentive to participate and to put forward observations and ideas for consideration and assessment.

Entrepreneurship in firms and markets

The question of what, exactly, is "entrepreneurship" has been addressed many times in economics, sociology, entrepreneurship studies, and business and management literature, and quite a long list of definitions and characterizations have been proposed. Peter Klein has classified the extant perspectives on entrepreneurship[29] as either occupational (dealing with the characteristics of "entrepreneurial" individuals), structural (dealing with characteristics of "entrepreneurial" firms), or functional (dealing with the characteristics of "entrepreneurial" processes). The functional category is more general in terms of the locus of entrepreneurship,[30] but within this category the entrepreneurial process has been characterized in various ways: as alertness, as judgment, as innovation, as coordination. Reasonable arguments can be made for all of these, and there is a large literature making, discussing, and comparing the particular cases. One is tempted to invoke the parable of the blind men and the elephant[31] here, but a more interesting resolution, suggested by the theory of the anticipatory firm, is that there is not just a single elephant to consider.

Let us define an entrepreneurial process as any of the processes leading from knowledge to decision under uncertainty in an anticipatory system. There are a number of processes which take place within an economy that can be labeled as entrepreneurial under this definition. And these can operate at the level of the individual, the level of the firm, and the level of the market. For individuals, these processes are normal brain functions, and it can legitimately be said that individual entrepreneurial behavior, i.e., behavior resulting from entrepreneurial processes, is ubiquitous.[32] But that is hardly helpful, and it makes more sense to single out for attention a subset of individual entrepreneurial behavior as that which constitutes the driving force, the efficient cause, of entrepreneurial processes in a social system. In the model of the anticipatory firm, those processes are labeled as "innovation" and "judgment", and so behavior contributing to the innovation process (innovative behavior) and behavior contributing to the judgment process (exercising judgment) are both entrepreneurial behavior, albeit in different contexts within the firm.[33]

Entrepreneurship can also be discussed in terms of the market in which firms are embedded. From the perspective of the market system, the entrepreneurial processes are those of market-level innovation and judgment which may, but do not necessarily, take place within firms, and entrepreneurial behavior is the activity of individuals whose actions constitute the efficient causes of these processes. It is at the market level that innovative ideas judged to be viable may result in the creation of new firms.

In tying entrepreneurship to uncertainty, there is no implication here that uncertainty is monolithic – short planning horizons face lower uncertainty than longer ones and, generally speaking, plans with contingency provisions face less uncertainty than more specific ones. These are margins of adjustment for entrepreneurs, as Koppl & Butos (2001, pp. 83–84) point out.

To summarize, entrepreneurship is behavior furthering any social process which bridges existing knowledge and forward-looking decision in an environment of uncertainty. It is clearly manifested within firms, but it is also obviously manifest at the market level, not least in the creation of firms. It is observed at both the firm level and the market level, and it appears in innovation-type processes and in judgment-type processes. This multiplicity of perspectives and contexts has made it impossible to convincingly pin it to particular characteristics of individuals or firms, or to uniquely describe it as a particular process.

Money and banking

Banks are firms, but they are special in one respect: their on-demand liabilities function as money. It is widely assumed and actively contended that the provision of money in a market economy is necessarily a function of government, administered by a central bank with a monopoly of note issue, with ordinary banks constrained as to the nature and minimum amount of the reserves required to back their checking deposit liabilities. But this is a mistaken view,[34] as it is quite possible to conceive of a banking system quite independent of government, capable not only of intermediating credit and providing money but also of reacting to – and anticipating – the varying overall demand of market participants to hold money balances.

In describing such an anticipatory banking system, we rely on the work of "free banking" theorists, especially White (1984a, 1984b) and Selgin (1988, 1997), who emphasize the incentives inherent in an unregulated banking system that encourage adjustment of the supply of money (in the form of bank notes as well as checking balances – "inside money") to the demand of holders of these liabilities without inflationary or deflationary effects stemming from the banks' activities. The underlying structure of the system is as follows:

- Bank notes, identifiable as liabilities of the issuing bank, and checks, drawn on specific deposit accounts, are redeemable on demand for a commodity reserve money[35] ("outside money") at a predetermined fixed rate of exchange (although customer withdrawals from checking accounts would normally be paid in bank notes).

- Banks have no prespecified requirements for holding reserves of outside money against their liabilities; redemptions of checks and notes are processed through a clearing house where claims of rival banks are netted out against each other at regular periods and individual banks are presented with net clearing amounts for payment denominated in outside money.
- There is no requirement for banks to accept the notes of rival banks at par or even to accept them at all.
- Banks are free to accept deposits, make loans, and set interest rates as they deem fit.
- There are no regulatory entry or exit constraints or requirements.

The system's apprehension and anticipation of changes in money demand, and its resulting adjustments of monetary output, are made by the accumulated activities of individual banks, each acting competitively as profit-seeking enterprises, with their own understanding of local conditions augmented by the more global knowledge of note redemption volumes and net clearings provided by the clearing process. How successfully individual banks respond, given the uncertainty inherent in the incomplete information at their disposal, depends on their entrepreneurial abilities.

Figure 6.3, following the general model of an anticipatory system, shows the organization of the sets of processes animating this type of banking system.

Clearing is the process through which the banking system learns of the market demand for inside money and the financial stability of individual banks. A general increase (decrease) in money demand will manifest itself in the clearing process as a gross decrease (increase) in the volume of clearings without any change in net clearings. An increase (decrease) in the demand to hold liabilities of a particular bank will manifest itself as a decrease (increase) in the net clearings for that bank. A persistent experience of adverse clearings for a particular bank is a signal that either the bank's reputation for financial stability among market participants has suffered or that the bank has attempted to issue more liabilities than the market chooses to bear.[36]

In this way, the clearing process generates knowledge of the banking system itself in terms of the pressures on and performance of member banks and of the monetary environment that the system is currently facing in terms of changes in the desire to hold checking and banknote liabilities. Banking entrepreneurs can use this knowledge in proposing and deciding on changes in reserve levels, loan and deposit interest rates, and loan management and other banking services intended to most profitably address anticipated future monetary conditions. Some of this knowledge – including note-discounting data, for example – may also be published outside the banking system, providing market participants with information on the characteristics of individual banks.

The knowledge generated in the clearing process serves not only as a picture of the current monetary environment and of developing trends, but also as an indicator of the success or otherwise of entrepreneurs' previous actions. It can supply direct negative feedback to individual banks in that the consequence of overissue

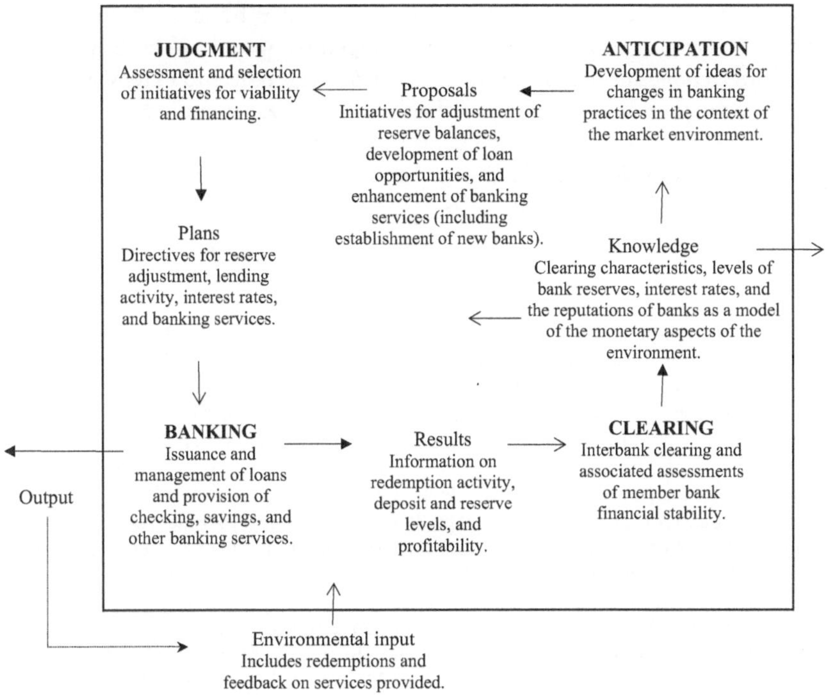

Figure 6.3 Process organization in a free banking system.

leading to adverse clearings is loss of reserves, increasing the perceived riskiness of the bank and providing an incentive to reduce liabilities. Even in the unlikely case of overissue by all banks in the system in concert, there will be negative feedback in the form of the increased variance of clearings as a result of the larger volume of clearances, indicating that an increase in reserves would be prudent and that the excess issue was ill-advised.[37] In cases where a bank is experiencing net favorable clearings and as a result its reserves are growing in excess of what the bank considers prudent to hold as precaution against redemptions, the obvious indication would be that the bank is in a position to issue more liabilities. It should be noted, however, that these are not mechanical reactions; they are an input to the entrepreneurial processes of envisioning possible *future* monetary environments, proposing strategies for how to most profitably operate in those hypothetical environments and, given the uncertainty inherent in any prediction of the future, exercising judgment in selecting actual courses of action. Without an efficient, centralized clearing process, the reaction of banks to money demand changes would be more cumbersome and slower. Also, the knowledge generated within the banking system, including as it does information about the state of competitor banks and not simply the state of one's own bank – and therefore giving a more global picture of the monetary environment – serves to reduce (but not eliminate) the uncertainty that attends future-directed planning.

Although such a banking system nowhere exists, it is based on historical episodes[38] of relative free banking involving competitive note issue by banks. And, apart from lacking the ability to issue notes and being subject to extensive regulation, the operation of modern deposit banks is recognizable in the above description. The point of dealing with it here is that it provides a benchmark of system operation against which the effects of government intervention can be assessed, a task taken up in a later chapter.

Notes

1 This chapter contains text previously published in McQuade & Butos (2005) with permission from Springer, and in McQuade (2019, 2023).

2 See, for example, Barry (1982, par. B.112): "In a market there is a mechanism, the price system, which does co-ordinate the actions of economic agents to produce an efficient order … but there is no similar mechanism at work in a legal system."

3 In line with the high level of abstraction that characterizes this discussion, the legal, security, and financial institutions which underpin the processes of production and exchange and are vital for their proper functioning are not included here – they are assumed to be operative in the background and to function adequately enough for it to be unproblematic to focus only on the higher-level processes they support.

4 The term "emergent" is used here informally to refer to a systemic property which arises from the interactions of system components. But it is not a simple concept. For an examination of the subtly different ways in which the concept is applied in economics and social theory, see Harper & Lewis (2012) and the articles in the volume for which that is the introduction.

5 Of course, other widely understood appraisals, like brand reputation, also emerge in this way, and calling the emergent mapping "the price structure" is not intended to imply an oversimplification of its complex structure. Less obvious, but no less important as a component of that mapping is what Lachmann (1956, p. 53) has called "the capital structure", the sensitive and shifting arrangement of capital goods as entrepreneurially appraised complements and substitutes for each other. The identification of the capital structure as a component of a mutable model of the environment is consistent with Horwitz's (2008) analysis.

6 The price structure has been characterized as a "classification" of environmental inputs – see McQuade (2007, p. 62): "The … transactions (characterized by transfers of goods and observable exchange prices) between the market participants … are induced by stimuli from environmental conditions conditioned by the preferences and creativity of the market participants themselves. They … result, indirectly, in a classification of the various stimuli currently impinging on the market system, a classification embodied in the array of market goods and their market prices." A classification of a set of phenomena is no more nor less than a type of model of the phenomena.

7 See McQuade & Butos (2005, pp. 343–344): "The market has, in effect, functioned as an anticipatory mechanism triggered by a current stimulus … that has conditioned it to respond in ways that take account of the future. … While it is clear that part of the process involves regular human insight into the future, it is at the market level … that we observe a manifestation of the anticipatory aspects of the system as it responds to environmental change. … For the market economy, these adjustment responses are instantiated by market mechanisms in which entrepreneurial activity and time markets play decisive roles."

8 As Harper (1996, p. 286) puts it, highlighting the bottom-up nature of the process in Popperian terms: "the refutation of entrepreneurial conjectures is a highly decentralized activity which does not involve an organized group or collective body representing consumers. Rather it results from a sufficiently large number of targeted consumers individually deciding not to purchase an entrepreneur's product offering."

9 Hayek (1945, p. 526) illustrates this point in the course of pointing out the efficacy of the price system in providing, in a usable form, information as to circumstances about which most market participants would have no means of knowing otherwise.

10 It is to be emphasized that this is a high-level picture of the functional organization of a market system, not of the movement of physical things within the system. It can be contrasted with the old standard circular flow diagram, which depicts an economy solely in terms of the movements of materials – goods and money – and in so doing represents the economy as a purely mechanical system.

11 As Schumpeter (1942, p. 86) eloquently put it, in the context of describing how the standard economic theory treats "competition within a rigid pattern of invariant conditions, methods of production and forms of industrial organization" in an equilibrium setting, and thereby misses the dynamic creative and destructive aspects of real-world competition: "Now a theoretical construction which neglects this essential element of the case neglects all that is most typically capitalist about it; even if correct in logic as well as in fact, it is like *Hamlet* without the Danish prince."

12 See Schumpeter (1954, p. 530): "[Although he] did not see all its analytic possibilities [J.B. Say] did realize, to some extent, that a greatly improved theory of the economic process might be derived by making the entrepreneur in the analytic schema what he is in capitalist reality, the pivot on which everything turns."

13 See Schumpeter (1942, p. 83): "[Capitalism is a process] that incessantly revolutionizes the economic structure *from within*, incessantly destroying the old one, incessantly creating a new one. This process of Creative Destruction is the essential fact about capitalism. It is what capitalism consists in and what every capitalist concern has got to live in."

14 Mises (1920, pp. 34–35) exposed the utopian nature of socialist theorizing: "All socialist systems … proceed from the assumption that in a socialist society a conflict between the interests of the particular and general could not possibly arise. Everybody will act in his own interest in giving of his best because he participates in the product of all economic activity. … But even if we for the moment grant that … each individual in a socialist society will exert himself with the same zeal as he does today in a society where he is subjected to the pressure of free competition, there still remains the problem of measuring the result of economic activity in a socialist commonwealth which does not permit of any economic calculation. We cannot act economically if we are not in a position to understand economizing."

15 According to Roberts (2004, p. 283), "in a firm of any size, the knowledge of how things really work, how customers really behave, how choices really interact, is highly dispersed." While this is true in general, there is no assumption that the knowledge is dispersed uniformly, and different firms will very in this respect. There are, indeed, very well-known (but rare) instances of large firms in which the behavior of the firm is dominated by an entrepreneurial individual – Apple in the Steve Jobs era being an example.

16 Foss & Klein (2014) properly dismiss the idea that a systemic description implies some sort of a group mind: "Thus, the notions that firms or whole economies are distributed knowledge systems mean that the set of agents comprising these entities somehow can be said to collectively possess knowledge that no single agent possesses. This does not amount to asserting the existence of mysterious supra-individual 'collective minds'. Knowledge still ultimately resides in the heads of individuals; however, when this knowledge is somehow combined, it means that considered as a system, the agents possess knowledge that they do not possess if separated. However, nobody possesses all this knowledge in its totality." This totality, this individual knowledge "somehow combined" by interactions comprising the processes within the firm, is what is regarded here as the firm's knowledge.

17 Weber (1922, p. 214) having described bureaucracy as an "ideal type", and aware that implementations of it can fall short of the ideal, stressed its superiority to alternate administrative structures, claiming that fully developed bureaucracy compares with them "exactly as does the machine with the non-mechanical modes of production.

Precision, speed, unambiguity, knowledge of the files, continuity, discretion, unity, strict subordination, reduction of friction and of material and personal costs – these are raised to the optimum in the strictly bureaucratic administration."

18 Merton (1940, p. 565): "If the bureaucracy is to operate successfully, it must attain a high degree of reliability of behavior, an unusual degree of conformity with prescribed patterns of action. Hence, the fundamental importance of discipline … Discipline, readily interpreted as conformance with regulations, whatever the situation, is seen not as a measure designed for specific purposes but becomes an immediate value in the life-organization of the bureaucrat. This emphasis, resulting from the displacement of the original goals, develops into rigidities and an inability to adjust readily. Formalism, even ritualism, ensues with an unchallenged insistence upon punctilious adherence to formalized procedures. This may be exaggerated to the point where primary concern with conformity to the rules interferes with the achievement of the purposes of the organization, in which case we have the familiar phenomenon of the technicism or red tape of the official."

19 Tullock (1965, pp. 148–152) uses the game of "whispering down the lane" to illustrate the distortions in information transfer in a hierarchy in either direction.

20 According to Roberts (2004, p. 2): "Falling barriers to international trade and investment, the rise of information technology (especially the Internet), and improved transportation mean that a firm's competitors are not just the old local rivals, but may be from anywhere. With more competition, the need to improve performance increases. These same developments also open new opportunities to do business far from home, and the new organizational designs support taking advantage of these opportunities. Capital markets, too, are increasing the performance pressures on firms. Especially in the United States, but increasingly elsewhere as well, the increased power of institutional investors and their increased willingness to use this power are pushing companies to do better." Another factor often cited – for example, by Drucker (1970), Pinchot & Pinchot (1993), and de Geus (1997) – is the emerging importance of "knowledge workers" who chafe under the rigid bureaucratic strictures and whose productivity is enhanced if given more freedom to use their imaginations.

21 See the case studies detailed in Bahrami (1992), de Geus (1997), Fulmer (2000), Roberts (2004), Ruigrok *et al.* (1999), Whittington *et al.* (1999), and Pettigrew *et al.* (2001). The latter is the introduction to a full journal issue on studies of organizational experimentation. The thrust in this research project is to get beyond platitudes and investigate the implementations of "new forms of organization". As Ruigrok *et al.* (1999, p. 41) put the challenge they are addressing: "According to one persistent argument, we are currently witnessing a major break from the multidivisional form of organisation seen in the past. Emerging organisational forms … would be characterised in particular by less horizontal and vertical differentiation, and by more ad hoc internal linkages. However, beyond certain well-known examples …, the incidence and international diffusion of these new organisational forms or new modes of organising have yet to be established."

22 Peter Drucker was an early exponent of hierarchy dismantling, and he emphasized the virtues of, and necessity for, communication throughout an organization. Drucker (1970, p. 19) asserts that "Communications in organization demands that the masses, whether they be employees or students, share in the responsibility of decisions to the fullest possible amount." And (p. 22): "Communications in organization … are not a *means* of organization. They are a *mode* of organization."

23 Roberts (2004, pp. 1–2) gives a good overview of the types of organizational rearrangements that are being tried: "They have eliminated layers of management and associated staff positions, redefined the units into which they divide themselves internally, dispersed functional experts to the business units, and increased the authority and accountability of line managers. By these measures, coupled with improved information and measurement systems and redesigned performance management systems, they have sought to increase the speed of decision-making and to tap the knowledge and energy

of their employees in ways that have not been tried before. To facilitate coordination and learning, they have experimented with linking people in different parts of their organizations directly, so that communications are more horizontal and not just up and down the hierarchy. Many have also tried to redefine the nature of the relationship they have with their employees while redesigning jobs and the very nature of work."

24 Obviously, the various individuals within a firm will possess tacit knowledge and skills which cannot be explicitly communicated. But who they communicate with, and what they communicate about, and how they communicate it will be influenced by this knowledge, and so it will indirectly contribute to the knowledge-generating process.

25 Grant (1996) provides a good overview of considerations of transferability and appropriability of the explicit and tacit knowledge of individuals within a firm. He develops a "knowledge-based" theory of the firm in which the emphasis is on how individual specialized knowledge is integrated and applied in the firm's production processes.

26 There is an obvious parallel here with Hayek's (1945) picture the market process which enables the significance of "the particular circumstances of time and place", which are only known individually to "the man on the spot", to be made available, in the form of the price system, to market participants in general.

27 Foss *et al.* (2019, p. 53) describe this sort of management activity as "designing incentive schemes, monitoring systems, means of resolving disputes, and other mechanisms", contrasting it with management by command.

28 Kollmann *et al.* (2020) show that what they call "entrepreneurial orientation" can be present in firms in management teams below the top management levels. It emerges, as the theory in this paper would predict, where there is a shared "transactive memory" – a knowledge base that combines what the individuals know themselves with the knowledge of who knows what, which arises through communication and interaction with other individuals in the firm.

29 See Klein (2008) and Foss *et al.* (2019). To give specific examples of different perspectives: Cantillon (1755) pointed to risk tolerance and the exercise of judgment, Knight (1921) to judgment under uncertainty, Mises (1920) also to judgment under uncertainty but particularly in the form of "economic calculation", Marshall (1920) to business acumen and management ability, Schumpeter (1926) to innovativeness, Kirzner (1985) to alertness, Casson (1995) to self-confidence, Harper (1996) to drive for achievement, and Langlois (1998) to ability to communicate a vision. Shane (2003), defining entrepreneurship (p. 4) as "an activity that involves the discovery, evaluation and exploitation of opportunities to introduce new goods and services, ways of organizing, markets, processes, and raw materials through organizing efforts that previously had not existed", lists (pp. 61–177) a range of personal attributes for which there is empirical evidence that individuals engaged in activity fitting that description may possess, and (pp. 194–249) discusses strategies available to such individuals for developing and exploiting new opportunities in the face of uncertainty and information asymmetry. See also Alvarez & Barney (2007).

30 Klein (2008, p. 177) makes the point as follows: "The entrepreneurial function can be manifested in large and small firms, in old and new firms, by individuals or teams, across a variety of occupational categories, and so on. By focusing too narrowly on self-employment and start-up companies, the contemporary literature [dealing with occupational and structural concepts of entrepreneurship] may be understating the role of entrepreneurship in the economy and business organizations."

31 See https://en.wikipedia.org/wiki/Blind_men_and_an_elephant.

32 "Alertness to (subjectively perceived) opportunities" is simply a way of describing a characteristic of this ubiquitous behavior.

33 There are other contexts within the firm in which entrepreneurial behavior can be recognized. The model of the firm presented here assumes the firm's existence, and specifies the processes within the firm necessary to support anticipation. It does not address the formation of the firm, the creation and adjustment of the forms of interaction supported within the firm, the coordination of production, or the acceptance of

individuals into, and ejection of individuals from, the firm. These all involve processes leading from knowledge to decision under uncertainty, and thus qualify as entrepreneurial.

34 For a trenchant criticism of government involvement in money and banking, see Yeager (1983). Not one to mince words, Yeager begins: "On reflection, our existing monetary system must seem preposterous. It is not difficult to understand how individually plausible steps over years and centuries have brought us to where we now are, but the cumulative result remains preposterous nevertheless." See also Horwitz (2013).

35 For a conjectural history of the spontaneous emergence of commodity moneys (particularly gold and silver), see Menger (1892). The natural scarcity value of the commodity serves as the system's anchor to real factors.

36 As Selgin (1988, pp. 42–47) explains, the signal indicating overissue of banknotes by a particular bank depends on there being a significant number of banknote holders who discriminate by brand. Evidence from actual historical cases of competitive note issue (pp. 45–46) indicates that the norm is that there is an adequate level of discrimination for the overissuing bank to be identified through adverse clearing.

37 Selgin (1988, p. 82) refutes the widely held view that there are no economic forces in a free banking system to check a concerted expansion by member banks. "Under in-concert expansion no member of a system of banks expanding in unison (and in the face of an unchanged demand for money) will experience any increase in its average net reserve demand; the change in expected value of its clearing credits will be exactly equal to the change in expected value of its clearing debits. But the growth in total clearings will bring about a growth (though perhaps less than proportionate) in the *variance* of clearing debits and credits, which increases the precautionary reserve needs of every bank. Thus, given the quantity of reserve media, the demand for and turnover of inside money, and the desire of banks to protect themselves against all but a very small risk of default at the clearinghouse at any clearing session, there will be a unique equilibrium supply of inside money at any moment. It follows that spontaneous in-concert expansions will be self-correcting even without any 'internal drain' of commodity money from bank reserves."

38 The major episodes of relatively free banking cited by White, Selgin, and other free banking theorists are Scotland between 1792 and 1845, Sweden between 1831 and 1902, China between 1644 and 1911, and Canada in the 19th century. In all cases, government regulations (including restrictions on entry, reserve requirements, and branching) and grants of monopoly in note issue fundamentally altered the character and operation of the systems.

Bibliography

Alvarez, S.A. & J.B. Barney 2007. Discovery and creation: alternative theories of entrepreneurial action. *Strategic Entrepreneurship Journal* 1, pp. 33–48.

Bahrami, H. 1992. The emerging flexible organization: perspectives from Silicon Valley. In P.S. Myers (ed.), *Knowledge management and organizational design*, pp. 39–53. Butterworth-Heinemann, 1996.

Barry, N.P. 1982. The tradition of spontaneous order. *Literature of Liberty* 5 #2, pp. 7–58. http://www.econlib.org/library/Essays/LtrLbrty/bryTSOCover.html.

Böhm, S. 1994. Hayek and knowledge: some question marks. In M. Colonna, H. Hagemann, & O.F. Hamouda (eds.), *Capitalism, socialism, and knowledge: the economics of F.A. Hayek* II, pp. 160–177. Edward Elgar.

Buchanan, J.M. 1979. What should economists do? In *What should economists do?* pp. 9–17. Liberty Press.

Buchanan, J.M. & V. Vanberg 1991. The market as a creative process. *Economics and Philosophy* 7 #2, pp. 167–186.

Cantillon, R. 1755. *Essay on the nature of trade in general.* H. Higgs (tr. & ed.). Macmillan, 1931.

Casson, M. 1995. *Entrepreneurship and business culture.* Edward Elgar.

De Geus, A. 1997. *The living company: habits for survival in a turbulent business environment.* Harvard Business School Press.

Drucker, P.F. 1970. *Technology, Management, and Society.* Harper & Row.

Foss, N.J. & P.G. Klein 2014. Hayek and organizational studies. In P. Adler, P. du Gay, G. Morgan, & M. Reed (eds.), *Oxford Handbook of Sociology, Social Theory, and Organization Studies: Contemporary currents*, pp. 467–486. Oxford University Press.

Foss, N.J., P.G. Klein, & M. McCaffrey 2019. *Austrian perspectives on entrepreneurship, strategy, and organization.* Cambridge University Press.

Fulmer, W.E. 2000. *Shaping the adaptive organization.* Amacom.

Grant, R.M. 1996. Toward a knowledge-based theory of the firm. *Strategic Management Journal* 17, pp. 109–122.

Harper, D.A. 1996. *Entrepreneurship and the market process: an enquiry into the growth of knowledge.* Routledge.

Harper, D.A. & P.A. Lewis 2012. New perspectives on emergence in economics. *Journal of Economic Behavior & Organization* 82, pp. 329–337.

Hayek, F.A. 1945. The use of knowledge in society. *American Economic Review* 35 #4, pp. 519–530.

——— 1975. *Kinds of order in society.* Institute for Humane Studies.

——— 1976. *Law, legislation, and liberty 2: The mirage of social justice.* University of Chicago Press.

Horwitz, S.G. 2008. Analogous models of complexity: the Austrian theory of capital and Hayek's theory of cognition as adaptive classifying systems. *Advances in Austrian Economics* 11, pp. 143–166.

——— 2013. An introduction to US monetary policy. *Mercatus Research Papers.* https://www.mercatus.org/system/files/Horwitz_MonetaryPolicy_v2.pdf.

Kirzner, I.M. 1985. *Discovery and the capitalist process.* University of Chicago Press.

Klein, P.G. 2008. Opportunity discovery, entrepreneurial action, and economic organization. *Strategic Entrepreneurship Journal* 2, pp. 175–190.

Knight, F.H. 1921. *Risk, uncertainty, and profit.* August M. Kelley.

Kollmann, T., S. Hensellek, C. Stöckmann, J.M. Kensbock, & A. Pesch 2020. How management teams foster the transactive memory system-entrepreneurial orientation link: a domino effect model of positive team processes. *Strategic Entrepreneurship Journal* 14, pp. 683–710.

Koppl, R.G. & W.N. Butos 2001. Confidence in Keynes and Hayek: reply to Burczak. *Review of Political Economy* 13 #1, pp. 81–86.

Lachmann, L.M. 1956. *Capital and its structure.* Sheed Andrews & McMeel, 1978.

Langlois, R.N. 1998. Personal capitalism as charismatic authority: the organizational economics of a Weberian concept. *Industrial and Corporate Change* 7, pp. 195–213.

Marshall, A. 1920. *Principles of economics.* Macmillan, 8/e.

McCloskey, D.N. 2010. *Bourgeois dignity: why economics can't explain the modern world.* University of Chicago Press.

McQuade, T.J. 2007. Science and market as adaptive classifying systems. In E. Krecké, C. Krecké, & R. Koppl (eds.). *Advances in Austrian Economics* 9: *Cognition and Economics*, pp. 51–86. Elsevier.

——— 2019. Organization, anticipation, and closure in markets and science. *Cosmos + Taxis* 6 #6&7, pp. 1–18.

——— 2023. Entrepreneurship and the anticipatory firm. *Cosmos + Taxis* 11#1&2, pp. 54–70.

McQuade, T.J. & W.N. Butos 2005. The sensory order and other adaptive classifying systems. *Journal of Bioeconomics* 7 #3, pp. 335–358.

Menger, C. 1892. On the origins of money. Economic Journal 2, pp. 239–255. Reprinted by The Ludwig von Mises Institute, 2009. https://cdn.mises.org/On%20the%20Origins%20of%20Money_5.pdf.

Merton, R.K. 1940. Bureaucratic structure and personality. *Social Forces* 18 #4, pp. 560–568.

Mises, L. 1920. *Economic calculation in the socialist commonwealth*. Mises Institute, 1990. Also in F.A. Hayek (ed.), *Collectivist economic planning: critical studies on the possibilities of socialism*, pp. 87–130. Routledge, 1935.

——— 1949. *Human action*. Henry Regnery, 3/e, 1966.

Pettigrew, A.M., R.W. Woodman, & K.S. Cameron 2001. Studying organizational change and development: challenges for future research. *The Academy of Management Journal* 44 #4, pp. 697–713.

Pinchot, G. & E. Pinchot 1993. The rise and fall of bureaucracy. In P.S. Myers (ed.), *Knowledge management and organizational design*, pp. 39–53. Butterworth-Heinemann, 1996.

Roberts, J. 2004. *The modern firm: organizational design for performance and growth*. Oxford University Press.

Ruigrok, W., A.M. Pettigrew, S. Peck, & R. Whittington 1999. Corporate restructuring and new forms of organizing: evidence from Europe. *Management International Review* 39, pp. 41–64.

Schumpeter, J.A. 1926. *The theory of economic development*. R. Opie (tr.). Harvard University Press, 2/e, 1934.

——— 1942. *Capitalism, socialism, and democracy*. Harper & Row, 3/e, 1950.

——— 1954. *History of economic analysis*. Routledge.

Selgin, G. 1988. *The theory of free banking: money supply under competitive note issue*. Rowman & Littlefield.

——— 1997. *Less than zero: the case for a falling price level in a growing economy*. Institute of Economic Affairs.

Shane, S. 2003. *A general theory of entrepreneurship: the individual-opportunity nexus*. Edward Elgar.

Tullock, G. 1965. *The politics of bureaucracy*. Public Affairs Press.

Weber, M. 1922. Bureaucracy. In H.H. Gerth & C.W. Mills (eds.) *From Max Weber: essays in sociology*, pp. 196–244. Oxford University Press, 1946.

White, L.H. 1984a. *Free banking in Britain: theory, experience, and debate, 1800–1845*. Cambridge University Press.

——— 1984b. Free banking as an alternative monetary system. In *Competition and currency: essays in free banking and money*, pp. 13–47. New York University Press, 1989.

Whittington, R., A.M. Pettigrew, S. Peck, E. Fenton, & M. Conyon 1999. Change and complementarities in the new competitive landscape: a European panel study, 1992–1996. *Organization Science* 10, pp. 583–600.

Yeager, L.B. 1983. Stable money and free-market currencies. *Cato Journal* 3, pp. 305–326.

7 Science systems[1]

The basic working hypothesis in the economics of science has long been that that the activities of scientists in the production of scientific knowledge can be understood in market terms, deploying some variation of the method of optimization under constraint. This has been conventional wisdom ever since the pioneering forays of Nelson (1959) and Arrow (1962).[2] It is true that the crude characterization of science as "the marketplace of ideas" is not a feature of more modern work, and certainly writers in the "new economics of science" such as Dasgupta & David (1994) hardly mention markets at all except in the context of technological development (which they sharply differentiate from science). In their concentration on individual incentives played out in contexts of imperfect information, they incorporate observations of the actual incentives encountered by scientists, and bring to bear some sophisticated economic tools in analyzing this new domain.[3] But, in characterizing the interactions as exchanges and invoking a benchmark of efficiency that if it is to be meaningful at all must assume a complex of goods production and exchange in an idealized competitive environment, they are effectively characterizing the new domain as a type of market without actually using the word. But while it is perhaps inevitable that economists will tend, like the man with a hammer who sees every problem as a nail,[4] to take every social arrangement they contemplate to be a market of some sort, this is not necessarily the most helpful approach. The obvious downside is that, by forcing our model of science into conformity with that of market, we will have to downplay the differences and, if these differences include phenomena that are important to the operation of science, then we impoverish our ability to understand science as a social system in its own right.

There is no question that one can easily point to similarities between the social domains of market and science. Both are populated by self-interested people – self-interested, that is, in the sense of forming (and acting based on) subjective appraisals of the costs and benefits of their actions and plans, so that behavior at the margin is sensitive to incentives. In both, the people involved are constrained by scarcities of resources, by the inability to do many things at once, and by the cognitive limitations of their brains in the context of a complex environment.[5] There are repeated, institutionalized interactions between the participants; interactions which can be quite indirect and often involve complete strangers but are essential to the individual pursuit of happiness. And, in both, specialization, competition,

DOI: 10.4324/9781003336150-7

and entrepreneurial or calculated risk-taking behavior are major forces in the operation and growth of the social network. When one looks at the overall structure of these two social arrangements, one sees no central locus of control in either case, and yet there is voluntary participation, driven by the positive feedback from the subjectively perceived benefits of participation, and general adherence to the rules of interaction. In cases in which the rules are violated, both incorporate negative feedback processes that keep defection at a tolerably low level.[6]

Yet, despite all these similarities, the differences are stark – and fundamental.[7] Most obviously, in the domain of science, there are no market prices. And, since market prices are an emergent phenomenon of the market system, their absence in science points to deep dissimilarities in the processes of interaction through which, in the case of markets, market prices are formed. The relevant institutions of interaction are in fact different, and they are different for a good reason: the content of the interactions (the goods, services, and money in the case of markets and the published articles and citations in the case of science) have very little in common. Published scientific articles, and whatever it is about their content that may be citable, are not regarded as property; the publication process necessitates interaction not with those who may cite the article but with an editor assisted by referees and therefore to call the publication–citation sequence an "exchange" is to take great liberties with the meaning of the word; and the acceptance of articles for publication may be based on appraised significance or interest or the author's reputation or connections, but not on expected profitability. In short, the major forms of interaction in science do not involve property, do not involve exchange, and do not involve economic calculation.

The definition of science as a type of market compels one to look for the science analog of marketable goods, and most authors on the topic argue that, despite the obvious problem of quantification, it is found in the knowledge or information content of the scientific publication. But this cannot be so. If there is "knowledge" in a published article, it would have to be the author's individual knowledge, but individual knowledge, being the current classificatory capability of an individual brain, cannot possibly be a thing separate from the individual involved. If there is "knowledge codified as information" as Dasgupta & David (1994) describe it, with information regarded as a signal subjectively appraised, one is out of that frying pan but has fallen into a nearby fire – the need to account for, as a separate process, the emergence of the corpus of current scientific knowledge as a classification distinct from the knowledge of the individual scientists who are parties to the information transfer. This codified individual knowledge, the purported analog of a market good, is not the final product, and it is a gross error to conflate it with scientific knowledge. Scientific transactions are not simply a matter of "theory choice" – as portrayed by Brock & Durlauf (1999) – in which the chosen bits of individual knowledge add up to the current state of scientific knowledge. Scientists use aspects of each other's work, modifying, adapting, criticizing, reinterpreting, and perhaps (from the point of view of the original author) misinterpreting it as they develop their own work. Repeated applications of this process are observed to tend to result in a commonly accepted conception (at least within particular schools, but sometimes in whole disciplines, and especially in those disciplines where empirical reproducibility is considered to be significant),[8] and this transformed conception, this tacit agreement as to the classification of phenomena in the subject domain (temporary and mutable though it may be), is what we call scientific knowledge. If one wanted to look for an analog of scientific knowledge in the market domain, the spectrum of current market prices for goods and services would be a reasonable candidate since both are emergent attributes of their respective systems, both have counterparts in the individual transactions of the system with which they are often confused,[9] and both provide information to the participants of the system that is vitally useful for the pursuit of their individual ends.

Science is not a market, but science and market, as social systems, have much in common. They are related fraternally rather than filially, and the conceptual parental figure is the anticipatory system. Science has its own distinct and characteristic closed set of self-supporting processes. Fundamental transactions in science involve publication in various forums and citation when invoking the work of others. These transactions are affected by the results of experiments and observations and are conditioned by the preferences and creativity of the scientists themselves. They result, indirectly, in the theoretical and taxonomic corpus of established scientific knowledge[10] and in the generally recognized reputations of individual scientists.[11] An individual may intend to develop and expound on a particular theory, but no individual determines how, and in what form, the insights of this theory are incorporated into the current body of scientific knowledge. An individual may deliberately seek scientific reputation, but no individual is in control of the emergence of the overall assessment of his reputation which reflects appraisals of the value and usefulness to others of his contributions. Yet science could not survive as a coherent system unless the body of scientific knowledge were, to some extent, a useful classification of natural phenomena, and its operation would certainly be seriously hampered if the general assessment of reputation persistently ignored important contributions.

The emergence of modern science

While people have engaged in activity that could be called "scientific" before the dawn of recorded history, it is only relatively recently that the phenomenon of modern science has emerged as a radically new social arrangement in the form of a self-maintaining system of scientific processes, an arrangement that, as we shall show, can be formally described as an anticipatory social system.

Over the course of the 17th century there occurred remarkable changes in the mode of understanding and the methods of investigating natural phenomena. Historians of science refer to this multifaceted transition as "the Scientific Revolution", and the capitals and the definite article are there with good reason.[12] This was certainly a "golden age" of scientific development, but there had been significant periods of scientific development before – in Greece from about 4th to the 2nd century BCE stemming from the philosophical schools of Plato and Aristotle, in China at roughly the same time in the era of the Hundred Schools of Thought, in northern India from about the 4th to the 6th century, in the Middle

East from about the 9th to the 12th century as Greek manuscripts were translated into Arabic and studied, and in medieval Europe in the 12th to the 14th century as Arabic manuscripts, including those Arabic translations of Greek manuscripts, were in turn translated into Latin.[13] All of these periods of progressive intellectual activity came to an end – either they simply lapsed into intellectual stasis, as was the case with the Greek[14] and medieval European episodes, or they were not resilient enough to survive societal changes (political regime change in the cases of China and northern India, and religious in-turning as a result of external threats in the case of the Middle East). In contrast, the intellectual revolution of the 17th century has initiated a form of scientific activity which has continued to grow, in discoveries, in active participants, in application, and in societal acceptance and prestige, to this day, and which, despite major political upheavals, shows no signs of tapering off.[15] But what was different about this particular revolution, what explains its staying power? The hypothesis developed here is that the system of science as we know it originated from a coalescence of methodological, epistemological, ideological, and institutional innovations that emerged during the 17th century, forming a radically new social arrangement: a self-maintaining system of scientific processes. These innovations are well known, and all have been cited as causes of the Revolution.[16]

For both Immanuel Kant and William Whewell, the key figure was Francis Bacon (1592; 1620a, b), whose elaboration of the experimental-inductive method marked the clear break from Aristotelean science. Ernst Mach points to Galileo's revolutionary method of forming an abstract mathematical model and submitting its consequences to experimental test. For Eduard Dijksterhuis, the Revolution was set in motion by Copernicus, whose inspired placing of the Sun at the center of the universe, despite the work being very much in the tradition of Greek mathematical astronomy, led to the decisive innovations of Kepler and Galileo in mathematizing natural phenomena. Alexandre Koyré saw the essence of the Revolution as the emergence in the work of Galileo and Descartes of a new conception of motion which sheared it of the purposefulness with which Aristotle had endowed it and replaced that with the idea of different states of bodies in a mathematically described space, which fit together with a new emphasis on precise measurement. Edwin Burtt also pointed to the emergence of a new mathematically oriented world view which, in the work of Copernicus and Kepler, and finally Galileo, resulted in the replacement of Aristotle's formal cause with mathematical description. Rupert Hall downplayed the empirical innovations and emphasized the new ideas involving the embrace of mathematics in describing nature in terms of law-like regularities, a method which had possibilities for application to sciences other than astronomy and physics. Thomas Kuhn divided the sciences into two groups: the "classical sciences" (such as astronomy and physics) had their mathematically oriented upheaval in the conception of how the world is to be described, while the "Baconian sciences" (such as magnetism and chemistry) had their empirically oriented upheaval in methods of investigation. And Richard Westfall saw as crucial the integration over time, culminating with Newton, of the two separate ideals of exact mathematical description and a worldview in which the underlying causes of phenomena could be deduced from experiment in terms of the motions of particles. All these authors cite, with varying degrees of emphasis, causes involving radically new conceptions of knowledge and experiment.[17]

Another group of authors cite causes external to the content of science, causes involving ideological and institutional changes, as necessary for the Scientific Revolution to take place. Included here are those who highlight the emancipation from religious dogma, such as Andrew White, whose polemical account of the "warfare of science with theology" had a run of popularity in the early 1900s. In contrast, Reijer Hooykaas saw an ideological shift conducive to experimental science in the aftermath of the Reformation, when the idea that scripture could be studied individually independent of authorities led to the attitude that God's other book, nature, could be approached similarly and that the answers found therein had to be humbly respected. Hooykaas also pointed to the downstream effects of the voyages of discovery in changing social attitudes in favor of an investigatory approach to nature. Robert Merton's study of the relation between science and the society in which it was embedded in the 17th century led him to point to aspects of the "Puritan ethos" – its utilitarianism, its empiricism, and its antitraditionalism – which altered social attitudes in the direction of making the new empirical approach of science commendable. Although Merton did not make the claim explicitly, his thesis has been taken as describing a driver of the Baconian side of the Scientific Revolution. George Clark proposed that the experimental method had its origin in procedures used in the emerging industrial processes and in the quantitative thinking necessary in business accounting, as well as in the new utilitarian religious attitudes. Elizabeth Eisenstein saw the availability of the printing press as enabling the wide communication and follow-up, a crucial feature of modern science not possible in a scribal culture. And Joseph Ben-David asked how it came to be, in the 17th century, that a socially acceptable and respectable vocation of science emerged and found his answer in science's compatibility with a developing ideology of progress in rational political and educational reform, an attitude shared by the sorts of men who were instrumental in forming the informal, and later formal, scientific societies.[18]

Floris Cohen (2015, pp. 262–269) has invoked most of the aforementioned causes in a comprehensive story of the rise of modern science in the 17th century. He stressed the revolutionary changes that the three innovations of mathematically precise laws, exploratory experimental methods, and corpuscular conceptions of reality introduced. Significantly, these were changes not only in the content of science but also in the conception of what constituted knowledge and how it was to be sought. As something of an afterthought, he noted the various aspects of the current societal environment which increased the chances that these developments would be pursued. When explaining the Revolution's survival, his major points were, first, that the Revolution was not snuffed out by religious and political forces thanks to the openness to innovation provided by the Reformation and the political stability following the Peace of Westphalia and the English Restoration, and second, that the potential for application (initially more hope than reality) resulted in both political endorsement in the chartering of scientific societies and societal acceptance in the growing industrial economy. If one regards, as Cohen does, the Revolution as a circumscribed episode that culminated with Newton, then that is possibly all there needs to be said, but what is not explained is the remarkable aftermath in which the science born in the 17th century has grown unabated into the cultural mainstay it is today.

In summary, with regard to the emergence of modern science, what we are left with are elaborations of necessary conditions; there is no compelling argument as to which set of them might be sufficient. And there is no viable explanation of why this particular upsurge in scientific activity, unlike all those that preceded it, has not lapsed into scientific stasis – instead, it shows continuous, even exponential, growth. So, rather than championing any particular necessary cause or set of necessary causes as providing sufficiency, the sufficient cause could be looked for in interactions between these causes. If the confluence of innovations of the 17th century resulted in the formation of a mutually supporting set of scientific processes, and if this system of processes was organized such that its interactions with its environment were adaptive in facilitating its own maintenance and growth, then the Scientific Revolution could be seen as the spontaneous formation of a radically new order of scientific endeavor and its remarkable continuance explained.

The structure of science systems

Perhaps the most fundamental of the scientific innovations of the 17th century was the radical change in the conception of scientific knowledge. No longer was knowledge thought of in terms of deduction from an overarching authoritative scheme, and no longer could ingenious and elaborate constructions designed to "save the appearances" be acceptable as providing an understanding of phenomena. Instead, nature was to be actively investigated by probing experiment. The plans for such experimental action could be based on suggested mathematical generalizations or on inductions from previous observation, but whatever the source it was the reaction from nature that was to determine whether the suggested understandings were plausible or defective. A strong indication that the idea that active experiment was the final arbiter of truth had taken hold in the minds of the scientists of the time is evident in the Royal Society's motto, "*Nullis in verba*", which was dismissive of speculation not backed up by experiment.

If knowledge were to be discovered and not simply deduced, then knowledge was mutable, and could be added to or corrected, depending on how the experimental results were understood and assessed. And here is where the genius of the Oldenburg innovations can be seen. There is an inevitable subjective component in the assessment of experiments – the results could be questioned, the apparatus judged unreliable, the experimenter considered incompetent, or complicating phenomena identified. Or the results could be ignored or dismissed out of hand because they did not conform to ingrained expectations. The resolution that Oldenburg provided for this pervasive problem was to enable the wide publication among scientists of experimental results and commentaries on them, so that assessment could take place in open discussion, and when (or if) a consensus emerged, it could be taken (at least provisionally) as an update to existing scientific knowledge. Without the availability of the printing press, this wide and timely distribution of purported facts and probing opinions would have been much more difficult, to the point of impracticability. This arrangement instantiated a decentralized process of systemic learning from experience in which there was no overriding personal authority, although reputational effects (which, in principle at least, reflected previous reliability) would mean that some assessments were more influential than others.

The access to widely distributed publication also played a large part in both fostering and constraining scientific entrepreneurship. Hypothesizing about scientific matters was certainly not a new activity in the 17th century, but its character changed with the new conception of knowledge and the new immediacy of exposure to criticism. Newton was famously dismissal of hypothesizing in the sense of loose speculation – "I feign no hypotheses" was the credo he added to the second edition of the *Principia* – and he insisted that scientific propositions be inferred from, and consonant with, the phenomena. Further constraining speculation was the acknowledged success of the use of mathematics for formulating coherent hypotheses, and this influenced the reception that published hypotheses met with in the scientific community. On the other hand, with the concepts of discovery and discoverer at play, there were rewards to be had for putting forward a viable hypothesis (and being the first to publish it), and this induced a competitive element into the process. For the first time in such an organized manner, scientific hypothesizing became the process of formulating anticipations of empirical phenomena based on an existing (and growing) base of knowledge,[19] an activity consistent with the age-old drive of curiosity but now hedged about with the possibility of both reputational costs and benefits.

With the new focus on experiment, both informal groups and, later, formally organized ones such as the Royal Society provided facilities where scientific experiments could be carried out. This, again, was the implementation of an entrepreneurial process, motivated of course by curiosity but also by the reputational rewards of discovery. Hypotheses (whether published or developed personally by the experimenter) can provide the rationale for experimental plans, but experimentation is neither a cost-free activity nor one certain of success, and so, given such constraints and likely faced with more hypotheses than can reasonably be addressed, a process involving selective judgement in the face of uncertain future outcomes is required. And again, the new institution of publication within the scientific community of results and hypotheses and the commentary on them is a vital innovation, for it provides considered reasons why particular hypotheses might or might not be confirmable and thereby reduces the inherent uncertainty of the selection process. The practice of vetting submissions for approval for publication (a process which has grown into the now-familiar refereeing procedure) was also a helpful element in the culling process.

The final components for completing this system of science, for adding a driving force to the closed cycle of social processes just described – investigation, assessment, anticipation, judgment, investigation – and for imbuing the system with the propensity to grow, are to be found, respectively, in Oldenburg's innovation of ensuring credit to authors of publications, and in the societal attitudes promoted by Bacon through which scientific work came to be seen as a respected and valuable activity. There may be several motivations for a person to adopt science as a vocation, and possibly the major one – certainly the one most often cited by scientists themselves – is curiosity and the promise of pleasure in its satisfaction.[20] But reputation amongst one's peers is also a natural motivation, whether openly acknowledged or not, and is the criterion of success in science (even if sometimes, unfortunately, it is only achieved posthumously), and the explicit recognition of personal contribution (an innovation which has grown into the norm of citation) is crucial for grounding that motivation in a tangible form.[21] The new system of science thereby presented strong incentives for intelligent people to enter a profession which was socially valued and supported, and which offered realistic opportunities for pursuing satisfying endeavor and obtaining recognition of success. And shortage of work for a growing number of participants was not likely to be a problem – in stark contrast to a system of knowledge based on deductions from an authoritative source, a system in which knowledge is based on experiment is open-ended, as technological innovations stemming in part from that experimental activity allow for more and more extensive and finely detailed investigation of what is an effectively (and may be actually) infinite nature.

The characteristics of this new system of science suggest that it can be modeled as an anticipatory social system, a closed system of processes whose outputs include a structure which can serve as the system's internal model of itself and its environment and which can be updated based on internally assessed experience of the environment. The body of scientific knowledge – a mutable complex of current consensus assessments of theories and methods – and scientific reputations – is that structure which serves as that internal model. The hypotheses and judgments of scientific entrepreneurs (which are the anticipatory element of the system affecting its research propensities), the environmental feedback from investigations, and the assessments of hypotheses in the light of that feedback are all transmitted within the system by the agency of repeated publication and citation transactions through which scientists engage with each other.

Figure 7.1 is a schematic representation of the fundamental process organization of science as an anticipatory social system, showing the self-sustaining cycle of social processes just described – investigation, assessment, anticipation, judgment, investigation – together with their critical inputs and outputs. As before, processes are shown in bold within the system boundary; process outputs are indicated by closed-headed arrows and inputs by open-headed ones.

It is to be emphasized that this is a model of the organization of the processes within the system, not of the system's members. There is no necessary one-to-one association of members and processes – individuals may, and often do, participate in more than one of these processes. While the process organization is quite straightforward, the network of relationships and interactions between members can be a complex one of both competition and cooperation as members pursue their own interests under the constraints of the norms of behavior that emerge within the system and the modes of interaction provided by the system's processes.

As with the market system, it is the purposeful agency of the scientists, in the course of acting according to their subjective preferences and motivations, which provides the motive force animating the processes in the system. Scientists interact

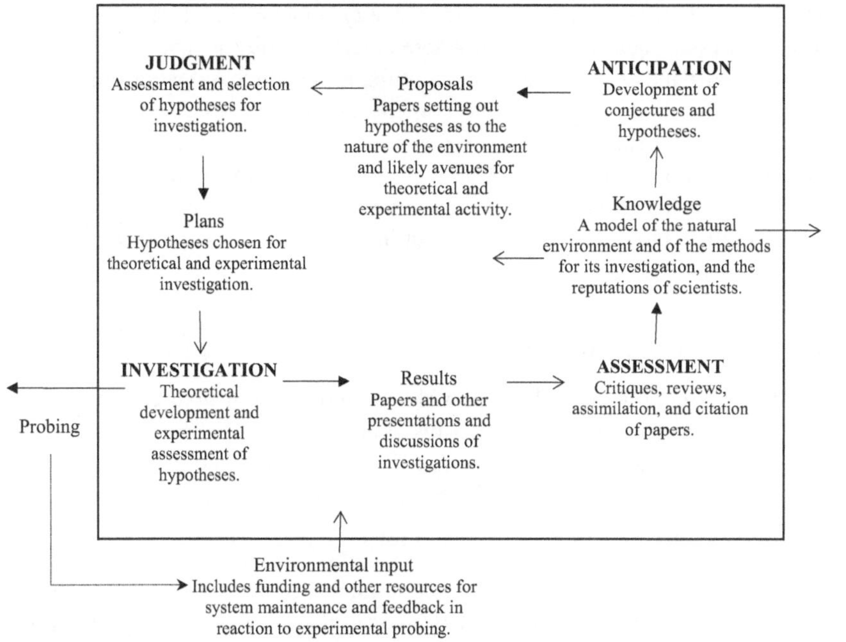

Figure 7.1 Process organization in a science system.

by participating in assessment, anticipation, judgment, and investigation under the norms of publication and citation – a set of processes which, given the system's material openness, are each necessary for the function of the others, and which together are sufficient to enable the system's existence and continuance as a self-maintaining entity.

The 17th century in Western Europe saw a significant phase change in social space, out of which emerged a new social order – the system of modern science – that was stable, closed and self-maintaining in its process structure (but open to the environment for material resources obtainable from a growing and liberalizing economy), and possessing an inbuilt propensity to grow.[22] The methodological, epistemological, ideological, and institutional innovations that were developed and adopted during that century combined to enable the formation of such an order. None of them was sufficient in itself, but together they provided the building blocks for a social arena in which people with an exploratory attitude, executing the procedures that formed the new arrangement, could pursue their interests with reasonable hope of some positive return. The success of this social arrangement has been such that, today, any discipline with pretensions to be scientific organizes its community of practitioners along the lines pioneered in the 17th century and first fully realized in the sciences of physics and astronomy.

In fact, all modern academic communities are organized with a similar process structure. Where they differ is in the investigative process. For the sciences, this process operates as a probe of the environment from which the environmental responses are taken as strong evidence in assessments of hypotheses about the environment. It is the system's anchor to reality, and for the physical sciences in particular it holds tight. For sciences whose objects of study are complex systems – climate science and (even more so) economics, for example – the bottom is much sandier, and the interpretation of experiments and observations subject to correspondingly greater latitude. For the humanities, the grip may be even more tenuous, and the possibilities for restraint on speculation much more attenuated. Mathematics is a hybrid case in which investigations are often conditioned by findings in the well-anchored sciences, but in which internal conceptions of what is interesting are also operative.

Empirical considerations

The basic model developed above provides an underlying structure within which a wide range of situations can be described, but in looking for observable implications we focus particularly on the sorts of incentives embodied in the mechanism that allow pattern prediction of likely trends. Several different lines of investigation immediately suggest themselves:

Communication. The major means of communication in science for reporting investigations, setting out entrepreneurial hypotheses, and assessing and using other scientists' work, is the act of publication. To be successful, the publication has to be noticed, since it is an unsolicited signal of a contribution. And it has to be noticed by people likely to make use of it and therefore to cite it favorably. Many details of the structure of the publication process can be shown to be geared to enhancing the signaling effectiveness in relation to the characteristics of the audience. Most obviously, growth in the numbers of scientific publications being generated leads to a strong tendency toward journal specialization, as journals cannot continue to command the attention of the whole of an audience increasingly diverse with respect to their scientific interests. Division of journals is probably as fundamental in science as is the division of labor in market-oriented production. Similar factors impel journals to become increasingly selective with respect to the publication of articles received, and to provide an explicit certification function by virtue of such selectivity. These topics have received some attention in the sociological literature, especially the phenomenon of prestige hierarchies in journals – see, for example, Cole & Cole (1973) and Whitley (1984). But we think that the unifying idea of the need for signal strength could usefully integrate this area of research, especially if it were to be connected with observations as to the accompanying changes in the characteristics of the knowledge generated.

A significant factor in determining signal strength has been observed to be the prior reputation of the author. As Merton (1973, p. 443) puts it: "… eminent scientists get disproportionately great credit for their contributions to science while relatively unknown scientists tend to get disproportionately little credit for comparable contributions". He has named the phenomenon "the Matthew effect", alluding to a famous biblical passage. This flair for description and naming probably overemphasizes the effect, however – a study that puts the issue more in perspective is that of Johnson (1997), who finds that prior reputation (measured as the number of citations per article in the past five years – self-citations not counted) has a "significant but small" effect in generating citations to later articles. Nonetheless, the model developed here would predict a positive effect of prior reputation at the margin simply on the assumption that author reputation is one selection factor considered by potential users of published work.

Considerations of signal strength also provide one basis for an explanation of the frequently observed tendencies toward fragmentation of scientific disciplines. Within a scientific group – a number of otherwise separate researchers all grappling with a particular problem or working within a common framework – the signals from researchers are likely to be stronger or more germane to those within the group than to those outside it. Those outside the group may lack the interest, specialized knowledge, or simply the time to maintain close interactions with members of the group. Citations of group members may be dominated by other members of the group. The formation of such "research groups" provides important focus, expertise, and feedback effects that justify high degrees of specialization often necessary for the growth of knowledge. Groups of this kind constitute spheres or "islands" of interaction within science that promote chopping up questions into more manageable pieces. The relation between such groups and the wider scientific community may be entirely compatible and synergistic. But not all scientific groups perceive themselves in this way. Instead, the rationale of the group may reflect discord along any number of different fault lines. In economics, these may involve serious philosophical, methodological, analytical, or policy differences. Because the production of knowledge will in general have less currency outside the group, incentives exist for groups, especially when they coalesce around a "school of thought", to build their own instruments to increase the value of their contributions, institutionalize their commonality, and expand their influence (mainly through "recruitment"). These may take on more formal characteristics – new journals and conferences, for instance – once the group reaches a certain size or attains a distinctive identity. Such arrangements further "within group" citation, which can help foster the emergence of "stars" who would presumably have been less successful if they were competing for citations outside their group.

However, whereas the value of reputation is directly related to the size (or prominence) of a scientific group, a premium exists for those who can transcend their "home group" by appealing to larger and better-established groups. This increases the flows of knowledge among groups, modifying (perhaps only marginally) each group's own identity and providing the basis for further cross-group exchanges. Whether such tendencies in fact exist depends on several factors, including the initial degree of separation and the importance to each group of remaining true to itself on whatever "foundational" issues it deems essential. The strength of forces pushing toward group "mergers" and cross-fertilization must be compared to those forces promoting isolation. In economics, casual observation suggests that the reputational gains from merging may be substantial for the great majority of researchers. Nonetheless, economics demonstrates the capacity to support a fairly large number of subgroups, despite their relative inaccessibility to the high-profile positions at important research universities and publication outlets. According to the analysis presented here, the survivability of such groups cannot be disassociated from the reputation-enhancing opportunities participation in the group makes available to researchers and which otherwise would have been unavailable without the group. If we assume that the likelihood of error-correction increases with exposure before a wider audience, researchers whose work remains largely within the confines of their own group will benefit from that in-group engagement; but the value of their signals to the wider scientific community is not likely to be as high. In any case, our underlying model provides a vehicle for connecting various lines of inquiry in this area.

Finally, consideration of the signal strength effect could provide some useful insights about the possibilities for the development of "internet journals". Attempts to replace the existing journal structure with more informal internet postings are not likely to succeed unless some method is found to maintain the signal strengths of individual publications. Although it is probably hazardous to speculate about exactly how this might be achieved from the safe vantage point of an armchair, one fairly obvious signal-enhancing feature that an internet journal could supply would be a much more sophisticated indexing feature so that potential users could conduct rather specific searches to find articles of interest.

Competition. Scientists, whether individually or as members of a research team, seek to persuade others. Theories, explanations, and facts do not present themselves; rather, they form aspects of an argumentative context in which scientists compete to persuade other scientists, funding sources, and even the general public to see reality in a particular way. But the inherently rivalrous character of scientific activity is nothing other than the flip side of reputation. Success in one would be expected to be associated with success in the other through bidirectional feedback loops.

Two ways (among others) that competition is played out in science is through specialization and access to publication outlets, especially journals. Authors build reputation through the quality, frequency, and impact of publications and citation. In so far as specialization allows researchers to pursue their own interests or take advantage of specialized knowledge or skills, this will enhance the signal strength of publications. At the same time, however, specialized research is exclusionary in terms of the audience to which it appeals and, consequently, would tend to exert a diminished reputational impact beyond the immediate research community. But some of these costs to specialization can be reduced by adding some institutional complexity, such as the increasingly familiar "review essay". Such innovations provide reputational benefits to both those specialists cited and to the authors of review essays. But nonspecialists may also benefit because knowledge is made available and put into a form that may be relevant for their own research. Menger's (1871, p. 217) insight about how "need for competition itself calls forth competition" is pertinent here, although the coordinating mechanism is not economic profit but reputation.

The payoff from specialization requires, however, the existence of publication outlets. Researchers, in effect, must compete for the available publication slots. If we assume that specialization is necessary for the growth of knowledge, an important part of that process will refer to the arrangements governing the number of journals (and presses) and their reputation-enhancing characteristics.[23] The rate of journal space accretion is constrained by significant start-up and operating costs. New journals also require an existing and identifiable body of scholarship to justify their appearance at all. Together, these considerations suggest that the introduction of new journals would be expected to lag new research specialties.[24] If so, this may retard the ability of new specialties to insinuate themselves into the institutionalized structure of science, at least without first demonstrating their value to the wider scientific community. Until then, such constraints provide gatekeeper functions that increase the reputational value of publication, given the available journal space. While all researchers want outlets for their work, they also must surely realize that their research has value in part because journal space precludes that option for others. This may account for attempts to replace the existing journal structure with more informal internet postings. However, as we have noted, these are not likely to succeed unless some method is found to maintain the signal strengths of individual publications, lest the arrangement slides into a case study of Gresham's Law.

Citation. The recordings of citations and citation counts could be a source of empirical data, and citation studies have a long history in the sociological literature, dating at least from Garfield (1955) and Price (1963). Economists have also invoked citation counts as determinants of journal and school rankings as well as researcher salaries – see Liebowitz & Palmer (1984) and Diamond (1986), for example.[25] Studies by Stigler & Friedland (1975) and Quandt (1976) include rankings of individual economists based on citation counts. Biddle (1996) has used citation data to probe the question of what particular aspects of Wesley Mitchell's work were most effective in establishing his reputation.

Several workers in this area have commented that the practice of simply counting all citations as equivalent is unsatisfactory. Stigler & Friedland (1975, p. 488) disaggregate their citation counts into "favorable", "unfavorable" and "neutral", and this is certainly consistent with the desire to relate citation quantities to reputation. But if we wish to be able to use citation data in analysis of contributions to scientific knowledge, then further disaggregation seems to be called for. There are positive "use cites", positive "review cites", positive "recognition cites", zero-effect "self cites", negative "argument cites", and negative "criticism cites". For building a reputation (and for contributing positively to current scientific knowledge), use cites are the most important (but probably with an effect that diminishes with quantity); for reducing a reputation, criticism cites are effective, and probably have a unit effect greater in absolute magnitude than use cites and increasing with quantity.

In short, for citation data to be useful in providing tests for our institutional model, a simple compilation of data published in citation indices will not be adequate. For example, an interesting study might be to pick a pair of scientists with comparable total numbers of citations but significantly different standing in the scientific community (an informal assessment of reputation). The prediction would be that disaggregation of the cites would show either fewer use cites or more criticism cites for the lower-reputation person.

Suitably disaggregated citation data could also be used in investigating trends in standards induced by external "nonscientific" influences. We have already noted that science, like government, is dependent for its survival as an order on the productive capabilities of an underlying market order. The methods by which scientists are supported – by employment for teaching purposes, provision of "expert opinion", and marketable product development, or by donation or government grant – will obviously have an effect on the productivity and direction of research. Competition for funding of various sorts or the emergence of new funding possibilities can also lead to "professionalization" of a discipline which should show up as a narrowing of the criteria for successful publication and a trend toward cumulative-style use-citation. Accompanying this might be fragmentation of the discipline as the "losers" in this competition dissociate from the "mainstream" winners. Comparisons might be made between citation spectra of sixteenth-century natural philosophy and modern physics, or between economics before and after World War II.

It is clear that there are practical difficulties here – assessing citations article by article is (we can report from experience) extremely tedious work. And there is also the issue of the appropriate weights to be assigned. This may be less of a problem than it seems at first blush, given the fact that we are largely interested in comparisons and trends in citation counts, not absolute values. But a more vexing issue is whether a criticism citation is actually negative in reputational terms. This may vary with the field. It could be the case (at least in some fields) that any recognition is better than none, but it may also be necessary to disaggregate negative citations into those associated with a demonstration of error and those associated with respectful disagreement.

Knowledge generation. The generation of scientific knowledge from this reputation-driven arrangement depends on reputation being primarily enhanced by useful contributions of scientific ideas – useful, that is, in the sense of actually being used by others (often competitors) in their own work. As we have noted above, this criterion conditions the characteristic attributes of the knowledge produced. Further, the proportion of use cites to total cites should be a measure that distinguished different scientific fields and the knowledge they produce with respect to the tendency toward cumulativeness of that knowledge.

Perhaps due to the nature of the subject matter, but more likely due to the state of its development and the nature of the equipment or techniques considered necessary for its investigation, different scientific fields differ in their criteria for contribution recognition and, therefore, we predict, in their ratio of use-citations to the other positive citation categories. And a field in which there is specific (and expensive) equipment involved or one in which very specific methods (often mathematical) have been developed would tend to have very specific recognition criteria for "normal science" publications, a relatively high proportion of use-citations, and a slowly cumulative type of knowledge generation. Kuhnian paradigm shifts would be possible, but rare. Fields in which these criteria are not met would probably tend to have relatively more review, recognition, and argument-type citations and less cumulativeness in knowledge generation.[26]

The hypothesis that direct *use* of a publication's scientific contribution is necessary for positive citations to be forthcoming needs to be amended for the case of review articles. Reviews, which can be regarded as intermediaries between publishers of scientific contributions and users of them, are a prominent feature of the scientific publication scene, increasingly so as the volume of published work in a field outstrips the ability of those in even closely related fields to stay abreast of it. Such articles in themselves are not direct contributions to scientific knowledge, yet scientists go to considerable trouble to write and publish them. Our model would predict that this would only be the case if the citation (and therefore reputational) returns from review publication were sufficient to bring forth the review effort, and this indeed seems to be the case. Not surprisingly, Laband (1990) has found that review articles are high on the list of cited articles.

Stability and evolution. When we look at science as an anticipatory system, it is necessary to analyze it in terms of the interactions from which it emerges and to avoid importing purposes to it apart from the separate aims of its constituent elements. Neither market nor scientific systems have goals. Science, then, cannot be assumed to fulfill some larger purpose or, in particular, to pursue knowledge (notwithstanding the happy side-effect that curiosity and the drive for reputation generates novel byproducts in the form of reliable and codifiable knowledge). Instead, we look to reputation as the relevant aim of individual scientists and thus infer that the stability of the system matters because the random awarding of reputation would unhitch the preferences of scientists from outcomes. For the system to function smoothly, procedures and incentives must come into play consistent with achieving an alignment between individuals' expectations and the outcomes it generates. This will likely involve arrangements to credential and monitor scientists by screening, certifying, and assessing their research, and to administer prevailing standards, such as citation conventions and intellectual honesty precepts, within the order, as Hull (1988) describes.

But self-organizing and regulating arrangements within scientific communities may also extend beyond those boundaries to partly intersect with market systems. Such interactions are unavoidable because the pricing system of the catallaxy provides science with inputs it could otherwise not produce on its own. Supporting the organization of science, from labs to scientists, requires the productive capabilities of an underlying market order. The delivery of this support, whether by university donors or government grant, will have an effect on the productivity and direction of research, as Kealey (1996) shows. The stability provided by the market to science exerts its fullest impact in areas of intersection and it is here that the (market) value of scientists and their output can be most easily established. Stability would be expected to increase as the scope of these intersections broadens.

The evolution of the scientific order will reflect changes in the interactions among scientists. Such changes will arise endogenously within science and exogenously from changes in the broader social framework, including the market order, the legal system, and the public sector, within which science is nested. The (evolutionary) mechanisms at play here are obviously complex. While analyzing these critically important issues would take us far beyond the scope of the discussion in this book, our emphasis on reputation may provide some leads here. The emergence of an increasingly complex scientific order, such as we observe in modern times, requires the extension and application of reputational mechanisms consistent with maintaining the viability of the overall order. Because reputation is associated with the generation of knowledge, ascertaining the value of that knowledge will figure prominently in the determination of reputation. This, of course, is often difficult in science because scientific knowledge may have no obvious value beyond that assigned to it by research communities and because it may itself be a byproduct of altogether different processes, such as technological advancement, as suggested by Kealey (1996) and Nightingale (1998). The ability of science to expand and deepen its reach will depend on its success in attracting resources, which in turn will be affected by demonstrating the value of its endeavors. In this regard, the extension and application of property rights, wherever possible, to science and its organizations will promote the marketization and commercialization of scientific activity and allow scientists to capture more readily the benefits of their endeavors beyond the accumulation of reputation. The foregoing listing and discussion of research possibilities intentionally raises more questions than it provides answers. We envision a program of research built around the concept of science as a particular instance of an anticipatory social order, and centered on the identification of self-interest within the order in terms of the earning of reputation. The model portrays the various procedural modes of interaction between scientists in which ideas, judgments, observations, and assessments are communicated and processed via the publication, use, and citation of scientific papers, but it is in the exploration of the individual incentives thrown up by this arrangement that the interesting empirical implications arise. We have given a rather brief exposition of the possible lines of investigation that could be followed – but it is a detailed enough one, we think, to show that this line of research has definite promise.

Issues in the philosophy of science

One of the characteristics of modern (postpositivist) philosophy of science is the adoption of an appreciation for the relevance of actual scientific concepts and findings, especially about human beings, and the history of actual scientific discoveries and the methods by which they were produced. A second feature is the appreciation for the relevance of social factors in the generation of knowledge, a concern that lends itself to a naturalistic approach. Entangled with both of these developments is the question of whether or not a normative stance, the traditional stance of epistemology, is still feasible. And further stirring the postpositivist pot is the question of whether, in the absence of any *a priori* foundation for a normative stance, the way is left open for a relativism in which any sort of belief formation is warranted.

For the purpose of bringing anticipatory systems theory to bear on this wide field of philosophical activity, it is useful to categorize the varieties of postpositivist naturalism into individually-oriented and socially-oriented, and to divide each of these further according to whether or not their thrust is normative.

	Individualist	*Social*
Nonnormative	Quine, Churchland	Barnes, Bloor
Normative	Laudan	Goldman

Here is some elaboration on each of the four possibilities:

- The original nonnormative individualist naturalism is that of Quine (1969), who suggested that traditional concerns about justification of beliefs confused two separate issues: explanation and legitimization. The latter is a matter for cultural studies; the former, focusing on a causal understanding of an individual's belief formation, is the province of psychology. This either eliminates any role for traditional epistemology, or reduces and reorients it as a branch of psychology. It is not a popular stand among postpositivist philosophers, although it has had some downstream influence. From the point of view of Hayek scholars, a particularly interesting variant of nonnormative naturalism is that of Churchland (1995), based on a theory of mind as patterns of activation in a recurrent Hebbian neural network which, although apparently pursued in complete ignorance of *The Sensory Order*, has much in common with Hayek's work – while going beyond it in adding considerable neurobiological detail, experimental grounding, and philosophical sophistication.
- Far more mainstream is normative individualist naturalism, of which the work of Laudan (1990) is an influential example. Here, the findings of science and the history of science are mined for clues as to what constitutes good reasons for belief and good practice. Instead of seeking to formulate *a priori* standards against which to evaluate scientific work, scientific activity is taken as paradigmatic of rational behavior. The aim is to pick out, from what scientists have actually done, the strategies which have made possible the emergence of science as a successful enterprise. The naturalistic fallacy – the construction of "ought" from "is" – is skirted by keeping any proposed norms strictly hypothetical.
- A prominent example of nonnormative social naturalism is the philosophical stance of Barnes (1974), Bloor (1976), and their followers in the Edinburgh School of sociology. Their claim is that they provide an exclusively descriptive account of scientific knowledge while adhering to their four general tenets:

causality (the intent to uncover the causal origins of beliefs), impartiality (the commitment not to privilege particular belief-generating systems), symmetry (the explanations of beliefs considered false invoking the same causal mechanisms as those of true beliefs), and reflexivity (the acknowledgement that the beliefs of the investigator are subject to the same analysis as those of the investigated). Knowledge is socially constituted in that norms of rationality emerge in specific social contexts and subject to the effect of interests from outside of science as well as inside, and knowledge is taken to be whatever beliefs are collectively endorsed in a particular social context. This relativist conception of knowledge would seem on its face to have ignored the rather important matter of the constraints imposed by the physical world itself, but Bloor (1976, p. 7) does acknowledge, if somewhat vaguely, that "naturally there will be other types of causes apart from social ones which will cooperate in bringing about belief".

- Probably the best-known normative social naturalism is Goldman's (1999) "social epistemics". Goldman proposes to associate a "veritistic value" to states of belief, where belief in a truth rates highest on the scale. He is a strong realist about truth; something is true if it conforms to what is observed to be so. Practices (including norms, rules, and forms of interaction) in a scientific (or any other) community can have positive instrumental veritistic value if they tend to increase the mean veritistic value across the members of the community, and this measure allows for a comparative assessment of existing and proposed practices. The evaluative standards proposed – reliability, power, fecundity, speed, and efficiency, according to Goldman (1987, pp. 128–129) – are universal ones, not relative to any particular community, although their respective weights may differ in different communities. And Goldman does not imply that some particular practices are always to be used, for a range of diverse practices operative within a community may turn out to score higher on the veritistic scale than uniformity of practice.

Since anticipatory systems theory deals with individuals embedded in a social system, studied in a way that has more in common with anthropology and sociology than epistemology as traditionally understood, it is no surprise that it would be closer in spirit to social naturalism than to individualist naturalism, and more in sympathy with nonnormative naturalism than with normative naturalism. However, there is no argument with nonnormative individualist naturalism as far as it goes, for understanding the behavior and reactions of individuals engaged in knowledge-generating activity is clearly important for understanding the system as a whole. This is particularly true with respect to Churchland's work, since this is, in effect, carrying further Hayek's work on which the generalization to social systems pursued here is based. Similarly for its normative counterpart – investigations of individual scientific practice, past and present, are useful inputs to a theory of science even if the motive for pursuing them is to unearth some normative pronouncements.

Nonnormative social naturalism is the species of postpositivism closest to anticipatory systems theory. But there are considerable differences between the two both in emphasis and in substance. The Strong Programme has been taken to task, for example by Goldman (1987, p. 112), for its concentration on factors influencing knowledge generation external to science, particularly ideological and political influences, and on its neglect of the world itself as a major factor. But from the perspective of anticipatory systems theory these objections miss an essential point – that it is not so much the interests and motivations of the individual scientists that determines what emerges as knowledge but the fact that these interests and motivations have to be played out in the context of interactions which incorporate very specific feedback effects on those individuals. They are the "invisible hand" of science. And these interactions, particularly the fundamental ones surrounding publication and citation, do not simply influence scientists' decisions and choices or constrain them to do the right thing, but are an integral part of the process by which individual contributions are transmuted into scientific knowledge. The adaptive system of science is built from *both* the individual scientists and their knowledge-generating interactions, and these in combination determine the external phenomena to which the system as a whole is sensitive and to which it adapts. With an emphasis on usefulness based on empirical success built into the basic interactions, the physical world is certainly top of the list, but social factors, including, for example, funding, can have their effect as well. Where anticipatory systems theory radically departs not only from Bloor and Barnes but also from all of the above naturalisms is in its insistence on a categorical difference between individual knowledge and scientific knowledge, between knowledge instantiated in the internal structure of a brain and knowledge instantiated in the internal structure of the social system of science.

What all of the above forms of postpositivism have in common (to widely varying extents and levels of emphasis) are the philosophical claims of "underdetermination" (of theory by data), "incommensurability" (of prior and current or of competing scientific theories), and "theory-ladenness" (of data and methods). But these claims are always given an individualistic interpretation, whether in the context of theory choice (by individual scientists) or the analysis of observation (again, by individual scientists). However, from the perspective of anticipatory systems theory, they are also systemic characteristics of scientific knowledge – they are a consequence of the way in which scientific knowledge is generated and the form in which it is instantiated in the structure of the social system. All of them arise from the way in which new inputs, incompatible with the system's current knowledge structure, to the extent that they are not simply ignored, result first in local adjustments, only leading to deeper readjustments of the system's knowledge after prolonged exposure of the system to more sustained experience of anomaly.

- Underdetermination of theory by observation is a consequence of the fact that the assimilation of empirical data is only part of the story in the systemic knowledge-generating process. Even given that empirical adequacy is a major contributor to the perceived usefulness of scientific contributions and therefore an important factor in the assimilation process, the assimilation has to proceed, not simply by scientists choosing to incorporate new empirical results but through the progressive rearrangements of transaction patterns that such choices initiate. Since these rearrangements are rearrangements of an existing structure, it is most likely that piecemeal, local adjustments would take place. The resulting global classifications of the system would show only minor change, giving the appearance of a Duhemian reaction to new data.

- Incommensurability of past and present scientific knowledge is not surprising in the face of the major rearrangements of the classificatory categories which can result, after a prolonged assimilation process, from the incorporation of significant new inputs. The extent of the incommensurability will depend on the extent of the differences between the past and present classifications, a difference which is likely to grow as more time passes and the system undergoes further adaptation. The case of the incommensurability of currently competing theories is also a matter of the difficulty of making comparisons from points of view based on different classifications, only here the classifications are more local – representing different schools of thought within science.
- Theory-ladenness of observation is the science analog of what Butos and Koppl (2007, pp. 29–30) have called the *pons asinorum* for *The Sensory Order* (i.e., Hayek's insight that memory is antecedent to sensation) applied to science rather than to the brain. An anticipatory system's reactions to input depend on *both* the input and the operative classifications, where the latter are the contingent result of the system's past experience and determine not only how current observations are to be interpreted but also which observations are to be considered relevant.

In short, viewed as systemic attributes of knowledge, underdetermination, incommensurability, and theory-ladenness are all natural consequences of the way in which the differentially mutable structure of an adaptive system reacts to its environment.

We can summarize the epistemological implications of anticipatory systems theory as follows. Scientific knowledge is not just a selection from the best offerings of individual scientists; it is the outcome of an extended, institutionalized, social process of publication, criticism, interpretation, citation, argumentation, promotion, rejection, reinterpretation, assimilation, and even (from some participants' points of view) misinterpretation of those individual contributions. It is not inherently propositional (although aspects of it can be usefully expressed in such terms) and is not any simple summation of individual contributions chosen for inclusion by participating scientists (although individual contributions are obviously essential elements in the system's knowledge-generation processes). Knowledge generation in science cannot be separated from the procedures through which scientists interact and through which individual efforts are transmuted to become accepted as scientific knowledge, and to attempt to characterize "scientific knowledge" apart from "scientific process and institutions" is a dualism on par with separating mind from matter. It is not simply that the norms of science, having emerged out of past interactions between scientists, have a determining effect on which individual contributions are acceptable contributions to knowledge – it is that such norms, procedural as well as prescriptive, are themselves part of the process through which individual scientific contributions are transmuted into emergent scientific knowledge. Not all social effects are simply influences on individuals on a par with personal interests; the particular transactional forms involved in the absorption of individual contributions are an integral part of the process of knowledge generation. Individuals and their scientific interactions together form a networked system, and scientific knowledge is an emergent side-effect of the activity within that system. To be more specific, scientific knowledge is a classification by the system of science of the environment to which that system is sensitive and to which it adapts – indeed, "knowledge" in general should refer to the classification produced as a side effect of the adaptation to its environment by *any* adaptive system.

Knowledge, thus construed, does not exist apart from particular knowledge-generating systems, and the capacity for knowledge is determined by the structure of the system. The individual brain performs a classification on events of the external world detected by the sense organs – a classification that Hayek (1952) characterizes in terms of "rules of action" that are the propensities for responses to these events. Individual knowledge *is* this classification. Hayek (1978, p. 40) is clear that "it is meaningless to speak of perceiving or thinking except as a function of an acting organism in which the differentiation of stimuli manifests itself in the differences of the dispositions to act which they evoke". Analogously, the sort of knowledge generated by a market order, or a scientific order, or even a political order, being the result of external events impinging on those complex objects undergoing a process of categorization unique to the particular type of order involved, depends both on the sorts of events being classified and on the internal structure of the system doing the classification.

We are so used to thinking of knowledge as something "out there" to be tapped into as best we can that its necessary connection to the system in which it is generated, and the fact that it cannot be talked about sensibly independently of that system, is easily overlooked. Even Hayek, especially in his earlier work, seems to overlook it, as, for example, when (1945, p. 520) he speaks of "the utilization of knowledge not given to anyone in its totality". This way of putting the matter fosters the notion that there actually is such a thing as that totality, and that the problem is how best to access it. This can be contrasted with his later statement quoted above (1978, p. 40) emphasizing the contingency of individual knowledge with respect to the structure in which it is generated, and, perhaps even more pointedly, with his statement (1952, p. 4) that "a question like 'what is X?' has meaning only within a given order". The lack of clarity evident from the juxtaposition of these appraisals of the status of knowledge has its root in the failure in the 1945 statement to distinguish between different sorts of order-dependent knowledge. Individual people know "the particular circumstances of time and place" (knowledge generated in the context of a sensory order), but this is not knowledge in the context of a market order. Individuals deploying their individual knowledge with respect to useful goods and services in the interactive context of a market generate knowledge in the market sense – market prices, reputations, and brand names. Individual knowledge is not accumulated and made manifest at a market level in this process; it obviously conditions the individual interactions, but what emerges as a side-effect of these interactions is something entirely different – not a summary of individual knowledge, but a transformation of it which can be seen as a classification of events in the market system's environment. From the point of view of individuals, this market knowledge feeds back as inputs from which enhanced individual knowledge can be generated. The market, however, does not make evident those particular circumstances of time and place any more than the sensory order makes evident the events in the external world as they "really are" – it classifies them, produces an abstract representation of them, in a form that individuals can use to their advantage by generating new propensities for action and thereby adapting more successfully to their own environment.

Learning from this confusion over the identification of knowledge, we can say that the pursuit of a study of the knowledge-generating class of objects called anticipatory systems should begin by being clear, for any particular type of system, exactly what is being classified, what categories are being produced by this classification, and how is it that this classification is taking place. The "how" involves elucidating the structure behind the order: what are its constituent elements, what are the relevant characteristics of these elements for the functioning of the structure, how do the elements interact, and how does this interaction give rise to a knowledge-generating apparatus? Such an approach would have epistemology become more like a positive natural science and less of a branch of normative philosophy.

Notes

1 This chapter contains text previously published in McQuade & Butos (2003) with permission from Springer, in McQuade (2007) with permission from Elsevier, in McQuade (2010) with permission from Emerald, and in McQuade (2019, 2022).

2 See, for illustration, the collection *Science Bought and Sold* edited by Mirowski & Sent (2002).

3 For a clear exposition of Dasgupta's and David's work as it relates to "the economics of scientific knowledge", see Hands (2001, pp. 374–378).

4 Maslow (1966, pp. 15–16), in the context of a discussion of the difficulties confronting a scientist who turns his attention to the investigation of a new domain: "I suppose it is tempting, if the only tool you have is a hammer, to treat everything as if it were a nail". This adage is probably not original to Maslow – one occasionally sees a very similar quote attributed to Mark Twain, but it may well be older than that.

5 This latter characteristic, treated extensively by Simon (1945, 1957), has been characterized as "bounded rationality".

6 Wible (1998, pp. 43–60) contains a short overview of some famous instances of fraud in science. But rather than looking at the specific institutions of negative feedback, he analyzes the phenomenon in "economic" terms, by which he means a rational-choice model of optimal individual decision-making under uncertainty.

7 For an extended discussion on the differences (and similarities) between markets and science, see Butos & Boettke (2002). Also, Mäki (1999) argues (on generally different grounds from those discussed here) that free market economics does not provide a useful basis for understanding science.

8 For a careful discussion of this "invisible hand" process, see Leonard (2002).

9 In market theory, the conceptual difference between an exchange price and a market price needs to be kept in mind; in science theory, the error of failing to recognize the conceptual difference between individual knowledge (even as expressed in a published paper) and scientific knowledge (the outcome of the integration of aspects of some published work into the existing framework) is a common one. Note, however, that our distinction between "exchange price" (the specific terms of exchange in a

particular transaction) and "market price" (the emergent general appraisal of the going price for a particular good) may cause terminological difficulties for Mises scholars – Mises (1949, p. 245) defines "market price" to be precisely what is referred to here as "exchange price", and talks (p. 338) about "the price structure" as the emergent outcome of the market process.

10 Characterized by Kuhn (1962) as a "paradigm" in the sense of the current state of science or of a branch of science, and by Kitcher (1993, pp. 87–89) as "consensus practice".

11 This emergence of a reputational assessment in science is the feature of the system that makes the seeking of reputation a significant motivating factor for the individual scientist. For other arguments for the cogency and usefulness of modeling scientists as self-interested reputation-seekers, see Hull (1988, pp. 281 & 305–310) and McQuade & Butos (2003). To forestall the usual objection that it is a gross oversimplification to portray scientists as being motivated only by reputation, we quote from that latter paper (pp. 141–142): "It is, without doubt, a simplification to represent science purely in terms of the pursuit of reputation. But it is an approach analogous to the one economists make in representing firms as profit-seekers. Anyone who has ever been in business knows that the actual motivations of businessmen are much more complex than that, but it is, nonetheless, a suitable abstraction because, whether or not profit is the specific aim, the only firms that survive are those who do, sooner or later, make profits. Similarly with scientists – the only ones who survive *as scientists* are those who, sooner or later, earn some reputation." On the other hand, it might be claimed that income is the actual motivating factor, but we would point out that, in science, income is usually a byproduct of reputational assessment.

12 According to Cohen (1994, ch. 2), although the revolutionary character of the period was recognized as early as 1756 in d'Alembert's *Encyclopédie*, it was first Koyré (1939) and then Butterfield (1949) who gave the singular term currency with historians of science, even though the boundary dates, particularly the starting date, vary considerably from author to author. Wootton (2015), for example, picks Tycho Brahe's observation of a nova in 1572 as his starting date. But the idea has not been without controversy. Kuhn (1962) finds at least four separate revolutionary "paradigm shifts" in the 16th and 17th centuries, but in a later work Kuhn (1977, ch. 3) returns to the concept of a single scientific revolution as a paradigm shift but encompassing only the classical physical sciences. Shapin (1996, p. 1) cast scorn on the notion that any single event could initiate a decisive change in how natural knowledge was perceived or obtained. In the same skeptical vein, it has been questioned, for example by the historian Jan Golinski in 1988, as quoted by Cohen (1994, p. 499), "whether the notion of a coherent, European-wide, Scientific Revolution can survive continued historiographical scrutiny" as more detailed historical research has uncovered difficulties in explanations based on it. However, Cohen (2015), dealing explicitly with such difficulties, has developed a detailed and convincing account of the Scientific Revolution as a unique confluence of a specific *series* of developments during the 17th century.

13 An obvious omission from this list of "golden ages" is the European scientific Renaissance of the 16th century, triggered by the fall of Constantinople which enabled the release and subsequent translation of original Greek documents including, significantly, some works of Archimedes. Butterfield (1949) includes this period as part of the Scientific Revolution, dating its beginning at 1500. Maier (1949) considers the Renaissance (coupled with the earlier medieval European developments) as (p. 5) "the first stage of a grand development process of which the second and decisive stage falls in the 17th century". See also Maier (1982). For the purposes of this chapter, it matters not whether the scientific developments of the 17th century constituted a separate revolution, marking a clear break from Renaissance thinking, as Cohen (2015) argues, or the second and final stage of a longer series of changes – what is important is that the 17th-century developments were decisive in establishing a revolutionary new regime of scientific activity.

14 Cohen (2015, p. 26) dates the end of Greek science's golden age at the death of Hipparchus in about 150 BCE. He does not claim that there were no original Greek thinkers subsequent to this – Ptolemy and Galen in the 2nd century certainly stand out – but these were isolated cases. There were similar cases after the end of the other golden ages, but none of these represented a sustained revival in intellectual progress.

15 Cohen (2015, p. 263) is clear about the uniqueness of this revolution: "The enduring survival of the new nature-knowledge broke with all historical precedent. What we have become used to in our day, the unbroken growth of the scientific enterprise, is the big exception in world history and as such demands an explanation."

16 The following one-sentence descriptions of the views of various historians writing on the subject of the causes of the Scientific Revolution are obviously totally inadequate at capturing the detail, the nuance, and even the contradictions of these views, but they are an attempt to capture what seems, admittedly subjectively, to be their most important point.

17 For a summary and comparative discussion of the contributions of Kant, Whewell, Mach, Dijksterhuis, Koyré, Burtt, Hall, Kuhn, and Westfall, with references to and quotations from their original works, see Cohen (1994, pp. 21–150). Also discussed are the contributions of Pierre Duhem, who located the birth of modern science in a 13th-century proclamation by the Bishop of Paris allowing for some freedom in theorizing about the nature of the world, and who found in the impetus theory of Buridan and others in the 14th century a direct forerunner of the concept of inertia; Anneliese Maier, who contested Duhem's conflation of the ideas of impetus and inertia and regarded the Scientific Revolution as a gradual repudiation of Aristotelianism occurring in two phases, a preliminary one in the 14th century and the decisive break coming in the 17th century; Herbert Butterfield, whose historical survey gave intellectual heft to the concept of "the Scientific Revolution" which he also, like Maier, regarded as a long process with a decisive phase initiated by Kepler and Galileo; and Auguste Comte, who proposed a stage theory of scientific development and identified the 17th century as the period in which the combination of Galileo and Bacon moved astronomy and physics into the "positive" stage in which quantitative mathematical laws were discovered.

18 For a summary and comparative discussion of the contributions White, Hooykaas, Merton, Eisenstein, and Ben-David, with references to and quotations from their original works, see Cohen (1994, pp. 308–377).

19 Polanyi (1967, pp. 540–541): "This is what the existing body of scientific thought offers to the productive scientist: he sees in it an aspect of reality which as such is an inexhaustible source of new and promising problems."

20 A Pew Research Center survey, posted online at https://www.pewresearch.org/fact-tank/2016/10/24/as-the-need-for-highly-trained-scientists-grows-a-look-at-why-people-choose-these-careers/ shows clearly that curiosity as to how the world works and the expectation that it can be satisfied (often planted in childhood by parents, teachers, and books) is given by a large majority of the scientist respondents as a motivating factor for their entering a scientific career.

21 Evidence that the desire for reputation is a strong driver motivating scientific activity is seen in the competitive behavior of scientists. In his study of scientific competition which focuses on the danger of being anticipated in a discovery, Hagstrom (1974, p. 3) notes that "competition is severe when being anticipated means losing all or nearly all recognition for one's work" and that (p. 8) "these results demonstrate the sensitivity of scientists to proper recognition of their work".

22 Stability and growth are not guaranteed, however, for science is an open system and not only is it dependent on the surrounding society for resources but it also requires that the surrounding society respect the integrity of its processes, for these are the geese that have laid the golden eggs of scientific knowledge.

23 Our discussion will highlight the quantity of journal slots. The importance of journals and other publication outlets in terms of quality is evident enough. Researchers are

ordinarily aware of the reputational differences among journals in their discipline and such differences seem to play an increasing role in evaluating productivity for promotion and tenure in academia.

24 This does not imply that the rates of increase in journal space and author numbers necessarily diverge. Also, a significant portion of journal revenues are third-party (university) payments; this distances the value of journals from their ultimate users thereby tending to increase the number of journals that are financially viable.

25 A short (and incomplete) survey of the use of citation counts in economics articles is given by Johnson (1997).

26 Fuchs (1992) discusses such phenomena and characterizes them in terms of two different characteristics of a scientific field: the extent of "mutual dependence" of workers in the field on each other for recognition and rewards, and "task uncertainty" in the sense of the amount of disagreement in the field with respect to the proper ways of doing research. He notes (p. 85) that highly standardized research practices will emerge in the context of a combination of high mutual dependence and low task uncertainty, and cites evidence to that effect developed by Collins & Restivo (1983), who compare the different emphases on formal symbolism and logical rigor between Greek and modern mathematics. This elaboration of the conditions of "use" and its connection to the characteristics of the field are quite compatible with our model and certainly suggest some interesting research into the origins of the differences between different scientific fields.

Bibliography

Arrow, K.J. 1962. Economic welfare and the allocation of resources for inventions. In R.R. Nelson (ed.), *The rate and direction of inventive activity: economic and social factors*, pp. 609–625. Princeton University Press.

Bacon, F. 1592. In praise of knowledge. In *The works of Lord Bacon* 1, pp. 216–217. Henry G. Bohn, 1854.

——— 1620a. *Novum organum, or true suggestions for the interpretation of nature.* J. Devey (ed.). Collier, 1902. http://oll.libertyfund.org/title/1432.

——— 1620b. *Novum organum, or true suggestions for the interpretation of nature.* J. Devey (ed.). Collier, 1626. *New Atlantis, a worke unfinished.* Reprinted by Project Gutenberg, 2000. https://www.gutenberg.org/files/2434/2434-h/2434-h.htm.

Barnes, B. 1974. *Scientific knowledge and sociological theory.* Routledge & Kegan Paul.

Biddle, J. 1996. A citation analysis of the sources and extent of Wesley Mitchell's reputation. *History of Political Economy* 28 #2, pp. 137–169.

Bloor, D. 1976. *Knowledge and social imagery.* Routledge & Kegan Paul, 2/e, 1991.

Brock, W.A. & S.N. Durlauf 1999. A formal model of theory choice in science, *Economic Theory* 14, pp. 113–130.

Butos, W.N. & P.J. Boettke 2002. Kirznerian entrepreneurship and the economics of science. *Journal des Economistes et des Etudes Humaines* 12 #1, pp. 119–130.

Butos, W.N. & R.G. Koppl 2007. Does *The Sensory Order* have a useful economic future? In E. Krecké, C. Krecké, & R. Koppl (eds.) *Advances in Austrian Economics* 9: *Cognition and economics*, pp. 19–50. Elsevier.

Butterfield, H. 1949. *The origins of modern science 1300–1800.* Macmillan. Free Press, R/e, 1965.

Churchland, P.M. 1995. *The engine of reason, the seat of the soul: a philosophical journey into the brain.* MIT Press.

Cohen, H.F. 1994. *The scientific revolution: a historiographical inquiry.* University of Chicago Press.

——— 2015. *The rise of modern science explained: a comparative history*. Cambridge University Press.

Cole, J.R. & S. Cole 1973. *Social stratification in science*. University of Chicago Press.

Collins, R. & S. Restivo 1983. Robber barons and politicians in mathematics: a conflict model of science. *Canadian Journal of Sociology* 8, pp. 199–227.

Dasgupta, P. & P.A. David 1994. Toward a new economics of science. *Research Policy* 23, pp. 487–521.

Diamond, A.M. 1986. What is a citation worth? *Journal of Human Resources* 21, pp. 200–215.

Fuchs, S. 1992. *The professional quest for truth: a social theory of science and knowledge*. SUNY Press.

Garfield, E. 1955. Citation indexes for science. *Science* 122, pp. 108–115.

Goldman, A. 1987. Foundations of social epistemics. *Synthese* 73, pp. 109–144.

——— 1999. *Knowledge in a social world*. Oxford University Press.

Hagstrom, W.O. 1974. Competition in science. *American Sociological Review* 39 #1, pp. 1–18.

Hands, D.W. 2001. *Reflection without rules: economic methodology and contemporary science theory*. Cambridge University Press.

Hayek, F.A. 1945. The use of knowledge in society. *American Economic Review* 35 #4, pp. 519–530.

——— 1952. *The sensory order*. University of Chicago Press. Reprinted in Hayek (2017, pp. 113–316).

——— 1978. *New studies in economics, politics, philosophy, and the history of ideas*. University of Chicago Press.

Hull, D.L. 1988. *Science as a process: an evolutionary account of the social and conceptual development of science*. University of Chicago Press.

Johnson, D. 1997. Getting noticed in economics: the determinants of academic citations. *The American Economist* 41 #1, pp. 43–52.

Kealey, T. 1996. *The economic laws of scientific research*. St. Martin's Press.

Kitcher, P. 1993. *The advancement of science*. Oxford University Press.

Koyré, A. 1939. *Galileo Studies*. J. Mepham (tr.). Humanities Press, 1978.

Kuhn, T.S. 1962. *The structure of scientific revolutions*. University of Chicago Press, 2/e (enlarged), 1970.

——— 1977. *The essential tension: selected studies in scientific tradition and change*. University of Chicago Press.

Laband, D.N. 1990. Is there value-added from the review process in economics? Preliminary evidence from authors. *Quarterly Journal of Economics* 105 #2, pp. 341–352.

Laudan, L. 1990. Normative naturalism. *Philosophy of Science* 57, pp. 44–59.

Leonard, T.C. 2002. Reflection on rules in science: an invisible-hand perspective. *Journal of Economic Methodology* 9 #2, pp. 141–168.

Liebowitz, S.J. & J.P. Palmer 1984. Assessing the relative impacts of economic journals. *Journal of Economic Literature* 22 #1, pp. 77–88.

Maier, A. 1949. *Die Vorläufer Galilei im 14 Jahrhundert: Studien zur Naturphilosophie der Spätscholastik*. Edizioni di Storia E Letteratura. Selected extracts translated in Cohen (1994, pp. 56–59).

——— 1982. *On the threshold of exact science: selected writings of Anneliese Meier on late medieval natural philosophy*. S.D. Sargent (tr.). University of Philadelphia Press.

Mäki, U. 1999. Science as a free market: a reflexivity test in an economics of economics. *Perspectives on Science* 7, pp. 486–509.

Maslow, A.H. 1966. *The psychology of science: a reconnaissance*. Harper & Row.

McQuade, T.J. 2007. Science and market as adaptive classifying systems. In E. Krecké, C. Krecké, & R. Koppl (eds.). *Advances in Austrian Economics* 9: *Cognition and Economics*, pp. 51–86. Elsevier.

——— 2010. Science and *The Sensory Order*. In W.N. Butos (ed.), *Advances in Austrian Economics* 13: *The social science of Hayek's "The Sensory Order"*, pp. 23–56. Emerald.

——— 2019. Organization, anticipation, and closure in markets and science. *Cosmos + Taxis* 6 #6&7, pp. 1–18.

——— 2022. On the emergence of modern science. *Cosmos + Taxis* 10 #3&4, pp. 33–51.

McQuade, T.J. & W.N. Butos 2003. Order-dependent knowledge and the economics of science. *Review of Austrian Economics* 16 #2&3, pp. 133–152.

Menger, C. 1871. *Principles of economics*. J. Dingwall & B.F. Hoselitz (trs.). The Free Press, 1950.

Merton, R.K. 1973. *The sociology of science*. University of Chicago Press.

Mirowski, P. & E.-M. Sent (eds.) 2002. *Science bought and sold*. University of Chicago Press.

Mises, L. 1949. *Human action*. Henry Regnery, 3/e, 1966.

Nelson, R.R. 1959. The simple economics of basic scientific research. *Journal of Political Economy* 67, pp. 297–306.

Nightingale, P. 1998. A cognitive model of innovation. *Research Policy* 27, pp. 698–709.

Polanyi, M. 1967. The growth of science in society. *Minerva* 5, #4, pp. 533–545.

Price, D. 1963. *Little science, big science*. Columbia University Press.

Quandt, R.E. 1976. Some quantitative aspects of the economics journal literature. *Journal of Political Economy* 84 #4, pp. 741–755.

Quine, W.V. 1969. Epistemology naturalized. In *Ontological relativity and other essays*, pp. 69–90. Columbia University Press.

Shapin, S. 1996. *The scientific revolution*. University of Chicago Press.

Simon, H. 1945. *Administrative behavior*. Macmillan, 1957.

——— 1957. *Models of man*. John Wiley.

Stigler, G.J. & C. Friedland 1975. The citation practices of doctorates in economics. *Journal of Political Economy* 83 #3, pp. 477–507. Reprinted in G.J. Stigler, *The economist as preacher and other essays*, pp. 192–222. University of Chicago Press, 1982.

Whitley, R. 1984. *The intellectual and social organization of the sciences*. Clarendon Press.

Wible, J.R. 1998. *The economics of science: methodology and epistemology as if economics really mattered*. Routledge.

Wootton, D. 2015. *The invention of science: a new history of the scientific revolution*. HarperCollins.

8 Government systems[1]

"Government" is an umbrella term for a linked collection of systems, differing in origin, structure, and evolutionary history. Legislatures are but one of these; others include executive arrangements, bureaucracies or ministries, systems of legal enforcement, military systems, and so on. Each has unique features in terms of internal processes and aspects of the environment (including other social systems) to which they are sensitive and on which they impact. What unites these government systems is that their impacts on other social systems and individuals can involve the legitimized use of force by government itself (although the use of such force has the tacit consent of most of the governed).

We have learned from many sources that the epistemic capabilities of legislators and bureaucrats are insufficient to the task of accurately evaluating the fitness for purpose of the legislation and rules they propose, let alone of accounting for the costs or benefits of the secondary consequences that might follow from their application.[2] In addition, as Buchanan & Tullock (1962) and others have pointed out, legislators and bureaucrats are self-interested (in a not necessarily pejorative sense) human beings who face a range of incentives, not all of which point to action geared to the wellbeing of the country in general, or even of specific constituent groups. It is widely presumed that the current mechanisms of democratic politics are very poor at conveying to policymakers in more than vague terms what constituents want or need[3] (and this is complicated by the fact that constituents express diverse and incompatible needs and wants); at least, they certainly do not convey in any practical detail how to realize policy in action. To bolster this rather dismal picture, there has been extensive documentation of what is characterized as "government failure".[4] And yet – and here we have a paradox – government, of which a legislature and a working bureaucracy are vital components, is one of the most successful social arrangements ever to appear, in terms of survival and growth of influence.[5] How is this possible, if legislators and other government actors are inherently unable, in most cases, to fulfill promises made, and even when attempts are made at implementation, are unable to gauge the consequences, so that, even given the best intentions and despite the fact that there are always some beneficiaries of any particular item of legislation or rule, a considerable amount of economic and social damage is inevitable?

It is obvious that this paradox can be resolved by asserting that the forms of government that have succeeded have done so because they have provided a net

DOI: 10.4324/9781003336150-8

benefit. The hypothesis is that if government in its current form were not a net benefit, if the directives produced were not in some sense "optimal", then there would be incentive to change it or even do away with it. Since there is clearly no significant movement in this direction, it must be that, when all costs (including transaction costs) and benefits (including intangible ones) are taken into account, there must be a net benefit. This is the argument put forward by many prominent economists, including Becker (1983), Stigler (1992), and Wittman (1989).[6] Unfortunately, no mechanism is given for how epistemically challenged and self-interested legislators could produce such optimal legislation, but it could be that each is "led by an invisible hand to promote an end which is no part of his intention". How this particular "hand" could work in the context of legislatures is considerably more mystifying than how Adam Smith's works in the context of markets, but this is something of a moot point, since the net benefit conclusion depends on the assessment of unquantified and unquantifiable costs and benefits in an assumed equilibrium, and so it is no more than an unjustified assertion, an untestable claim.

A much simpler resolution of the paradox would be to dispense with claims as to the net benefit or otherwise of the government systems and to hold that government is successful because, first, it provides clear and viable opportunities for the pursuit of happiness of internal participants (whether that be power and prestige, or wealth, or the promotion of societal ends thought worthwhile); second, it is an arrangement which is capable of sensing (and even anticipating) and reacting adaptively to certain features of its environment; and third, its product is such that, over time, it at least partially conditions the feedback from the environment toward favoring the system's sustainability and growth of effective authority. It is also worth noting that, while the reactions from the system's environment become more pointed from time to time in voting exercises, such feedback, to the extent that it is effective, is directed at those internal participants who face election and not at the systemic processes, much less at the system itself, so that only in very extreme cases of widespread rebellion would its existence as a viable system be threatened.

The question arises, then, of exactly what sort of "viable systems" comprise a government. An extensive literature in political science and public choice economics gives us excellent detail about how particular processes within legislatures and bureaucracies operate, but does not add up to an overall picture that addresses the issues of viability and adaptability of the systems as a whole. In order to address the question, it is necessary to focus on understanding how the various processes within the government systems interrelate so as to maintain system integrity and enable adaptability.

Legislatures

Legislatures are the legislation-producing component of democratic government. They are arrangements in which a limited number individuals, some of whom are elected as representatives and others of whom are private lobbyists whose business it is to influence legislation,[7] interact according to specific transactional modes, producing continually updated bodies of legislation.[8] Legislatures were conceived in a constructivist manner as organizations with fairly simple constitutional specifications, but they have evolved into much more complex arrangements and are more usefully characterized as spontaneous orders.[9] Any doubt as to their complex, adaptive nature should be quelled by a perusal of Riddick (1992), an exposition of the accumulated rules governing the activities of the US Senate, which describes over 10,000 precedents.[10] In analyzing such systems, then, it is not unreasonable to differentiate between planning and acting on an individual level and the emergent systemic outcomes which are a side-effect of that activity in a particular context.

Common parlance is an impediment to clarity about the systemic nature of legislatures. The terms used to refer to legislators, like "policymaker" and "lawmaker", contain the implication that it is the individual legislator who makes the legislation. But this is obviously not so. Legislators may draft bills, and may have clear ideas as to what specific legislation they would like to see passed, but they cannot individually enact it unilaterally. They must become participants in a process in which proposed legislation is discussed and amended, where it is subject to the vagaries of compromise and logrolling, where even when initially passed it is subject to further modification in the process of reconciliation in conference committees. The legislation that ends up being enacted is emergent from this process and may bear little relation to the initially proposed bill.

The characteristics and purposes of individual legislators and lobbyists, and their epistemic and other limitations, are important considerations in understanding their behavior, but for understanding the operation of legislatures it is necessary in addition to examine not only the processes involved in legislator and lobbyist activity and interaction but also their organization, because adaptation and growth are features of the system as a whole. Legislatures are systems which are obviously capable of adaptation in order to survive and prosper, but attributing to them goals appropriate for individuals is a serious misconception.

But there is nothing original in the observation that legislatures are not individuals.[11] It has been common in the past for economists, from Pigou to Samuelson, to characterize legislatures as if they were a powerful person (a benevolent dictator, for example) with motivations and goals such as would be reasonable or desirable (in the opinion of the analyst) for such a person.[12] However, this is now sometimes recognized as a metaphor that should at least be qualified, as much attention has been devoted to the study of the internal structure of legislative systems. Economists and political scientists in the "rational choice" tradition[13] have theorized about political arrangements in much the same methodologically individualistic way that most economists approach market arrangements – individuals, constrained by the given arrangements, choose the best of the expected outcomes from the available options according to their preferences, which are assumed to be comparable and transitively ordered, *i.e.*, they maximize expected utility.[14] The problem then becomes to examine how groups of individuals, faced with making a "group choice" will tend to react under different institutional arrangements. There is no assumption here that the group is merely the individual writ large; in fact one of the major findings of this line of research is that there exists no reasonable (which excludes dictatorial) way of forming a coherent group preference from the preferences of rational individuals.[15] Furthermore, theorists in this tradition, Buchanan and Tullock (1962), for example, explicitly reject naïve personifications of both the State and society at large; that is (p. 12), they reject the "organic conceptions" of the State as "some *überindividuell* entity" and the existence of a "general will" or an overarching "public interest".

What does not seem to have changed, however, is the unexamined assumption that legislatures have a purpose,[16] and that this purpose is to generally (on balance, at least) improve the lot of the citizens subject to the legislation produced. The legislative individual has faded into the background, but her purpose, like a Cheshire cat's grin, is still very much in evidence.

In what follows, the hypothesis will be put forward that a legislative system can be characterized as a materially open system with a closed causal cycle of processes, each of which provides the necessary output for the succeeding one. The output of one of these processes is a modifiable body of legislation which is the system's internal model of its environment but which also impinges directly on and constrains activity in that environment. This enables the legislative system to attach itself, parasitically, to its host, the market economy, and it is able to thrive and grow as long as that host is productive enough to sustain the extractions that are called for by the legislation produced. As a separate social system with its own internal components and processes, it is not purposeful in any sense other than to maintain its own survival and growth, and to ascribe to it the explicit purpose of benefiting the greater society, whether one thinks that it succeeds or fails in that respect, is a serious misconception, an error of anthropomorphism.

A legislative system as shown in Figure 8.1 encompasses the activities of people in their roles of legislators (and their staffs)[17] and lobbyists interacting according to specific transactional modes, which include lobbying, logrolling, agenda-setting, voting, and constituent relations, and engaging in the proposal, selection, and development of bills and resolutions (and amendments to these). Observable as the emergent result of this activity is a mutable body of enacted legislation. A mildly unorthodox aspect of this description is the inclusion of lobbyists as components of the system itself, as opposed to external influences acting on the system. This inclusion is suggested by the observation that lobbyists and legislators are in regular contact throughout the legislative process, and that lobbyists contribute to the development of bills and amendments along with legislators.[18] The general citizenry, on whom the legislation impacts, are part of the system's environment. The focus here is on the organization of the various processes within the legislative system involving the activities of legislators and lobbyists, and by "organization" is meant how the separate processes, their inputs and outputs, are related to each other, and how this organization results in a coherent, potentially long-living, materially open but efficiently (in the causal sense) closed, adaptive system.

The body of enacted legislation, largely stable but changeable (almost always by accretion) in reaction to new initiatives and reassessments, is the structure within the system that serves as a model of the system's environment – a model that is continuously updated by environmental feedback transmitted (and filtered) by the agency of repeated legislative transactions through which legislators and lobbyists

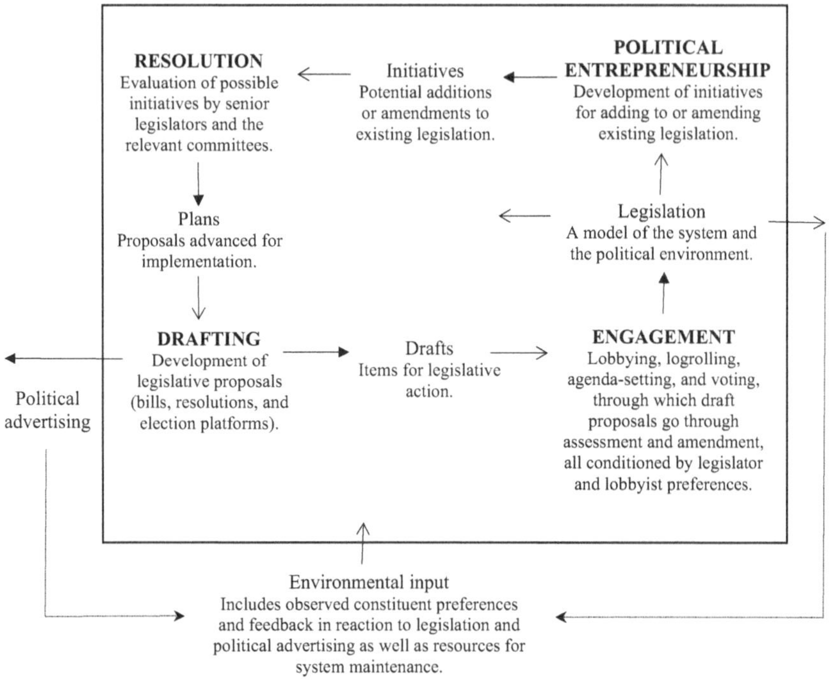

Figure 8.1 Process organization in a legislative system.

engage with each other. Political entrepreneurs within the system rely, at least in part, on this existing knowledge base in imagining new legislative initiatives and in assessing the feasibility of these surviving, at least in part, the encounter with other legislators and lobbyists, and thus act as an anticipatory process affecting the system's bill-and-resolution-drafting and platform-development propensities.[19] The "resolution" processes serve to cull from the legislative initiatives the ones viewed as actionable by those in control of these processes (committee chairs, for example). The "drafting" processes include formalization of legislative proposals for submission to the "engagement" processes, as well as explication of proposals and platform to constituents, an activity labelled here as "political advertising".[20] Out of repeated transactions (involving lobbying, logrolling, and agenda-setting with respect to the consideration of bills) between legislators and lobbyists (acting according to their individual subjective preferences but, for legislators, conditioned by perceived constituent preferences), and eventually terminated by voting, there emerges the structure of enacted legislation.

It is the purposeful agency of the legislators and lobbyists, in the course of acting according to their subjective preferences and motivations, which provides the motive force animating the processes in the system. Legislators and lobbyists interact by participating in engagement, entrepreneurship, resolution, and drafting under the institutions of legislative procedure – a set of processes which, given the system's material openness, are each necessary for the function of the others, and which together are sufficient to enable the system's existence as a self-maintaining entity.

To summarize, this organization of processes represents a legislative system as an anticipatory system incorporating and maintaining a working model of its environment, a model which can be accessed internally within the system to project the anticipated effects of future actions taken by the system. As with other social systems such as markets and sciences, the internal model of the environment has causal effects on the environment.[21] Reaction from the environment is taken into account in the processes which update the model, and this in turn provides an enhanced picture of the environment upon which entrepreneurial actors can base proposals which condition the propensities of the system to act on the environment.[22]

From the perspective of an individual within the system, participation has many potential benefits, both tangible and intangible: doing good for society, righting perceived wrongs, joining with others in promoting an ideological agenda, gaining power and influence, benefiting monetarily. From the perspective of the system, these motivations played out in the context of the particular transactions possible within it have the emergent effect of endowing the system with adaptability in the face of those reactions from its environment to which, for its own survival, it must be sensitive.[23]

One feature of this legislative system which differs markedly from market and science systems is the nature of its anchor to the world outside of it. Markets face real scarcity as a hard constraint; sciences (to varying extents) prioritize conformity with observation of real events. In contrast, the only serious fully external constraint on legislatures (besides constitutional constraints[24] and the input of market-generated resources) is the preferences of constituents, and these are notoriously divergent and usually expressed as generalities lacking in specificity as to both implementation and understanding of possible adverse consequences,[25] and can be conditioned to some extent by political advertising. It may be argued in addition that constituent preferences are taken account of only intermittently, at election time, but legislators, like monopolists attuned, as Wohlgemuth (1999) puts it, to the effects of their actions on possibilities for future competitive entry, are attentive to current moods as harbingers of possibilities for being voted out at future elections.[26] There is continuous political advertising aimed at conditioning constituent preferences. As public choice analysis has emphasized, the personal preferences of legislators and lobbyists loom large, but they are certainly always conditioned by perceived constituent preferences.[27]

In short, while constituent preferences are the legislative system's anchor to reality, and as such certainly do affect legislators' perceptions and behavior, that reality is not composed of hard and stubborn facts but is a shifting amalgam of diverse, abstract, inconsistent, and emotional ideas.[28] And yet, this shifting amalgam has an underlying coherence; its basis is in ideologies, the belief systems that all people adopt in order to simplify a complex reality and give meaning and sense to their social experiences.[29] The dominant ideologies in a society[30] are not static; they change over time as social experiences change,[31] and one major factor in those changes is the experience of living under legislation. There is two-way feedback between dominant ideologies and the legislative system.[32] Higgs' (1987) exposition of "the ratchet effect" highlights the particular role of societal crises and of the experience of surviving the crises while living under the legislative edicts introduced as the government's method of addressing the crises. With legislators attuned to dominant ideologies which take it for granted that a crisis requires legislation to authorize "doing something", the effect is that the legislature's disposition to deal with the crisis not only by expanding its scale but also by widening the scope of its activities is enhanced, and legislation enacted following such a disposition results in increasing legislative authority over aspects of society not previously subject to it. When the crisis passes, when the war is won, when the depression is over, when the pandemic is survived, there may be pressure to repeal the extraordinary measures, but the experience of living through the crisis under those measures and successfully returning to normalcy has the effect of validating to some extent those legislative advances, and repeal will be, at best, incomplete.[33]

It is not only as a result of crisis survival that the legislature's output conditions its ideological environment. The nature of legislation is such that any particular piece of legislation will result in (at least short-term) benefits to some and costs to others. As the quantity and scope of legislation increases, most constituents will experience both costs and benefits and can come to regard their benefits as a right. The presence of lobbyists within the system, together with the imperative faced by legislators to get reelected, conditions legislation to concentrate benefits and distribute costs,[34] and this property of legislation enhances in individuals a perception of general benefit (especially if the financing of the benefits can be achieved by borrowing or money creation), so that, even if (by some measure) it were possible that one could show net cost overall, it would be unlikely to be convincing at the individual level.

In short, a legislative system, like other adaptive social systems, has an anchor to reality, but the reality to which it reacts is ideological rather than physical. Systems anchored to physical aspects of their environment face hard constraints; and although it is conceivable that intangible constraints can be effective, in the case of legislatures the intangible constraint is subject to modification by the system's own output in a way that is favorable to the system's growth.[35]

A question not well answered in current political science is why, given its unlikelihood in the face of the severe difficulties characterized by Scheall (2020) as "the problem of policymaker ignorance", the significant possibilities for individual corruption detailed by political scientists, and the pervasive phenomenon of "government failure" documented by public choice scholars, the institution of the legislature has not only survived as an integral part of society but has been able to greatly expand its influence over society at large. A partial explanation has been given by Boettke *et al.* (2007), who point out that the political survival of individual legislators is not closely tied to whether or not the legislation they enable enhances economic efficiency.[36] Legislators are not ignorant of what is needed to succeed within the legislative system; it is just that economic knowledge is seldom helpful (and its application often distinctly unhelpful) in that regard. The feedback to the legislative system (and to individual legislators) from the economic effects of legislation is not direct but is filtered through an ideological lens; legislators rarely suffer political losses from economically inefficient or damaging legislation provided that the legislation can be characterized as conforming to the ideological presuppositions of the majority of constituents.

But this is not the whole story. The fact that individual legislators can prosper in the face of epistemic and other difficulties does not fully explain why the system as a whole should survive and prosper. To explain that, it is necessary to inquire into the organization of the system's processes and to show how these processes combine constructively to endow the system with the capability for adaptation to (and even anticipation of) environmental feedback which may threaten its integrity. The bases for this feedback are the ideological preconceptions prevalent in society, and those preconceptions are, over time, conditioned, by the experience of living under the very legislation the system produces, to favor the production of more of it. The ability to react adaptively to the external pressure of ideologies combined with the conditioning of those ideologies by legislation itself is how the legislative system is able to survive and grow in scope and influence. To get to the source and mechanism of the legislature's adaptability it is necessary to understand both its organization as a system of mutually supportive processes which generate emergent effects, and the reciprocal interactions between its emergent products and its environment.

Government bureaucracies

A government bureaucracy (a "department" or an "agency" within a department) has some superficial resemblance to a firm – both are organized groupings of people established initially in order to enable the production of some envisioned output. The organization of both will involve levels of hierarchy in which those people at a higher level may, to some extent, direct the activities of those at a lower level. But there are fundamental differences. The most obvious one, a difference Mises (1944) discusses in detail, is that the production of government bureaucracies is not subject to the discipline of profit and loss through market transactions.[37] While this is clearly a significant point of difference, it is inadequate by itself for understanding the working and operation of government bureaucracies, for these entities exist in an environment very different from that of a private firm. While both are subject to significant externally-imposed constraints on both their output and their internal operations, the rules and directives imposed on government bureaucracies by the legislative, executive, and judicial branches of government[38] are, in their pervasiveness and their inconstant and often-vague nature, such as to create a constellation of constraints and incentives that affect internal operations and output much more than do the regulations imposed on private firms.[39]

Government bureaucracies are set up as organizations charged with administering the implementation of specific items of legislation. But, like any social grouping in which there are long-term interactions between the people involved within the group, the participants, through their interactions and their efforts to pursue their own interests in addition to furthering the purported aims of the organization, will learn how the group actually works internally. The organization will not be that of a Weberian machine, if for no other reason than the fact, emphasized by Tullock (1965), that information flowing both up and down the hierarchy will be subject to distortion. There will be entrepreneurial initiatives within the group aimed at changing the group's procedures, its modes of interaction, and its output, and there will be judgments made by managers and executives as to the desirability of these initiatives in the light of their interpretation of the constraining legislation. There will possibly emerge within the group a shared sense of mission. In short, the organization, if left to itself as a "free bureaucracy", will take on the aspect of an anticipatory system with the designated legislation and its funding appropriation as its two major constraints.

However, the situation for actual government bureaucracies is considerably less "free". Legislatures and legislative committees impose detailed restrictions on the bureaucracies' internal procedures – specifying rules for hiring and firing of personnel, for purchasing of needed inputs, for dealing with suppliers and contractors, and for salaries and criteria for promotion. Presidents attempt to influence the operation and output of agencies by executive appointments, directives to "improve efficiency", and departmental reorganizations. Courts intervene in agency management, allowing challenges to particular aspects of agency outputs and even of agency procedures. No bureaucracy can serve three masters, and yet that is what they must do, or be seen to do. In addition, the impositions and requirements can change frequently, due to changes in political control, constituent-driven pressures on elected officials, or media highlighting of adverse effects of some aspects of the agency's outputs.

With these considerations in mind, Figure 8.2 represents a bureaucratic government agency as a hampered anticipatory system.

The pressures and controls exerted by the executive, legislative, and judicial branches of government have the effect of constraining (but not eliminating) the options for entrepreneurship within the agency – an effect indicated by showing the innovation and judgment processes in small type. The plans input to and the internal assessment of the results output from the action processes are shown as dashed arrows to indicate that the communications up and down the hierarchical chain will inevitably result in some loss of fidelity along the way, and so there is opportunity for lower-level managers and the operators who perform the tasks that constitute the agency's output to introduce their own individual preferences and dispositions and to exercise some discretion and situational flexibility in shaping the output. While the effects of the agency's output on its clients (those in the environment who are affected by, or interested in, the agency's actions) can be observed, and reacted to, by people within the agency, the major feedback from clients is indirect. Clients unhappy with agency procedures or actions can, and do, lobby the appropriate people in the executive and the legislature or pursue relief in the courts; those wishing to enhance or extend the agency's scope of operation can do the same. This sort of feedback goes on continuously, and it is relatively easy for politicians and judges to react to concentrated pressure by adjusting the agency's appropriations or by issuing rules and directives, whether or not the new rules and directives are compatible with existing ones. A major part of the entrepreneurial activity within the agency is focused on anticipating and reacting to this politically-induced uncertainty, and it is no surprise that there should be a tendency, in bureaucratic action, to err on the side of caution so as not to induce reactionary additions to rules and directives.

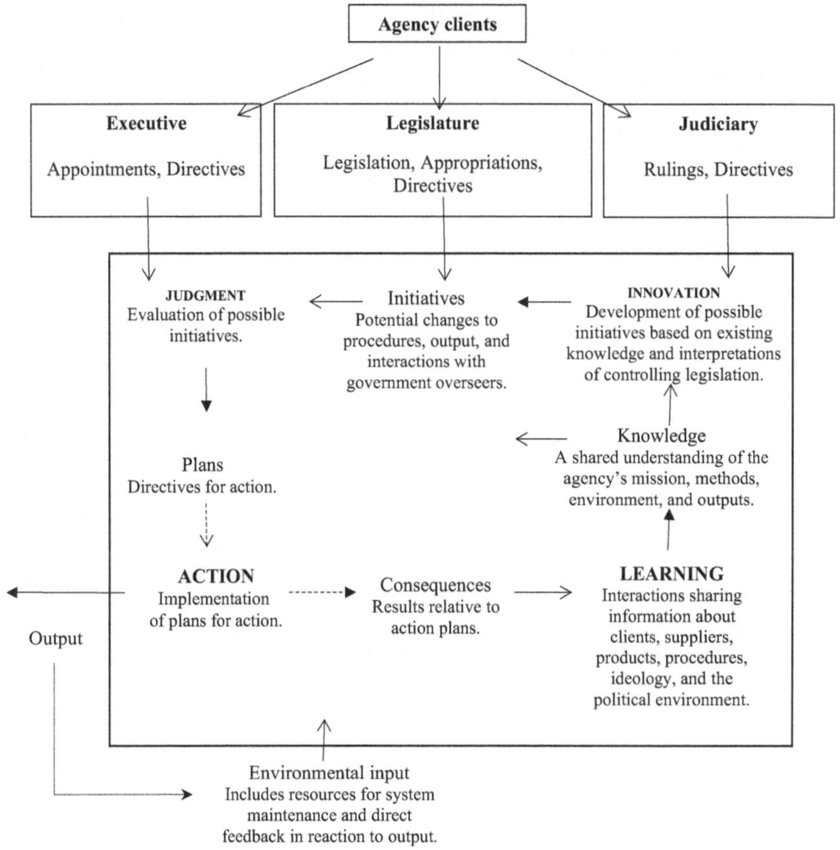

Figure 8.2 Process organization in a government agency.

Different agencies will experience these effects in different levels of intensity, depending on the characteristics of their enabling legislation, the interest legislators take in the agency's output, and the strengths of the reactions of the agency's clients. Wilson (1989, pp. 75–83) classifies agencies into four types based on such political considerations:

1 Client agencies, where the agency must deal with a single organized client group that benefits from the agency's activity. The costs of the activity are spread over a large, dispersed, and therefore unorganized group. The clients lobby to ensure the continuance of the agency and, if possible, its growth. And, especially if the enabling legislation is vague as to the specific task of the agency, the clients can shape the agency's activities to their own benefit. An example is the Commodity Credit Corporation, a USDA agency whose enabling legislation[40] described its tasks as "stabilizing, supporting, and protecting farm income and prices", "assisting in the maintenance of balanced and adequate supplies of agricultural commodities", and "facilitating the orderly distribution of agricultural commodities".

2 "Entrepreneurial" agencies, where the costs are concentrated in one group or locality and the benefits are widely dispersed. Such an agency would be politically difficult to create except in a case where the enabling legislation and support is the result of lobbying and effective media advertising on the part of specific policy entrepreneurs. An example is the National Highway Traffic Safety Administration, an agency of the US Department of Transportation, created in reaction to Ralph Nader's raising and promotion of the issue of car safety, and tasked with[41] providing "for a coordinated national safety program and establishment of safety standards for motor vehicles in interstate commerce".

3 Interest-group agencies, whose output imposes concentrated costs on one group and concentrated benefits on another. Here, the agency may find itself driven in one direction as one of the competing groups is able to influence the political majority, and then in another direction as the political climate changes. An example is the Occupational Safety and Health Administration, an agency of the US Department of Labor, originally tasked with developing and establishing recommended occupational safety and health standards.

4 Majoritarian agencies, whose costs and benefits are not borne by any organized client group. They are the result of majoritarian politics and, although they may face pressures as political majorities change, they have little or no organized client opposition. And, especially if the enabling legislation is broad and vague, the agency's output can be adjusted with experience to avoid creating a concentrated client opposition. An example is the Antitrust Division of the US Department of Justice, authorized, suitably vaguely, by the Sherman Act[42] "to protect trade and commerce against unlawful restraints and monopolies".

It is evident from this analysis of types of government bureaucracies that they constitute something of a menagerie. While "regulatory capture", as described by Stigler (1971) and others, is a very real phenomenon, it is neither simple nor universal, and depends for its effect on the extent to which client groups are able to bend agencies to their benefit through executive or legislative lobbying.[43] While the tendency for agency executives to attempt to increase their agency's budget, size, and scope as much as possible, as hypothesized by Niskanen (1971), is a very real phenomenon, it is not true of every agency since, depending on the types of clients affected, growth may result in increased oversight, constraint, and decrease of autonomy.[44] For a more comprehensive understanding of agency behavior it is necessary to impose on the basic bureaucratic organization the effects of the agency's main anchor to its environment – the external factor which most constrains its possible range of action – which is the activity of the legislature, whose output, as we have seen, is conditioned by the divergent, imprecise, and short-term-oriented input from its constituency.

Even agencies of the same type may diverge in the workings of their internal processes. There are factors, specific to the nature of the tasks with which agencies are charged, which influence the ways in which they operate. These are the ability of their main output to be readily measured or assessed and the ability of agency managers to monitor the activities of the operators responsible for producing the agency's output. Wilson (1989, pp. 158–171) identifies four modes of operation, based on combinations of these internal factors:

1 Production agencies, in which both operator activity and outcomes are observable, tend to operate efficiently as long as legislation endows the agency with a clear and unambiguous goal and the agency's output earns it political support. An example is the US Social Security Administration, whose main goal, to pay regular retirement benefits based on lifetime earnings, is clear, measurable, and has political and constituent support.
2 Procedural agencies, in which operator activity is observable but the outcome does not lend itself to measurement, tend to emphasize procedure and "red tape" over efficiency and fidelity of output. An example is any army in peacetime.
3 Craft agencies, in which operator activity is difficult to observe but outcomes are relatively easy to assess, tend to develop a strong sense of mission. An example is the US Army Corps of Engineers.
4 Coping agencies, in which neither operator activity nor outcomes are readily observable, tend to incorporate conflicting incentives facing managers and operators, with managers focusing on any aspects of output to which measurement can be applied and operators acting with some combination of doing what they think is right within the constraint of supplying the managers with acceptable statistics or simply (and often resentfully) letting the constraints define the output. An example is any police department, where policemen out in the community can choose to resolve situations without arrest or citation despite the pressure from supervisors to boost the department's statistics.

In summary, among government bureaucracies there is exhibited a wide range of adaptive responses to their environment and the constraints it imposes on them. Unlike market firms which, even if organized bureaucratically, are subject for their survival and growth to the clear forces of market discipline, government bureaucracies face constraints which, while more forgiving in terms of survival and growth, are, at the same time, both more invasive of their internal operations and more likely to change unpredictably. Given such differences, any exhortations that agencies would be more efficient if run like a business are naïve.

A major interest in what follows is the interaction between government and science, and this (in the US context) involves two major agencies, the National Science Foundation (NSF) and the National Institutes of Health (NIH). The NSF's primary task is to support basic scientific and engineering research, and that of the NIH is to support biomedical research and its applications. In terms of the classifications described above, these agencies are client agencies whose clients, the researchers who may apply for funding and their supporting organizations, clearly perceive a benefit from them. They are also production agencies, in that their output is readily observable, their assigned tasks, while broad, are sufficiently clear, and their activity enjoys widespread political support. It is no surprise that, as we shall see, these agencies have enjoyed sustained growth, and have become a major factor in funding – and influencing – scientific research.

Notes

1 This chapter contains text previously published in McQuade (2021).

2 See particularly Hayek (1989, p. 7): "If man is not to do more harm than good in his efforts to improve the social order, he will have to learn that in this, as in all other fields where essential complexity of an organized kind prevails, he cannot acquire the full knowledge which would make mastery of the events possible. … The recognition of the insuperable limits to his knowledge ought indeed to teach the student of society a lesson of humility which should guard him against becoming an accomplice in men's fatal striving to control society – a striving which makes him not only a tyrant over his fellows, but which may well make him the destroyer of a civilization which no brain has designed but which has grown from the free efforts of millions of individuals." According to Scheall (2020, p. 1): "The problem of policymaker ignorance is the simple fact that the success of purposeful political action is necessarily limited by the nature and extent of policymakers' ignorance and their capacities to learn. We cannot deliberately realize policy objectives beyond the ken and control of our political representatives. … Policymaker ignorance is the ultimate barrier that we cannot breach in our attempts to deliberately reform society and 'make the world a better place'."

3 The assumption of weak voter feedback is disputed by Wittman (1989), who argued that voters are sufficiently informed and legislators sufficiently disciplined by democratic processes that the legislation produced is wealth-maximizing. Among others, Boettke *et al.* (2007, pp. 136–141) have convincingly contested this view, at least in the extreme form put forward by Wittman. See also Boudreaux (1996) and Wagner (1996).

4 Since Buchanan & Tullock (1962) developed their theory of "collective choice" with the very reasonable assumption that individuals, when participating in the political realm, were no more nor less self-interested than when participating in the economic realm, a large literature has emerged under the rubric of "public choice" which has examined political institutions both theoretically (from a methodologically individualist perspective) and empirically. One result of this investigation has been the recognition that neither markets nor governments meet any standard of perfection and, further, that the shortcomings of government (even with respect to claimed intentions) are considerably more damaging than market failures. Keech & Munger (2015) present a comprehensive "anatomy" of government failure from a theoretical perspective, and Simmons (2011, pp. 185–320) provides an extensive catalog of case studies. Another list of examples, this time from an Austrian perspective and emphasizing the unintended consequences of government action is found in Gallaway (1998). See also Ikeda (1997).

5 Estimates by Tanzi & Schuknecht (2000, p. 6) of government expenditure as a percentage of GDP in a number of countries including the US indicate a growth factor between 1870 and 1996 of about 4.5. But expenditure is a very incomplete measure of the size and scope of government. As Higgs (1987, pp. 31–33) points out, the growth of regulation is not captured by the standard measures of growth, and "the long-run growth of governmental activity in the US economy has depended mainly on the scope of effective governmental authority over economic decision-making, not on the degree which existing governmental potential has been realized at any particular time". A rough indicator of the growth of legislative activity is given by an estimate by Govtrack (govtrack.us/congress/bills/statistics) that, since World War II, "Congress has typically enacted 4–6 million words of new law in each two-year Congress". Perusal of the *Federal Register*, which lists final rules (interpretations based on enacted legislation) of government agencies, shows a growth in such rules from about 4000 in 1993 to over 94,000 in 2015. For a readable history of the growth of government in the US, see Hughes (1991).

6 According to Stigler (1992, p. 459), "every durable social institution or practice is efficient, or it would not persist over time. … Tested institutions and practices found wanting will not survive in a world of rational people. … So I would argue that all social institutions, including common and statute laws, must be efficient." Wittman

(1989, p. 1421) makes a more pointed claim, implying that democratic methods are as capable of disciplining legislators as market methods are of disciplining producers: "Behind every model of government failure is an assumption of extreme voter stupidity, serious lack of competition, or excessively high negotiation/transfer costs. Economists are very suspicious of similar assumptions regarding economic markets. This skepticism should be carried over to models of government behavior." The Achilles' heel of this line of thought is the fact that political and economic institutions and transactions are radically different in the incentives offered and the type of knowledge produced.

7 While, conventionally, "legislature" refers to the body of elected politicians, I use it here as a synonym for "legislative system", *i.e.*, the system whose elements are the legislators, their staffs, and the lobbyists.

8 The usual characterization of legislators as "lawmakers" is inapt, as Hayek's (1973, p. 72) distinction between law (spontaneously evolved rules of conduct) and legislation (rules deliberately constructed) makes clear. The common misconception that all law is legislation is (p. 73) "a product of the intentionalist fallacy characteristic of constructivism, a relapse into those design theories of human institutions which stand in irreconcilable conflict with all we know about the evolution of law and most other human institutions".

9 A very clear statement describing the political sphere of society as a spontaneous order (as opposed to an organization) is given by Martin (2010). Also Butos & McQuade (2017, p. 14): "if social science is going to seriously treat the interactions of different complex systems (science and government, for example) then a first step is to include in the analysis that government is indeed a complex system with its own characteristic structure, internal transaction types, and emergent effects". Devins *et al.* (2015, p. 613) observe that "Legal institutions, designed to be economies [*i.e.*, planned and controllable entities, in their parlance], become spontaneous orders as they evolve in response to shifting political and social environments, unforeseen and unforeseeable by the designers of these institutions. All institutions, even the most seemingly fundamental, evolve so as to drift, even dislodge, from their original premises, so that attempts to engineer these institutions will always fall apart in the long run."

10. Such a characterization applies to legislatures not only in the US but also in democratic societies in which the legislature has considerable (but not necessarily total) independence from the other branches of government. It applies perhaps somewhat more clearly to systems in which individual players (including the executive) have limited control over the legislative agenda. It certainly does not apply to "puppet" legislatures controlled by authoritarian rulers in which the order is anything but spontaneous.

11 In fact, Bastiat (1848, p. 146) says, with his usual clarity: "I contend that this *personification of the State* has been in the past, and will be in the future, a fertile source of calamities and of revolutions."

12 Ascribing purposes and goals to the State as a unitary entity is done in an offhand manner, without analysis or even consideration that there might be anything controversial about it. For example, Pigou (1932, p. 142) states "It is, however, possible for the State, if it so chooses, to remove the divergence [between private and social net product] in any field by 'extraordinary encouragements' or 'extraordinary restraints' upon investments in that field. The most obvious forms which these encouragements and restraints may assume are, of course, those of bounties and taxes." In a similar vein, Samuelson & Nordhaus (2010, pp. 306–308) ask "What are the appropriate economic goals for government action in a modern mixed economy? ... A central economic purpose of government is to assist in the socially desirable allocation of resources. ... In addition, government tries to smooth out the ups and downs of the business cycle, in order to avoid either large-scale unemployment at the bottom of the cycle or high inflation at the top of the cycle." De Jasay (1985, p. 1), however, deliberately ascribes purposes and goals to the State in an "as if" sense: "Braving the risks of confusing institutions with persons and the difficulties of passing from the prince to his government, [my approach] chooses to treat the State as if it were a real entity, as if it had a will

and were capable of reasoned decisions about means to its ends. Hence it tries to explain the State's conduct towards us in terms of *what it could be expected to do*, in successive historical situations, if it rationally pursued ends that it can plausibly be supposed to have."

13 For a good introductory overview of the application of rational choice methods to politics, see Shepsle (2010).

14 A theorist is free to hypothesize the sorts of preferences that are likely to be uppermost in particular situations. For example, Riker (1962, p. 22) claims that "What the rational political man wants, I believe, is to win, a much more specific and specifiable motive than the desire for power. ... He wants to exploit each situation to his advantage, and he wants to succeed in a given situation." Riker viewed political science as a study of what he called "heresthetics", *i.e.*, strategic behavior aimed at winning rather than persuading, which includes particular behaviors such as agenda-setting, coalition-forming, and logrolling. See Riker (1977).

15 This result is known as Arrow's Theorem – see Arrow (1951). It means, in practice, that while group decisions may depend on individual preferences, they are manipulable by those with the power to set agendas for the process of translating individual preferences into group decisions.

16 An exception is Kohn (2004, p. 310), who in a critique of the dominant and long-lasting "value paradigm" of economic theorizing and its cornerstone assumption of trading equilibrium for its claim to be a general theory of economics, notes that "the interaction of these individuals within firms and governments is ignored by the value paradigm and the aggregates themselves are treated as though they had motives and intelligences of their own". See also Martin (2010, p. 234), who is clear that "policy is the result of an emergent process, not an object of choice. Ideas do not translate one to one into policies in the same way they would for an individual. Politics is not purposive; but political agents are."

17 According to US congressional statistics published by the Brookings Institution (2019), the number of congressional committee staff and personal staff employees has grown from 39 in 1891 to 9,947 in 2015 (reaching a high plateau of over 11,000 between 1980 and 2006). Salisbury & Shepsle (1981, pp. 563–567) point out that staffs enable legislators to pursue multiple goals at the same time: getting legislation developed and ushered toward enactment, seeking advancement within the system, and working toward reelection.

18 For in-depth studies of legislator–lobbyist interactions, see Baumgartner *et al.* (2009) and Godwin *et al.* (2013). According to Buchanan & Tullock (1962, p. 294), "Scientific progress in the analysis of politics cannot be made until this widespread activity [*i.e.*, special-interest lobbying] is fully incorporated in the analytical models." Also relevant is the literature on rent-seeking stemming from Tullock (1967) and Krueger (1974). There is also a large literature on legislator–legislator interactions, particularly logrolling and coalition-forming – see, for example, Buchanan & Tullock (1962, ch. 10 & 11), Weingast & Marshall (1988), Evans (1994), and Holcombe (2006). Buchanan & Tullock (1962, pp. 135–136) draw attention to an aspect of bill construction which they call "implicit logrolling". This involves the development of complex bills covering multiple issues designed to take advantage of the fact that a legislator who feels strongly about one of the issues may vote for the bill even the other issues in it, about which he feels less strongly, are not to his liking.

19 Martin & Thomas (2013, p. 23), citing a large literature in political science and public choice economics on political entrepreneurship, describe a political entrepreneur as an "individual who plays a key role in identifying policy problems, mobilizing supporting coalitions, and implementing policy change". This is a mixture of political entrepreneurship as described here (which focuses on ideas for legislative initiatives) and opportunistic behavior in the context of engagement with other legislators and lobbyists. They also describe another aspect of political entrepreneurship as being "directed at altering the institutional context within which entrepreneurship occurs". This is

certainly an important phenomenon, and it merits more attention than is given here. It definitely qualifies as entrepreneurship in a general sense, and it is a characteristic also of other social arrangements, including markets and science. It results in the slow but sure evolutionary changes within the system – it is the force behind the size and complexity of the rules and precedents that Riddick's (1992) compilation documents.

20 Political advertising can run the gamut between sincere expressions of intent and misleading and diversionary oratory. On the latter, Scheall (2020, p. 154) points out, "policymakers can often accrue the same benefits by merely pretending to pursue a policy goal as they can by actually pursuing it. … However, in the modern age of 24-hour news, overtly biased journalism, politicians with sizable media budgets, and deranged social media bombardments, it is perhaps easier than ever for those in positions of power to manipulate constituents into mistakenly thinking their interests are being pursued." Either way, political advertising, coming from individual legislators or their surrogates, is intended to influence constituent preferences.

21 In the case of legislatures, this is obvious; the legislative edicts are imposed on the population as a whole and are backed up by legalized force.

22 Devins *et al.* (2015, p. 624) give a very compatible description of the legal system: "Laws are set in motion and catapulted into an ever-evolving dance between the legal system and the entities it regulates. In turn, this dance creates ever-new 'opportunities' in an ever-changing but unintended adjacent possible [*i.e.*, unrealized but realizable system states] into which the legal system evolves and creates yet further adjacent possible opportunities. Laws are 'used' for purposes not intended or envisioned by those creating the laws. Often without intent or foresight, this evolution creates its own future possibilities and then expands into them. Rather like jazz or improvisational comedy, the system enables that which it becomes."

23 In the extreme, as Hobbes (1668, p. 68) put it, "the power of the mighty hath no foundation but in the opinion and belief of the people".

24 The subject of constitutional constraints on legislation is a huge one, far beyond the range of this chapter. It is worth pointing out, however, that a constitution becomes less of a binding constraint over time than it may appear. According to Devins *et al.* (2015, p. 629): "We assert that the history of the United States Constitution, and its gradual failure, provides a compelling demonstration that design does not work. Power structures, institutions, and people will find ways to subvert the initial intent behind institutions in furtherance of their own interests."

25 As Bastiat (1848, p. 140) put it: "The unfortunate State, like Figaro, knows neither to whom to listen nor where to turn. The hundred thousand tongues of press and rostrum all cry out to it at once: 'Organize labor and the workers.' 'Root out selfishness.' 'Repress the insolence and tyranny of capital.'."

26 Professional lobbyists can be much less attentive to voter preferences than can legislators, and this may well be a significant factor in accounting for the bias in legislation toward influential interest groups, a hallmark of "crony capitalism".

27 There is more than a sliver of truth in the quip (usually ascribed to H.L. Mencken) that a politician is an animal which can sit on a fence and yet keep both ears to the ground.

28 Constituent preferences for such (abstract) goals as "economic equality", "economic justice", "a level playing field", and "keeping undesirables out of the country" are loudly and unambiguously expressed, and do not constitute much of a problem for legislators to know them. And constituents, lacking (like most everyone else, including legislators) any coherent theory of society, think that they know the seemingly obvious concrete goals to pursue in order to realize these overarching goals: tax the rich, increase welfare, set minimum wages, subsidize local industry, impose tariffs, build a wall. And there is no big problem for legislators to know that constituents want these sub-goals pursued; indeed, they often agree that these are valid sub-goals for achieving the more abstract goals. What the constituents (chronically) do not know is that the obvious-seeming sub-goals are rarely, if ever, effective steps toward realizing the overarching goals. And not only do the sub-goals not work well, they in addition also tend to have

unintended consequences that can make things worse for some of those demanding constituents. According to Martin (2010, p. 236): "Politicians of all sorts *are* subject to popular control. But that control itself is exercised by those who have *no greater knowledge* of the conditions of the extended order than do the politicians."

29 Martin (2010, p. 240) correctly points out that "the extended order, by default, does not offer tight feedback [to policy-makers]", given that what he means by "tight feedback" is real effects such as scarcities. He does insist, however, on the importance of ideology in politics (p. 237): "The mental models that people have about society determine what sorts of arguments are valid or invalid when discussing policy options."

30 At any time there may be, and often is, more than one dominant ideology (or at least family of ideologies); currently there are two major ones, "the right" and "the left". These have different ideas concerning which areas legislation should address and the extent to which legislation should intrude into private life, but both are in general agreement that legislation of some sort is an appropriate way to address perceived social problems.

31 As Higgs (1991, p. 12) points out, "The world of 1901 differed in many pertinent ways from the world of 1989. Among other differences, people at the two dates had quite different ideas about what they wanted government to do. In the United States in 1901 many people still thought in terms of a variant of classical liberal ideology. ... In 1989, in contrast, most Americans had relatively inflated ideas about the range of social and economic 'problems' they wanted the government to 'solve'."

32 There is no suggestion here of a deterministic relation between ideology and legislation. As Letwin (1965, p. 54) notes, a legislature "is not a factory that mechanically converts opinion into statutes". The effect of any particular external ideology (which legislators themselves may share) is but one input (although a significant one) alongside the personal preferences of legislators and lobbyists into the systemic processes which produce legislation.

33 Higgs (1987, pp. 71–72) describes post-crisis ideological change as follows: "Suppose, for example, that in a great social crisis a command-and-control system displaces the free market. Experience under the new regime will generate learning of several kinds. To some extent government planners and bureaucrats will improve their means of manipulating the economy ... These improvements make the controls less obnoxious to aggrieved parties ... Citizens also learn that some of their prior beliefs about the impossibilities or dangers of governmental control now appear groundless ... Many of the conservatives' stock warnings about the prospective horrors of one thing leading to another are perceived by the masses as well as the elites as overdrawn ... Conceivably, then, ideological learning makes a discrete leap as a result of social crisis and the attendant expansion toward Big Government."

34 There is a large literature on what is called "pork-barrel politics" and "special-interest politics" which examines the stratagems by which legislators and lobbyists can maneuver and lobby to have inserted into legislative packages legislation benefiting targeted parties. See, for example, Buchanan & Tullock (1962), Ferejohn (1974), Stockman (1975), Shepsle & Weingast (1981), and Evans (1994). Such legislation, once in effect, creates a constituency for its continuance which has a strong incentive to resist any efforts at repeal. Tullock (1975) has labelled this phenomenon "the transitional gains trap". Selectorate theory addresses similar issues from a wider perspective in terms of the maintenance of winning coalitions, where, especially in democracies where the winning coalition is a relatively large portion of the electorate, the maintenance of a winning coalition requires a significant provision of so-called public goods in addition to private goods distributed to elites and insiders. See Shirk (1993) and Bueno de Mesquita *et al.* (2003).

35 This is not to say that survival and growth are assured. It is possible, in crisis situations, that the dominant ideological belief in the legitimacy of the system can change rapidly, such that the system cannot adapt (or cannot adapt quickly enough) to its new environment. See Linz (1978) for an extended discussion of the breakdown of democratic systems.

36 In their words, (p. 131): "knowledge generated in the political context may enable individuals to survive in the competitive environment of politics, but it does not lead them to exploit the opportunities for gains from economically beneficial trades and eradicate economic inefficiencies … The persistence of economically inefficient policy is not an illusion because it is possible for politically efficient policies to be economically inefficient. Whereas within a market system technologically possible projects are subjected to the economic test of profit and loss, the economic test of profit and loss is not employed in assessing political choices."

37 According to Mises (1944, p. 19, emphasis added): "Bureaucracy, its merits and its demerits, its working and its operation, can be understood *only* by contrasting it with the operation of the profit motive as it functions in the capitalistic market society."

38 In this discussion of government bureaucracy, we are focusing specifically on the arrangements in place in the US. These will differ in some respects from those in other countries – for example, in parliamentary democracies, the executive and legislative functions are closely combined. For a discussion of national differences, including the effects of cultural differences, see Wilson (1989, pp. 295–312).

39 Galbraith (1967) has argued that large corporations have strong similarities to government bureaucracies in that they are able to insulate themselves from market pressure. This hypothesis has not fared well, given the experiences of once-dominant corporations such as IBM and Polaroid. In contrast, Wilson (1989, p. 115) highlights the fact that, for government bureaucracies, "control over revenues, productive factors, and agency goals is all vested to an important degree in entities external to the organization … [so that] government management tends to be driven by the *constraints* on the organization, not the *tasks* of the organization".

40 See https://www.usda.gov/ccc.

41 See https://www.govtrack.us/congress/bills/89/s3005/text.

42 See https://www.ourdocuments.gov/doc_large_image.php?flash=false&doc=51.

43 As Stigler (1971, p. 5) put it: "We propose the general hypothesis: every industry or occupation that has enough political power to utilize the state will seek to control entry. In addition, the regulatory policy will often be so fashioned as to retard the rate of growth of new firms."

44 Halperin (1974, p. 51) claims to find that agencies "are often prepared to accept less money with greater control than more money with less control". See also Wilson (1989, pp. 179–195) for an extended discussion of the relevance of bureaucratic "turf".

Bibliography

Arrow, K.J. 1951. *Social choice and individual values*. Wiley.

Bastiat, F. 1848. *The State*. In G.B. de Huscar (ed.) & S. Cain (tr.), *Selected essays in political economy*, pp. 140–151. Foundation for Economic Education, 1995.

Baumgartner, F.R., J.M. Berry, M. Hojnacki, D.C. Kimball, & B.L. Leech 2009. *Lobbying and policy change: who wins, who loses, and why*. University of Chicago Press.

Becker, G.S. 1983. A theory of competition among pressure groups for political influence. *Quarterly Journal of Economics* 98 #3, pp. 371–400.

Boettke, P.J., C.J. Coyne, & P.T. Leeson 2007. Saving government failure theory from itself: recasting political economy from an Austrian perspective. *Constitutional Political Economy* 18, pp. 127–143.

Boudreaux, D.J. 1996. Was your high-school civics teacher right after all? Donald Wittman's "*The myth of democratic failure*". *The Independent Review* 1 #1, pp. 111–128.

Brookings Institution 2019. *Vital statistics on congress*. https://www.brookings.edu/multi-chapter-report/vital-statistics-on-congress.

Buchanan, J.M. & G. Tullock 1962. *The calculus of consent: logical foundations of constitutional democracy*. University of Michigan Press.

Bueno de Mesquita, B., A. Smith, R.M. Siverson, & J.D. Morrow 2003. *The logic of political survival*. MIT Press.
Butos, W.N. & T.J. McQuade 2017. Polanyi, Hayek, and Adaptive systems theory. *Cosmos + Taxis* 4 #1, pp. 1–22.
De Jasay, A. 1985. *The State*. Basil Blackwell.
Devins, C., R.G. Koppl, S.A. Kauffman, & T. Felin 2015. Against design. *Arizona State Law Journal* 47 #3, pp. 609–681.
Evans, D. 1994. Policy and pork: the use of pork barrel projects to build policy coalitions in the House of Representatives. *American Journal of Political Science* 38 #4, pp. 894–917.
Ferejohn, J.A. 1974. *Pork barrel politics*. Stanford University Press.
Galbraith, J.K. 1967. *The new industrial state*. Princeton University Press, 1985.
Gallaway, L. 1998. Some Austrian perspectives on unintended consequences. *Review of Austrian Economics* 10 #2, pp. 91–100.
Godwin, K., S.H. Ainsworth, & E. Godwin 2013. *Lobbying and policymaking: the public pursuit of private interests*. Sage.
Halperin, M.H. 1974. *Bureaucratic politics and foreign policy*. Brookings Institution.
Hayek, F.A. 1973. *Law, legislation, and liberty* 1: *Rules and order*. University of Chicago Press.
——— 1989. The pretence of knowledge: Nobel memorial lecture, December 11, 1974. *American Economic Review* 79 #6, pp. 3–7.
Higgs, R. 1987. *Crisis and leviathan: critical episodes in the growth of American government*. Oxford University Press.
——— 1991. Eighteen problematic propositions in the analysis of the growth of government. *Review of Austrian Economics* 5 #1, pp. 3–40.
Hobbes, T. 1668. *Behemoth, or the long parliament*. F. Tönnies (ed.), 1889. University of Chicago Press, 1990.
Holcombe, R.G. 2006. *Public sector economics: the role of government in the American economy*. Prentice Hall.
Hughes, J.R.T. 1991. *The government habit redux: economic controls from colonial times to the present*. Princeton University Press, 2/e.
Ikeda, S. 1997. *Dynamics of the mixed economy*. Routledge.
Keech, W.R. & M.C. Munger 2015. The anatomy of government failure. *Public Choice* 164, pp. 1–42.
Kohn, M. 2004. Value and exchange. *Cato Journal* 24 #3, pp. 303–339.
Krueger, A.O. 1974. The political economy of the rent-seeking society. *American Economic Review* 64, pp. 291–303.
Letwin, W. 1965. *Law and economic policy in America: the evolution of the Sherman antitrust act*. University of Chicago Press.
Linz, J.J. 1978. *The breakdown of democratic regimes: crisis, breakdown & reequilibration*. The Johns Hopkins University Press.
Martin, A. 2010. Emergent politics and the power of ideas. *Studies in Emergent Order* 3, pp. 212–245.
Martin, A. & D. Thomas 2013. Two-tiered political entrepreneurship and the congressional committee system. *Public Choice* 154, pp. 21–37.
McQuade, T.J. 2021. What is a legislature's purpose? *Cosmos + Taxis* 9 #7&8, pp. 26–40.
Mises, L. 1944. *Bureaucracy*. Yale University Press.
Niskanen, W.A. 1971. *Bureaucracy and representative government*. Routledge, 2017.
Pigou, A.C. 1932. *The economics of welfare*. Macmillan, 4/e.
Riddick, F.M. 1992. *Riddick's Senate procedure: precedents and practices*. US Government Printing Office.
Riker, W. 1962. *The theory of political coalitions*. Yale University Press.

——— 1977. The future of a science of politics. *The American Behavioral Scientist* 21, pp. 11–38.

Salisbury, R.H. & K.A. Shepsle 1981. US Congressman as enterprise. *Legislative Studies Quarterly* 6 #4, pp. 559–576.

Samuelson, P.A. & W.D. Nordhaus 2010. *Economics*. McGraw-Hill, 19/e.

Scheall, S. 2020. *F.A. Hayek and the epistemology of politics: the curious task of economics*. Routledge.

Shepsle, K.A. 2010. *Analyzing politics: rationality, behaviour, and institutions*. Norton, 2/e.

Shepsle, K.A. & B.R. Weingast 1981. Political preferences for the pork barrel: a generalization. *American Journal of Political Science* 25 #1, pp. 96–111.

Shirk, S.L. 1993. *The political logic of economic reform in China*. University of California Press.

Simmons, R.T. 2011. *Beyond politics: the roots of government failure*. The Independent Institute, 2/e.

Stigler, G.J. 1971. The theory of economic regulation. *The Bell Journal of Economics and Management Science* 2 #1, pp. 3–21.

——— 1992. Law or economics? *Journal of Law & Economics* 35 #2, pp. 455–468.

Stockman, D. 1975. The social pork barrel. *Public Interest* 39, pp. 3–30.

Tanzi, V. & L. Schuknecht 2000. *Public spending in the 20th century: a global perspective*. Cambridge University Press.

Tullock, G. 1965. *The politics of bureaucracy*. Public Affairs Press.

——— 1967. The welfare costs of tariffs, monopolies, and theft. *Western Economic Journal* 5, pp. 224–232.

——— 1975. The transitional gains trap. *Bell Journal of Economics* 6 #2, pp. 671–678.

Wagner, R.E. 1996. Review of Donald Wittman's *The myth of democratic failure*. *Constitutional Political Economy* 7, pp. 153–160.

Weingast, B.R. & W. Marshall 1988. The industrial organization of Congress; or, why legislatures, like firms, are not organized as markets. *Journal of Political Economy* 96, pp. 132–163.

Wilson, J.Q. 1989. *Bureaucracy: what government agencies do and why they do it*. Basic Books.

Wittman, D. 1989. Why democracies produce efficient results. *Journal of Political Economy* 97 #6, pp. 1395–1424.

Wohlgemuth, M. 1999. Entry barriers in politics, or: why politics, like natural monopoly, is not organized as an ongoing market process. *Review of Austrian Economics* 12 #2, pp. 175–200.

9 Interactions with government[1]

The picture we have drawn of an anticipatory social system – and illustrated with the cases of market, science, and government systems – identifies a closed set of process types (learning, expectation, selection, and action) as shown in Figure 9.1. Such a system is organized such that the output from a process of any type can serve as an input for other processes, including a process of the next type in sequence.

The system is materially and energetically open to the environment, on which it relies for resources necessary for the operation of the system's processes. But available resources are not the only component of environmental input – there are also effects on the system stemming from the outputs from other social systems. When the other system is a government system, these effects can include constraints on the operation of system processes and explicit control of the provision of material through legislation and bureaucratic rule-making.

Categories of effect

For the purpose of analysis, the effects of input, and changes in that input, emanating from government systems can be divided into three general categories:

1 Direction. Even in the absence of any external control, the distribution of resources to processes is not necessarily uniform, even among processes of the same type. And, since resources are scarce, some members of the system who desire to engage in some particular process may be unable to do so simply through lack of some particular resource. The knowledge generated within the system will, of course, be affected by the distribution of resources – the system will adapt to the current distribution and will attempt to adapt to any changes in it. So, it is no surprise that externally controlled changes in resource availability will induce adaptation. But exactly how the system will adapt is not predictable because the results of the entrepreneurial processes – the innovative alteration of dispositions in response to the resource change and the subjective judgments applied in evaluating these dispositions for action – are not predictable. However, if the externally-induced resource changes are such as to favor particular subgroups of processes relative to others, then the population of members involved in those subgroups is likely to increase and the generation of knowledge will increase in the direction of the favored activity.

DOI: 10.4324/9781003336150-9

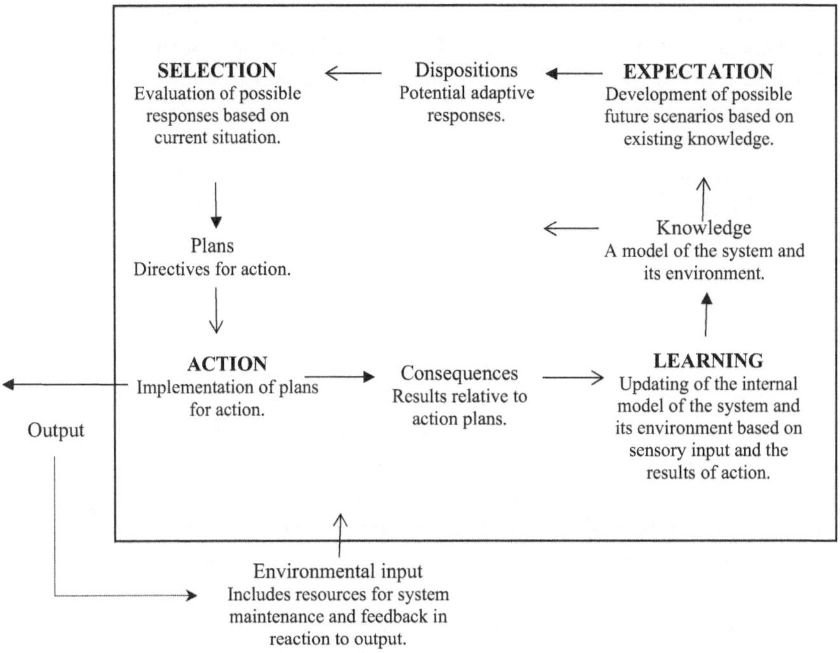

Figure 9.1 Process organization in an anticipatory system.

2 Destabilization. Resources are employed within the system not only for the maintenance of the people involved but also for the creation and maintenance of physical supplies and equipment – capital stock – necessary for the execution of the system's processes, especially processes of the action type. Adaptations which require alterations of the capital stock, both in building it up in response to increases in resource availability and in realigning it in response to decreases, are necessarily time-consuming. If a situation of expanding availability of a widely used resource, with the concomitant build-up of physical capital, is suddenly brought to an end (either through the cutting off of the availability of the resource or the inability to obtain complementary factors used up in the period when the resource was plentiful), the adaptation to the change will require widespread reallocations of capital, including liquidation of partially completed items, with adverse consequences for the owners of such capital. To the extent that such fluctuations can be expected to recur, entrepreneurial attention will be directed to the external social system inducing these fluctuations, and the anticipatory processes will include assessments of the external system's propensity to produce such effects. The system's anchor will be tied not only to those aspects of the environment to which the system is normally sensitive but also to an intangible factor (and as such a difficult one to anticipate), the behavior of the external social entity.

3 Distortion. If the external system has the power to interfere with the system's processes, either directly in precluding their normal functioning or indirectly

> in specifying constraints on their inputs or outputs, then such interference can be characterized as a distortion of the normal functioning of the system and a constriction of its evolved ability to adapt to its normal environment. The system will, of course, attempt to adapt to the interference, and how the system reacts will depend on the characteristics of the system's processes and the flexibility inherent in the system for workarounds to be discovered. The response may involve innovative changes in dispositions and is therefore inherently not predictable. The interference with the normal processes may even trigger the adoption of new process variants not subject to the interference, perhaps based on modes of interaction known to the participants in different contexts.

Directional effects are the least problematic, since the adaptive processes of the system operate in the same way as they would for any natural resource change. But directional effects can become destabilizing if they are prolonged beyond the availability of complementary resources or if the controlled resource provision is withdrawn more quickly than the system's adaptive processes can react. The effects of distortion can be particularly severe since they tamper with the system's knowledge-generating capabilities and therefore, to some extent, render the system maladaptive to its normal environment. The following are specific examples of government interactions with market and science systems which illustrate the operation of the destabilization and distortion effects, emphasizing the unpredictability inherent in system's reactions.

Effects on markets

The phenomenon of government intervention in markets has been the subject of an enormous literature which we cannot hope to even summarize here. Sufficient for our purposes, however, is to briefly point to some aspects of government intervention which the view of markets as anticipatory systems brings to the fore – in particular, effects which illustrate the plasticity inherent in anticipatory systems and, more generally, the phenomenon of "unintended effects". We note that the most prevalent form of government interaction that produces distortions in markets is regulation, which generally takes the form of rules which restrict behavior in some way, together with an enforcement mechanism to see to it that the rule is obeyed. Rules of this type inflexibly demand a certain response with respect to a controlled margin. Their inherent inflexibility precludes innovations and resulting adjustments at the controlled margin – adjustments which in the absence of the regulation would be made in the process of adapting to a changing environment. But innovative adjustments will be made at other margins,[2] and these adjustments are likely to be unintended consequences of the regulation and as such invite further regulation to control them.

One possible result of a restriction on the operation of a particular procedure will be a switch to participation in some available alternative, giving an interaction configuration not likely to be predictable by the intervener. Interventions that foreclose the use of some particular procedure will tend to provoke a move to the adoption of a "nearby" institution (one known to the participants in a different context) for the purposes served by the foreclosed one. Examples of this phenomenon are not hard to find. The adoption of the institution of "shoe money" (traditionally, a payment by *prospective* tenants to a middleman for help in negotiating a rental contract) in arrangements with *existing* tenants in the aftermath of Hong Kong's imposition of rent control in the 1920s, described by Cheung (1975), is a clear example. More generally, the phenomenon of the market's adjustments to the shutting down of existing transactional paths has been recognized elsewhere as "intervention breeding more intervention" – see, for example, Mises (1949, pp. 762–764) and Ikeda (1997). There *will* be a workaround subsequent to intervention (since adaptive systems can do nothing else but attempt to adapt) and, if (as often happens) the ensuing state of affairs is unsatisfactory to the intervening party and the response is further intervention, the result is simply further injury to the adaptive capability of the system.

For an example of government intervention generating uncertainty and systemic destabilization, consider the phenomenon of markets with "Big Players" as described by Koppl (2002), i.e., bureaucratic functionaries, such as central bankers or finance ministers with discretionary power to affect market conditions, who are outside the market system in that they are, in these roles, immune to the discipline of profit and loss. The presence of a Big Player introduces a prominent element into the environment of the market system, and so the resulting knowledge generation is an adaptation not only to the usual environmental conditions but also to the Big Player's actions. Especially in cases where the Big Player's activities affect the supply of money and credit (since money is a component in every transaction and many transactions, involving both capital and consumption goods, are dependent on credit) the market's adaptation is significantly affected by the actions of the Big Player. For a normal market participant, it is at least as important to predict the future behavior of the Big Player as it is to predict the "underlying fundamentals". If Big Players engage in discretionary policy, market participants are not likely to be able to adjust their transactional behavior quickly enough to the realities of the new (and ever-changing) environment and so the market-generated knowledge will be only a poor representation of the actual circumstances. Since, in the Big Player market, the market knowledge is much less useful for augmenting individual knowledge of the circumstances beyond those affected by the Big Player, the opportunities for market participants to adapt their individual knowledge to these circumstances is impaired. Their obvious incentive is to adapt their knowledge to the behavior of the Big Player, but this can be a difficult and error-prone process in a regime of discretionary policy. In looking for clues here, market participants are likely to form expectations heavily based on what others think the Big Player is going to do, thereby providing a rationale for "herding" behaviors, as Koppl (2002, pp. 129–130) argues.

Effects on money and banking

Having described a banking system free of government interaction, and noting that systems of central banking operate by replacing or curtailing some of the free banking processes with decisions made within the central banking bureaucracy, we can understand why the central banking system does not, and cannot, react quickly and appropriately to both local and global changes in the demand for money in the same way that a free banking system would be capable of reacting.[3] In monopolizing the production of banknotes, in eliminating the possibility of redemption of these notes in terms of a commodity money (and therefore effectively designating the central bank's notes as outside "base" money), and in specifying mandatory reserve requirements applicable uniformly to all banks, the central bank has a distorting effect on the system, removing possibilities for individual banks to act entrepreneurially in adjusting to their particular circumstances, and setting itself up as a "Big Player" immune from the constraints (particularly on note issue) that free banks would face.

The key feature of central banking is that a single entity – the central bank – has the capacity to dominate the system's responses, in both real and nominal terms. Relative to a decentralized free banking system, the central bank suffers from feedback and adjustment deficiencies. We can imagine several conditions that might give rise to such deficiencies – such as constraints or policies arising from political pressure, its incentives as a bureaucracy to respond in certain ways, or subservience to Treasury and government fiscal policies.[4] But we can simply frame the discussion in terms of the information available to the central bankers that induces them to take action, which corresponds to how effectively they can access and use relevant knowledge, and second, the kind of policy adaptation and response they implement, which corresponds to the kind of knowledge their actions generate. A brief overview of each will suffice to adumbrate the difficulties a central banking system encounters when there is an excess demand for money (in other words, a decrease in the velocity of money) at the prevailing constellation of prices.

If the velocity of money decreases, the central bank must identify that such a decline has in fact occurred, its likely magnitude, whether it is localized or systemic, and whether it is transitory or chronic. These questions, while ascertainable *ex post*, remain problematic in terms of when that information becomes available to the central bank. The inescapable uncertainties surrounding the future (or expected) movement of velocity and other economic variables over the relevant policy horizon pose serious dilemmas for central bankers.

To illustrate, we can examine the actions of the US Fed leading up to and during the onset of the financial crisis of 2008. Figure 9.2 illustrates that, from our *ex post* vantage point, the velocity of M2 in late 2007 began to fall. Its decline, however, was initially mild and even consistent with what could have appeared as a generalized continued downward trend since 2000.

While we know *ex post* that M2 velocity began to decline substantially in the fall of 2007, the information that might have convinced policymakers to head off the decline in velocity earlier in the recession was not available to them or unambiguous. Although MZM[5] velocity would have been *ex post* a better predictor of the decline in velocity during this episode, the Fed does not use that measure of money, perhaps because its volatility relative to M2 velocity is larger. So, despite its precipitous decline beginning in 2007, MZM's velocity, from the Fed's vantage point, is not reliable as a useful signal upon which to adjust monetary policy.

The question of whether the Fed could have better predicted the 2008 decline of M2 velocity is complicated by policies the government and the Fed began to

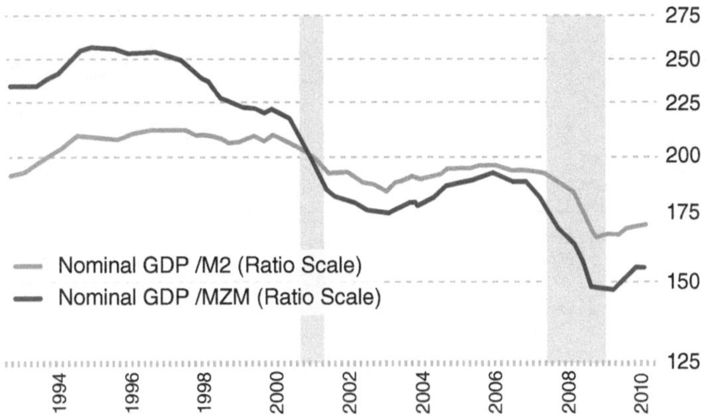

Figure 9.2 Money Velocity, 1993–2010.

Source: St. Louis Federal Reserve Bank.

implement in late 2007 to deal with the financial crisis and the recession. The policies themselves – e.g., the Fed's Term Auction Facility and other lending facilities that opened in late 2007 and early 2008, TARP (signed into law in October, 2008), and Fed-assisted bank bailouts of Bear Stearns – by which the Fed and Treasury got into the business of credit allocation to financial firms and later non-financial ones as well, may actually have had a negative effect on the economy due to inefficiencies associated with selective credit allocation programs. The induced uncertainties surrounding the hodgepodge of policy responses are factors that seem to have contributed to the continued fall in velocity through mid-2009.

Fed actions through the end of August 2008, from TAF lending and Fed funds rate reductions, increased loans to domestic (and foreign central) banks by $250 billion. However, the Fed kept the monetary base largely unchanged by purchasing an equal amount of Treasury securities. It was only later in the early fall of 2008, when the Fed dramatically increased its lending, that we saw an increase in the monetary base from about $0.5 trillion to about $1.25 trillion by January 2009. As seen in Figure 9.3, the increase in the monetary base had little impact on M2 velocity and even as the base approached $2 trillion in 2010, velocity leveled out at 1.7, suggesting that using velocity as a benchmark for changing the monetary base is not necessarily sufficient in all circumstances for reducing an apparent excess demand for money. About 18 months after the recession "officially" ended, the enormous expansion in reserves showed up as excess bank reserves and only in early 2011 did the banking sector show some tentative signs of increasing its lending. Indeed, it seems that while the plunge in M2 velocity was no doubt connected to the financial crisis and the recession, factors other than these were in play and contributed to their severity, including most particularly the various distortions and uncertainties induced by Federal Reserve and government policies.

Interpreting data and the lags in getting information affect the timeliness of Fed policy responses precisely because the decision-making is centralized. Information flows that originate at the level of individual banks or within specific sectors of the

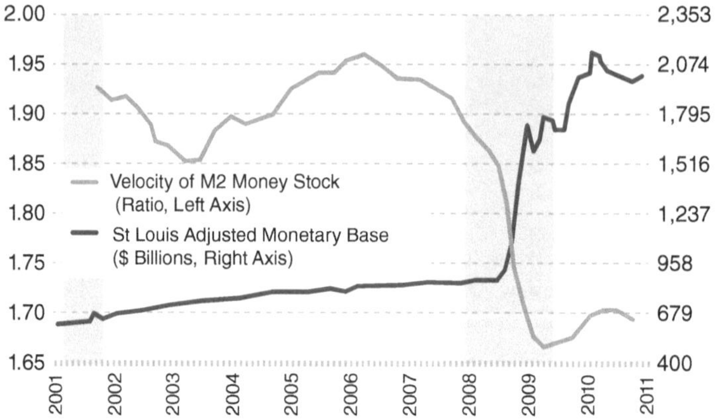

Figure 9.3 Money Velocity and Monetary Base, 2001–2011.

Source: St. Louis Federal Reserve Bank.

economy are aggregated into data thought to be essential for informed policymaking. Because policy mistakes affect the entire system and possibly the reputation of the policymakers themselves, we can understand why policymakers might have an incentive to wait for additional corroborating evidence before embarking on new policies. In contrast, the information flowing to banking institutions under free banking can be remediated quickly. Moreover, because these responses are highly decentralized, their effects are marginal and focused. The absence under free banking of *monetary policy* is a strength of the system.

What appears as macroeconomic problems are real enough, but solutions ordinarily center on addressing difficulties dogging interconnected individual markets. Let us call this "the macro-micro problem". Because policy measures principally are applied to the system at large, it is difficult to use the sorts of tools ordinarily available to policymakers to address subtle problems and market imbalances of a complex system and its multidimensional latticework of interconnected activities. An example is the 2008 housing crisis, which showed the difficulty of addressing an excess stock of housing and the accompanying drop in housing prices using monetary policy tools, especially when fiscal policies, which aimed to provide a floor for housing prices and to subsidize homeowners, very likely made these problems deeper and longer-lived.

Such "macro-micro problems" can be approached from a somewhat different vantage point by highlighting that given increases in the money stock by a free banking system and a central banking regime in response to an excess demand for money will have different effects on market outcomes. Even if we stipulate that nominal income (MV) increases by the same amount in each context, the way in which those increases are brought about cannot be the same. As noted earlier, under free banking, specific banks respond to the excess demand for their liabilities while the central bank responds systemically with a general increase in its liabilities coursing through the entire banking system. Under free banking the response, in contrast to that of a central banking regime, is decentralized, focused, and justifiable for those banks, and results in the elimination of an excess demand for money in particular areas of the economy. In addition, under central banking, and unlike free banking, there is no mechanism to ensure that the increase in the (aggregate) money stock will be directed to where it is most needed. The way new money is introduced into each system is qualitatively different; hence, the allocative effects on the economy will be different under each system. The transmission channels by which some evident excess demand for money is resolved will generate different outcomes in the economy, assuming the restoration of MV is the same under each institutional setting. While the unhindered processes of free banking have the prospect of providing incentives to address disturbances in specific market areas, the transmission channels available under central bank policy cannot replicate this. These differing allocative effects suggest that the accommodation of demand changes under central banking, such that the stream of MV is unaffected by an excess demand for money at the prevailing price level, will involve an underlying configuration of outputs and relative prices in the economy that is not the same as would have occurred under a free banking system. Even if a constant MV stream could be achieved under central banking, we cannot assume it will have eliminated the pockets of disturbance in all markets.[6]

The central bank's difficulties arise because incoming and outgoing flows of information operate at a highly centralized level. This arrangement, in turn, does not provide or possess the requisite feedback paths for timely and appropriate adaptive responses by the central bank to the economic conditions it seeks to manipulate. To put it simply, the central bank arrangement has an insurmountable knowledge problem. A recent (2022) case in point has been the Fed's Chairman Powell's insistence,[7] in the face of obviously rising prices, that this was just a "transitory" episode. Yet, as Figure 9.4 shows, the money supply was exploding (by

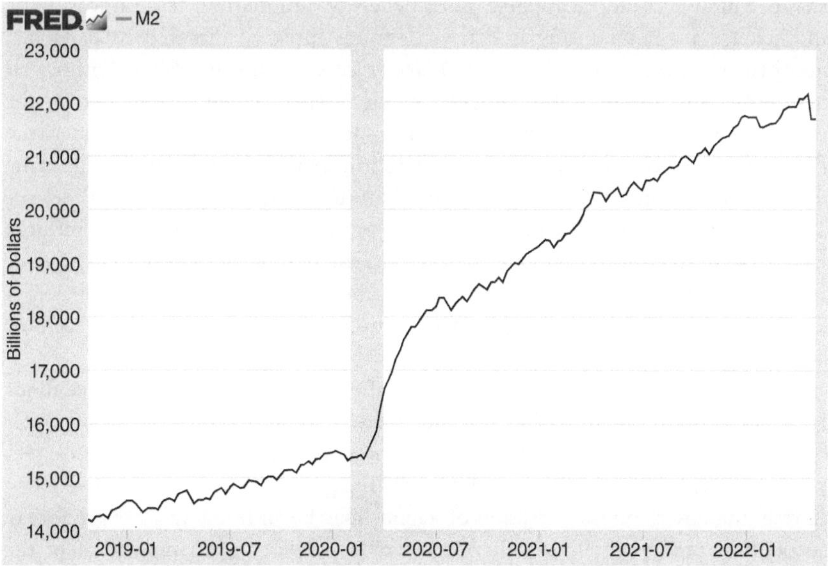

Figure 9.4 Money Supply (M2), 2018–2022.

Source: Board of Governors of the US Federal Reserve System.

about 40%) as a result of the Fed's assets purchases from 2018 to 2022. Powell held his ground until the inflationary trend was obvious to everyone. It was only in May 2022 that the Fed, seeing the inflation rate rising to a level not seen since the 1980s, started selling its assets, sending interest rates higher.

As noted earlier, a free banking regime, by its very structure, is able to more effectively solve the knowledge problem – both in using and generating relevant and appropriate informational flows, and in so doing to adapt with greater agility and to greater effect. Exhortations to urge central bankers to respond more quickly and forcibly are beside the point and do not solve the underlying problems confronting any centralized policymaking entity that attempts to make policy in real time amidst substantial uncertainty about the future. In fact, quick and decisive responses by the central bank may actually increase the frequency of discretionary interventions and also the number of interventions that will turn out to be over- or under-reactions. Milton Friedman's image of a truck driver over-steering down a narrow and twisting country road, careening from one side to the other, captures the point. Although we may rant at specific policymakers and their decisions, these deficiencies cannot be disassociated from the institutional context in which they operate. The problem resides with central banking and policymaking as such. The problem of central banking is an institutional one and only regime change can solve that.

Effects on science: boom and bust

Science, as a social order, is not self-supporting – it does not generate the revenue necessary to support itself and so is reliant on external funding. And such funding, being inevitably limited with respect to the potential scientific research projects to which it could be applied, is, of necessity, nonneutral. It is impossible to fund science in general; any injection of funds must be directed to particular scientists or institutions and to particular activities in specific fields within science. How this nonneutrality actually affects science depends not only on the procedures within science which react to funding but also on the characteristics of the sources of funding. A major consideration here for identifying destabilizing effects is the degree of decentralization of funding sources. If, for example, the pattern of funding involves a concentration of major funding in a small number of funding sources, as is the case for the current regime of government science funding, the pressures on science are likely to be quite different from those experienced in a regime of many dispersed, unrelated funders each with its own particular agenda.

Even providing an analysis of the directional effects of government science funding is not a simple matter. The specific flows of government funding involve a complicated process that includes various players within academia, the private sector, and intra-government funding clients seeking government funds. In some cases, the resulting effects on the direction of science may be an unintended byproduct of the political process itself; in others, they reflect deliberate manipulation of the funding process, the imposition of political preferences, the playing out of political pressures, directing funds to specific projects, and the pursuit of short- and long-run policy goals. This suggests that directional effects associated with the process of government funding should be analyzed in terms of the institutions comprising the interplay among the relevant players and the incentives that guide their behaviors – questions that would take us, however, far beyond the confines of this book.[8]

From the point of view of scientists and the universities, firms, and laboratories that house them, the pattern of funding is critically important. Scientists must associate success or failure with their ability to secure resources. Since a large proportion of basic science is performed by university-based researchers, scientists' professional careers and their incomes are connected to their securing grants. Indeed, for untenured researchers, their university posts in part hinge on securing grants. If the pattern of funding support changes, we expect scientists and universities to either reap benefits or bear costs as a consequence of the changes in the direction and magnitudes of funding. The full ramifications of such funding changes may well be subtle and empirically shadowy. Yet, such funding changes may empirically appear as changes in the allocation and scale of science inputs across specific areas of research, including capital expenses, employment of scientific personnel, the number of degrees awarded and areas of specialization of graduate students, as well as a connection between success in securing research grants and subsequent publications and citations.

Turning to destabilizing effects, a funding regime of a small number of large funding sources, the shifting priorities of the funding institutions may result in a phenomenon of "boom and bust" within scientific subdisciplines. The boom is initiated as generous funding policies make funding more generally available and easier to obtain, and as "popularity" (for both real and political reasons) of a particular subdiscipline makes funding for that subdiscipline easier to get. This generates a herding effect as the increased activity in the subdiscipline is observed by both researchers and funders, the result of which is that research projects that under earlier funding conditions would not have been attempted are now able to be funded. Individual researchers cannot know whether the boom is fueled by real or artificial factors or some combination of these and, even if they did deduce an artificial component, they could not reliably tell when its influence will end. Many researchers will follow the incentives of the science feedback loops, evaluated in the light of what they know about the current conditions of the subdiscipline and its funding, and only very few will have the reputational stability to avoid participating in the available possibilities for reputational enhancement in the short term.

Generous funding of a scientific discipline does not necessarily give rise to an unsustainable boom, and large increases in scientific activity in a particular area are not necessarily unsustainable.[9] So, funding by itself, even if directed to favor one hypothesis over another, is not the problem; the problem arises when the provision of funding allows for, or even encourages, the continuation of research and publication activities which undermine the operation of the feedback inherent in the standard procedures of science – feedback which performs the scientific analog of profit and loss in assessing the scientific value of publications and in furthering the scientific reputations of their authors.

The bust will come when it becomes apparent that many of the research projects in the subdiscipline enjoying the boom cannot be completed, either because, due to a shift of funding priorities, the funding for the projects is scaled back or terminated before the projects are completed, or because reality manifests itself in the form of lack of experimental validation, which makes continued participation more problematic. Failures are more likely in the riskier projects, which will tend to be those requiring capital investment a long time before useful results can be anticipated, or those which were funded with inadequate appraisal of the researcher's capability, the feasibility of his approach, or the likely usefulness to other researchers of his potential findings. To the extent that failures in a heavily funded subdiscipline damage the credibility of the organizations funding the failed projects, the subsequent withdrawal of funding due to these organizations' reduced ability to generate new funds can induce curtailments in areas outside that affected subdiscipline. Failures and curtailments of science projects result in increased unemployment and resource idleness, since the movement of people and resources to other projects and subdisciplines is a difficult and time-consuming process.

There is no shortage of candidate episodes for illustrating the phenomenon of science boom and bust. Two particularly prominent US examples are:

- The rush to fund basic physics, mathematics, astronautics, and space science in the wake of the Sputnik launch in 1957,[10] culminating in the moon landings, after which both interest and funding fell off markedly and NASA's budget fell from $26 billion in 1968 to $11.5 billion by 1974[11] (in constant 2007 dollars).
- The renewed attention paid to computer science (particularly artificial intelligence [AI]) prompted by the perceived threat of the Japanese "Fifth Generation" project begun in 1982, going as far as the establishment in the US of a major research consortium pooling the resources of several major corporations together with a major initiative by the Department of Defense to develop intelligent systems. With the failure of the Japanese project and disappointing results from artificial intelligence research, the wave of funding subsided considerably. Between 1984 and 1988, total Federal funding for AI research rose from $106 million to $274 million, according to NRC (1999, pp. 213–216). However, DOD's Strategic Computing Program, slated to spend $1 billion over 10 years on the nurturing of "strong AI", had to be discontinued as commercial developments in computer workstations rendered its LISP-based technology obsolete. According to McCorduck (2004, pp. 426–429), the funding for AI software was cut "deeply and brutally" as attention shifted to other areas of research.

These were relatively short-lived episodes, and the busts came when political interest (and funding) waned, due to the purported crisis no longer being seen as a pressing concern. More long-lasting were the booms in eugenics and in nutrition science and, currently ongoing, in climate science.[12] The eugenics boom, although very adequately funded, came to an end with the exposure of the eugenics-inspired atrocities of the Nazis, and the nutrition science boom has slowly (and quietly) given way to the gradual accumulation of empirical evidence difficult to fit within the government-favored hypothesis. In both of these cases, the object of study is a complex adaptive system, where the internal feedbacks are poorly understood and even incompletely identified, and where the sharp and detailed prediction possible in the hard sciences is not feasible, the scope for extra-scientific factors to enter into the assessment of hypotheses, and therefore the scope for Big Player involvement, is much higher. The role of scientific arbitrator can be pursued through application of force and intimidation, as was the case of the Soviet government acting as a Big Player in the Lysenko episode in biology,[13] or, more subtly, by any organization which, for political or ideological reasons, has been able to set itself up as a respected voice qualified to assess the state of science in a particular discipline. The UN's Intergovernmental Panel on Climate Change (the IPCC), aggressively championing the hypothesis of anthropogenic global warming (AGW),[14] has taken on that Big Player role in climate science, as will be described in more detail in a later chapter.

Effects on science: distortion

In the presence of distorting effects, the functioning of the scientific order becomes maladaptive to science's normal environment and the so-called knowledge generated in these conditions is tainted, if not totally invalid – in any case it has not emerged from the free operation of the procedures that are an inseparable aspect of scientific knowledge generation. An obvious example was the tragic fate of the biological sciences under Stalin, when the procedures of biological science were essentially replaced by brutally enforced Stalinist ideological criteria. However, one does not need to invoke such extreme political intervention to populate this category – distortions can arise from pressures coming from both inside and outside the science community.

Fraud and misconduct in science, discussed extensively by Wible (1992) and characterized as the deliberate attempt by scientists to plagiarize or to manipulate or falsify research data and results, is a distortion which may affect which articles are published and cited and hence affect the reputational status of researchers. The requirement for adherence to the scientific norms is an effective constraint on achieving success (recognition) in science; hence, we must acknowledge that incentives exist for scientists and funders to circumvent or subvert the normal procedures. To the extent that instances of fraud and misconduct remain hidden, other researchers may use such fabricated results in their own research, potentially inadvertently compounding the initial fraudulent research. As a result, the *wrong* science – wrong in the sense of violating scientific norms, not wrong in the sense of simply being in error – gets legitimated. Even if dishonest researchers are never unmasked, however, we would expect that eventually the work of other researchers will supersede the original fraudulent results. Because *some* fraud in science is likely always to be with us, the relevant issue becomes the speed at which non-fraudulent results weed out fraudulent ones or allegations of fraud can be assessed by scientists themselves. But as long as there is competition (or the threat of it) in the relevant scientific arena itself, there will be not only a strong deterrent to fraud but also an established procedure for unmasking it. Scientists and funders, of course, have an incentive also to uncover fraud, if only to protect their reputational capital; and, significantly, various sorts of arrangements have emerged from within science itself that work to maintain the integrity of the scientific order, such as review boards and university committees that investigate charges of plagiarism, fraud, and chiseling.[15]

It is worth emphasizing that we do not conflate *error* in science with *distortions* of science. Because knowledge is an emergent outcome of science, its generation will typically involve displacing existing knowledge by providing a more complete understanding of reality or identifying accepted knowledge as having been mistaken. The replacement of existing knowledge by new knowledge is precisely what we would expect the scientific order to accomplish. Even a modest assumption of fallibility implies that scientific error cannot be ruled out, and hence so-called new knowledge is not necessarily better knowledge. Yet, we do expect that, over some relevant time horizon, manifest errors can be eliminated. If that is to happen, however, our argument is that the scientific procedures must function on an ongoing and unrestricted basis if the knowledge-generating process of the scientific order is to be maintained. If it does not, then we cannot rule out that errors, which under normal functioning would tend to be weeded out, will survive as knowledge distortions with little prospect for their systematic elimination.

Our main concern, however, is the potential for distortion that derives from pressures external to science – in particular, those inherent in the characteristics of the funders and the degree of decentralization of the funding environment. In an environment composed of many funders, the effectiveness of any single one to interfere with the scientific processes and their operation is likely to be small. They lack the ability to impose their will on a significant segment of the scientific order. Thus, while there may be grounds for claiming that, no matter how dispersed the funding environment, science cannot fully insulate itself from distorting interferences, there is little reason to think that such impairments are likely to be systematic or injurious to the overall functioning of the scientific order.

But that is less likely to be true for more centralized funding arrangements. With funding lodged in a small number of related sources, actions by the funder (intentional or otherwise) that have the effect of compromising the scientific processes have the capacity to affect a large number of scientists and their activities. One channel through which unintentional distortion could occur in such an environment would be via an alteration of the incentives facing scientists. The ability to attract funding from a large and reliable source of funds confers prestige and administrative power to scientists who are successful in doing so. For these scientists, professional reputations now reflect not only their scientific accomplishments but also their ability to raise and dispense research funds. Given the tight connection between reputation on the one hand and influence over scientific research on the other, success in securing and controlling funding resources may itself exert a distorting effect on science. Reputation derived from funding success can substitute for or augment reputation derived from the production of useful scientific work, so that future scientific work is reviewed with less scrutiny and perhaps more readily accepted than it would have been were reputation based purely on scientific accomplishment. Also, in order to attract necessary funding, scientists may feel the incentive to produce results or shade conclusions in a way that they see as being in sync with, or furthering the aims of, one or more of the funding organizations. Again, this incentive will be present in any funding regime, but is much more likely to have systemic effects when the funding sources are concentrated.

On the face of it, one would not expect that a funding regime in which the majority of funding was provided with public funds would necessarily exhibit the characteristic of high concentration, because such funding is administered through a variety of funding agencies whose concentrations are in different fields and whose funding imperatives are independent of each other. But, to the extent that political considerations external to science play a part in funding decisions, there is the possibility that such government agencies will, motivated by the same political pressure, effectively act in concert – in other words, not only take on the appearance of a highly centralized funding arrangement but effectively act as one. In any case, from the point of view of a scientist in a particular field, the funding for that field may be dominated by a single agency. And, in the final analysis, with government funding, the ultimate source of funding and the interests of the ultimate funder are not dispersed, but concentrated in a single, if often fractious, entity, the legislature.

Concentration of the funding environment is not the only characteristic of public funding with distortion potential. Government funding of science comes equipped with political or even constitutional prerogatives for overseeing science not available to private funders, and these are ordinarily justified as providing the oversight and accountability taxpayers sometimes expect from government. The use of regulatory vehicles (with access to an arsenal of resources – staff, lawyers, and raw political muscle), such as Congressional hearings and access to media outlets, can, whether intentionally or not, exert an influence scientists' *scientific* reputations for good or ill, and can lead to the circumvention of standard evaluative procedures and criteria used to review and ascertain the publication worthiness of scientific work. There is a clear sense, then, in which the simple expedient of government funding science may generate incompatibilities with the institutions of science.

The Baltimore case is an interesting example of the distortion of science brought about by government regulation of the scientific process. David Baltimore, a high-profile 1975 Nobel Prize recipient in Medicine, collaborated with T. Imanishi-Kari (the principal author) and four other researchers on an immunology paper published in *Cell.* A post-doc lab assistant in Imanishi-Kari's lab disputed some of the published findings. Allegations of misconduct by Baltimore and Imanishi-Kari led to internal reviews of the paper by committees convened at Tufts University and MIT. The committees supported the paper, holding that any errors would be addressed by the normal processes by which science works. The whole matter was rapidly deflating until two National Institutes of Health (NIH) scientists at the Department of Health and Human Services (DHHS), Ned Feder and Walter Stewart, resurrected it as part of their ongoing, unauthorized, and self-appointed crusade to ferret out unethical behavior of government-funded scientists.[16] But the key escalation occurred when Feder and Stewart brought the case to the attention of Representative John Dingell of the House Energy and Commerce Committee. The Congressional investigations and hearings that followed under Dingell in the Subcommittee on Oversight and Investigations were legitimated by the oversight responsibility of Congress regarding the use of Federal funds. Baltimore and Imanishi-Kari soon found themselves targets of the full array of government assets – the NIH Fraud Unit, the Office of Scientific Integrity (OSI) of the DHHS, US Treasury document examiners, US Secret Service forensic specialists, and Subcommittee investigators and lawyers.

There are two aspects of the Baltimore Case that illustrate the connection between distortion effects in science and the funding source (here, the Federal government). One concerns the reputational effects on Baltimore and especially Imanishi-Kari arising from, as Kevles (1998, p. 185) put it, the Subcommittee's "show trial" use of "innuendo and rumors" to "harass, embarrass, and vilify" them. The tactics of Dingell and others severely impacted the professional careers of Baltimore (who, although never formally charged with misconduct, was pressured to resign as President of Rockefeller University) and Imanishi-Kari (who was found guilty of misconduct by the OSI, losing all NIH funding for ten years, only to be cleared of all charges by a HHS appeals panel in 1996). Eventually, Imanishi-Kari got her position back with tenure at Tufts; Baltimore is now a chaired professor at Caltech.

Once allegations of scientific misconduct had been made against Baltimore and Imanishi-Kari, the government had reason to exercise its oversight function for ensuring that taxpayer funds were properly used. Thus, it is not implausible to suggest that, once the case reached the hardball court of the Subcommittee, the accused, whether guilty or not, had implicitly exposed themselves to scrutiny (fair or not) by virtue of their acceptance of Federal monies. But this does not fully address the effect on science of the sorts of tactics, backed by the weight of an intimidating array of government resources, which can be brought to bear on scientists testifying before Congressional committees. The reputations of Baltimore and Imanishi-Kari *as scientists* were severely compromised, not as a result of the evaluative processes of science acting on their work, but because of their very public exposure to the adversarial investigation.

But an even more serious distortion of scientific procedure in the Baltimore Case came about because the Subcommittee's oversight prerogative was exercised in ways that moved beyond an investigation into misconduct and into, as Culliton (1988a, p. 1721) notes, the area of actually "auditing ... scientific disputes". The paper that thrust Baltimore and Imanishi-Kari into the national limelight had survived the journal's editor, peer reviewers, and two university committees of inquiry; nonetheless, determining whether it constituted *good* science emerged as relevant to Dingell's case because he equated scientific error with fraud. As biologist Robert Pollack's op-ed in the *New York Times* noted, Dingell, as quoted in Kevles (1998, p. 185), believed that "published science must be free of error, and that error itself indicates bad faith and fraudulent intent". The Committee's members and investigators set their sights on determining the quality of the science contained in the paper and in the laboratory practices used by Imanishi-Kari, as they really had to do if the charges of misconduct and data fabrication were to be sustained. In effect, it is not clear how the investigation of alleged scientific misconduct can be isolated and objectively analyzed without also making judgments about the scientific methods, choices, and interpretations inhering in scientific work.

To summarize: there are serious implications for science as an anticipatory system if the processes of that system and their constraints and feedback loops are seriously weakened. Scientific findings will be less reliable. The corruption of the processes of science would promote the spread and installation of ideas and findings that have not gone through the standard procedures of critical evaluation or acceptance by other scientists of contributions they find useful. Such effects are considerably more likely in an environment in which funding sources are concentrated (as is the case when government assumes a major role) compared to when they are decentralized. Further, when funding is accompanied by regulatory oversight, the possibilities for distortion are significantly increased.

Notes

1 This chapter contains text previously published in Butos (2012) with permission from The Mises Institute, and in Butos & McQuade (2012) with permission from De Gruyter.

2 Kahn (1988, p. 28), writing in the context of rate regulation, puts the point clearly: "If regulation limits competition, it must be because some competition would otherwise be feasible: the ability and will to compete are therefore present. And, if the regulation is effective, price will be held above at least some producers' or potential producers' marginal costs. In these circumstances, controls over price competition are subject to evasion by accentuated quality and service rivalry, limited only by the ingenuity of businessmen in seeking new methods of enticing customers. … Similarly, the elevation of price … sets up persistent temptations for new businessmen to come into the market, in turn creating the necessity for regulatory limitations on entry, and for extension of controls to unregulated firms."

3 For a thorough analysis of the shortcomings of central banking relative to free banking, see Selgin (1988, pp. 89–143).

4 These considerations are clearly germane to central bank policymaking, but are not considered here.

5 MZM is a monetary aggregate of "zero maturity assets" *i.e.*, M2 less time deposits plus money market funds.

6 In contrast to the "macro-micro" views expressed here, Horwitz & Luther (2010, pp. 14–15) couch their discussion of central bank policy in terms of aggregates: "In our view, monetary stability means continuously adjusting the supply of money to offset changes in velocity. Given the current monetary regime, where such adjustments are in the hands of the central bank, they should be made as mechanical as possible. … Given our monetary equilibrium view, we hold that the Fed should adopt a nominal income target. … Under a nominal income targeting regime, monetary policy would have the best chance to maintain our goal of monetary equilibrium, at least to the extent that central bankers can accurately estimate and commit to follow an aggregate measure of output."

7 In a press release dated April 28, 2021, posted online at https://www.federalreserve.gov/newsevents/pressreleases/monetary20210428a.htm.

8 Happily, such incentives and effects have been covered extensively by Cohen & Noll (1991), Martino (1992), Savage (1999), Kealey (1996), Greenberg (2001), Gough (2003), Hart (2003), Shane (2004), and Butos & McQuade (2006).

9 Molecular biology has been well funded in recent years, and the confirmed results have, if anything, exceeded expectations. Quantum mechanics saw extraordinary growth from the 1920s onward which, far from being unsustainable, has changed the world and continues to do so.

10 The "Sputnik crisis" led directly to the creation of NASA and the quadrupling of funding for NSF in 1958. Total Federal R&D in aerospace rose from $934 million in 1950 to $2.4 billion in 1960 – see Gilbert (1981). And, in addition to the influx of funds designed to immediately enhance space science capability, an initiative was launched to provide for more scientists in the future. As documented by Dow (1991), "the launching of Sputnik released a torrent of Federal funds. In 1958 the NSF increased its support for curriculum development at a rapid pace. … By 1960 the programs of the Education Directorate represented 42% of the NSF annual budget." Also, "the National Defense Education Act, the most far-reaching Federally-sponsored education initiative in the nation's history … authorized expenditures of more than $1 billion for a wide range of reforms including new school construction, fellowships and loans to encourage promising students to seek higher education, new efforts in vocational education to meet critical manpower shortages in the defense industry, and a host of other programs."

11 See Table 4.1 "Outlays by Agency" at http://www.whitehouse.gov/omb/budget/Historicals. Large swings within categories of NASA's R&D expenditures are often significant, as can be seen from Table II-12 at http://www.aaas.org/spp/rd/rdreport2010/tblii12.pdf. For example, from fiscal year 2008–2009, "Space and flight support" increased 64%, "Astrophysics" decreased by 13%, "Space exploration" increased 23%. These shifts reflect, in part, adjustments in Administration priorities, as evidenced, for example, by President Bush's support for the Constellation systems (which comprised in 2009 $3.5 billion of "Space exploration" or 27% NASA's budget), a set of programs whose funding was terminated in President Obama's 2010 NASA budget.

12 For a description of the eugenics episode, see Crichton (2004), Selden (2005), and Bashford & Levine (2010). For nutrition science see Taubes (2007), Butos & McQuade (2012), and Scheall *et al.* (2018). For climate science, see Butos & McQuade (2015).

13 The Lysenko affair lasted from the late 1920s to the early 1960s in the Soviet Union and other Eastern Bloc countries and was not only a serious setback for biological science in those countries but also its applications to agriculture exacerbated the effects of the disincentives inherent in communist management. See Soyfer (2001) and Graham (2002).

14 The AGW hypothesis holds that the overwhelming explanatory factor for the global warming observed during the past century, and particularly since 1970, is the forcing provided by the emission, as a byproduct of human activity, of carbon dioxide and other greenhouse gases.

15 The Federal government requires that institutional review boards adjudicate allegations of scientific impropriety for all publicly funded research and research involving human subjects. Oversight of these provisions is conducted by the Office of Research Integrity of the Department of Health and Human Services. See http://ori.dhhs.gov. For a critique of these mandated review boards, see Hyman (2007).

16 Culliton (1988b) notes that Feder and Stewart were employed as researchers at NIH. They received NIH approval to spend up to 20% of their time policing published scientific papers, endeavors that would actually absorb nearly 100% of their paid time. Stewart, Culliton emphasizes, "maintains that error, once known, should be explicitly corrected" by the reviewer, not a scientific board of inquiry, examining "the published literature for error". Also see Steele (1999).

Bibliography

Bashford, A. & P. Levine (eds.) 2010. *The Oxford handbook of the history of eugenics*. Oxford University Press.

Butos, W.N. 2012. Monetary orders and Institutions: a Hayekian perspective. *The Quarterly Journal of Austrian Economics* 15 #3, pp. 259–276.

Butos, W.N. & T.J. McQuade 2006. Government and science: a dangerous liaison? *The Independent Review* 11 #2, pp. 177–208.

——— 2012. Nonneutralities in science funding: direction, destabilization, and distortion. *Journal des Economistes et des Etudes Humaines* 18 #1, article 4. DOI: 10.1515/1145-6396.1262.

——— 2015. Causes and consequences of the climate science boom. *The Independent Review*, 20 #2, pp. 165–196.

Cheung, S.N.S. 1975. Roofs or stars: stated intents and actual effects of a rents ordinance. *Economic Inquiry* 13, pp. 1–21.

Cohen, L.R. & R.G. Noll 1991. *The technology pork barrel*. Brookings Institution.

Crichton, M. 2004. *State of fear*. HarperCollins. An excerpt dealing with eugenics is reprinted at http://www.michaelcrichton.net/essay-stateoffear-whypoliticizedscienceis dangerous.html.

Culliton, B.J. 1988a. A bitter battle over error. *Science* (ns.) 240 #4860, pp. 1720–1723.

——— 1988b. A bitter battle over error (II) *Science* (ns.) 241 #4861, pp. 18–21.

Dow, P. 1991. *Schoolhouse politics: lessons from the Sputnik era*. Harvard University Press.

Gilbert, J. 1981. *Another chance: postwar America, 1945–1968*. Temple University Press.

Gough, M. (ed.) 2003. *Politicizing science: the alchemy of policymaking*. Hoover Institution.

Graham, L. 2002. *Science and the Soviet social order*. Harvard University Press.

Greenberg, D.S. 2001. *Science, money, and politics*. University of Chicago Press.

Hart, D.M. (ed.) 2003. *The emergence of competition policy*. Cambridge University Press.

Horwitz, S.G. & W.J. Luther 2010. The Great Recession and its aftermath from a monetary equilibrium perspective. GMU Mercatus Center working paper #10–63. http://ssrn.com/abstract=1720138.

Hyman, D.A. 2007. The pathologies of institutional review boards. *Regulation* 30 #2, pp. 42–49.

Ikeda, S. 1997. *Dynamics of the mixed economy*. Routledge.

Kahn, A.F. 1988. *The economics of regulation, vol. 2: Institutional issues*. MIT Press.

Kealey, T. 1996. *The economic laws of scientific research*. St. Martin's Press.

Kevles, D.J. 1998. *The Baltimore case: a trial of politics, science, and character*. W.W. Norton.

Koppl, R.G. 2002. *Big Players and the theory of economic expectations*. Macmillan.

Martino, J.P. 1992. *Science funding: politics and porkbarrel*. Transaction.

McCorduck, P. 2004. *Machines who think: a personal inquiry into the history and prospects of artificial intelligence*. Peters, 2/e, 2019.

Mises, L. 1949. *Human action*. Henry Regnery, 3/e, 1966.

NRC (National Research Council) 1999. *Funding a Revolution: Government Support for Computing Research*. National Academy Press. https://www.nap.edu/read/6323/chapter/1.

Savage, J.D. 1999. *Funding science in America: Congress, universities, and the politics of the academic pork barrel*. Cambridge University Press.

Scheall, S., W.N. Butos, & T.J. McQuade 2018. Social and scientific disorder as epistemic phenomena, or the consequences of government dietary guidelines. *Journal of Institutional Economics* 15 #3, pp. 1–17.

Selden, S. 2005. Transforming better babies into fitter families: archival resources and the history of the American eugenics movement, 1908–1930. *American Philosophical Society* 149 #2, pp. 199–225.

Selgin, G. 1988. *The theory of free banking: money supply under competitive note issue*. Rowman & Littlefield.

Shane, S. 2004. *Academic entrepreneurship*. Edward Elgar.

Soyfer, V.N. 2001. The consequences of political dictatorship for Russian science. *Nature Reviews Genetics* 2 #9, pp. 723–729.

Steele, F.R. 1999. Review of the Baltimore case. *Nature Medicine* 5 #1, pp. 13–14.

Taubes, G. 2007. *Good calories, bad calories: challenging the conventional wisdom on diet, weight control, and disease*. Knopf.

Wible, J.R. 1992. Fraud in science: an economic approach. *Philosophy of the Social Sciences* 22 #1, pp. 5–27.

10 State-sponsored science[1]

With the rise of the modern nation state, science has been increasingly subject to government intervention in its funding and direction. This tendency's underlying driving force has been the growth of government itself. The governmental impetus to ensure politically determined adequate levels of scientific research and development (R&D)[2] and to manage such efforts took hold in the 20th century principally as a consequence of nationalistic hostilities or perceived threats of external aggression. This rationale was eventually augmented by more broadly based social agendas and by the "market failure" claim that academic economists advanced in the late 1950s (and since) with respect to the production of R&D, especially so-called basic research – see, for example, Nelson (1959), Griliches (1960), and Arrow (1962). The extent of US government engagement in science has trended upward significantly – with nondefense R&D spending rising from under $10 billion (in 2020 dollars) in 1961 to over $70 billion in 2021[3] – and the prevalent thinking of our times is that only fiscal constraints limit the magnitude of government funding of science.

There are serious reasons, however, for thinking that the liaison between government and science carries with it unrecognized dangers for the functioning and integrity of science as a reliable generator of knowledge. It is not so much that government seeks to exert a blatant and crude control over the content and direction of scientific inquiry – although such heavy-handed intrusion has precedents, most notably in the USSR – but that the structure and content of seemingly benign and generous government funding of science has side-effects that generate instabilities in scientific activity in the short run and corrode the structure and adaptability of the system of science itself in the long run.

The history of US government science funding

The US government has funded isolated scientific research projects (broadly conceived) since the early days of the Republic, as evidenced, for example, by the War Department's support of the Lewis and Clark Expedition and the congressional appropriation to support Samuel Morse's electric telegraph. The Civil War accelerated and broadened a Federal presence in science, including the use of scientific advisors for wartime purposes, and the congressional establishment of the National Academy of Science (NAS) in 1863. The Federal government established the

DOI: 10.4324/9781003336150-10

Department of Agriculture and the land-grant system of colleges, both of which provided institutional bases for government-funded scientific research that have persisted to this day. The Pure Food and Drug Act of 1906 established a permanent regulatory demand for scientific expertise. With the outbreak of World War I, the Navy Department constituted a naval consulting board (headed by Thomas Edison) to seek out applications of technologies for military purposes; it would become the Naval Research Laboratory after the war. President Wilson created the National Research Council (NRC) as an offshoot of the NAS to study the government's scientific needs. The NRC coordinated wartime projects in optics and gas warfare which involved the military, private contractors, and government-sponsored university R&D. At the end of the war, this government–industry–university establishment was largely dismantled, and although the NRC was given permanent status, its activities during the 1920s greatly diminished due to a lack of funding.[4]

Although a government presence in scientific and technological R&D was well established by the beginning of World War I, it was not based on a principled, coherent, or explicit "national science policy". Instead, government support for science served largely transitory wartime exigencies. But this situation would change under Franklin D. Roosevelt's administration with the continuation of the depression and the approach of war. In 1933 Roosevelt set up the Presidential Science Advisory Board and the National Planning Board (NPB) to enlist scientific expertise for solutions to the Depression. In 1934, the National Resources Board (NRB) replaced the NPB and subsumed within its jurisdiction the Science Advisory Board. As Feldman *et al.* (2002, p. 13) point out, "after all the organizational issues were settled, the Federal government recognized … that it had and would continue to have an important coordinating role to play in science and technology planning toward a national goal of economic well-being".[5]

Of special note was NRB (1938), entitled *Research – A National Treasure*, a comprehensive survey of government, industry, and university scientific activity that would provide the rationale and justification for a governmental science policy. The report argued that the government

1. is constitutionally obligated to support science and technology related to defense, scientific standards of weights and measures, and certain regulatory functions;
2. is more effective than the private sector in carrying out research, especially when private costs of research are high relative to its practical or social value; and
3. can stimulate industry research that is expensive and has unpredictable or delayed financial payoffs. See Feldman *et al.* (2002, pp. 13–14).

Once war broke out again, the government moved to harness scientific resources for military purposes. According to Feldman *et al.* (2002, p. 14), of the 92,000 working scientists prior to the war, about 19,400 were employed in the government, and more than 72,000 were employed, in roughly equal numbers, at universities and at the more than 2,200 industrial laboratories. In 1940, Roosevelt established the National Defense Research Committee, replaced in 1941 by the Office of Scientific Research and Development (OSRD), to organize scientific and technological resources for the war effort. Under the chairmanship of Vannevar Bush, the former president of the Carnegie Institution in Washington and a one-time vice president of MIT, the OSRD did not conduct research, but it did establish contractual relations – a protocontractual framework – governing collaboration between government funding agencies and university and industry entities that undertook and administered sanctioned research.[6]

As World War II drew to a close, no concerted effort was made to dismantle the government's wartime involvement in science, in contrast to the post-World War I experience. Instead, Roosevelt asked Bush to prepare a report analyzing how the OSRD's role could be played in *peacetime* collaboration of government and the scientific community for the purpose of achieving "improvement of the national health, the creation of enterprises bringing new jobs, and the betterment of the national standard of living".[7] Bush's report, published in 1945 as *Science – The Endless Frontier*, is perhaps the decisive document charting the institutional framework for science in the later part of the 20th century and into the 21st. The report claimed that government support of science is essential for medical advances, national security, economic welfare, and full employment. Bush (1945, p. 25) argued that attaining these goals required that the "Federal Government should accept new responsibilities for promoting the creation of new scientific knowledge and the development of scientific talent in our youth". And (p. 28) this "national policy for scientific research and education" was to be financed by government funds, making payments to industry and subsidizing research as well as undergraduate and graduate student scholarships in universities. In addition to recommending expanded support for research and applied work conducted by government laboratories, the report highlighted the special role that colleges and universities should play in basic research.[8] The institutionalization of the Federal government's reconfigured role was to be attained by the creation of a National Science Foundation (NSF), whose purpose was (p. 28) to "develop and promote" Federal science policy and to implement policies aimed at supporting "basic research in non-profit organizations". The report also charged the NSF with responsibility for developing scientific talent and for supporting long-range research with military applications.

Bush's central claim was that material progress depends on new scientific knowledge and that such knowledge, in turn, depends on what he called "basic research": research performed without thought of practical ends, as he defined it.[9] Implicit in this claim was the assumption that the Federal government must provide the dominant guiding, coordinating, and financing role for the growth of scientific knowledge. He rested this assumption on a constitutional claim (1945, p. 68) that the "Federal government, by virtue of its charge to provide for the common defense and general welfare, has the responsibility of encouraging and aiding scientific progress". The connection between national defense and military, scientific, and technological progress was not a new justification for an expanded role for government. Justifying this expansive role with reference to "public health, higher standards of living, conservation of national resources, new manufacturing which creates new jobs and investment opportunities, in short, the prosperity, well-being and progress of the American nation" reflected a vision that was reminiscent of, but surely more politically timely than, the 1938 report *Research – A National Treasure*. Although the claim that marshaling the amount of research money necessary to satisfy these objectives requires substantial Federal support appears throughout the 1945 report, no detailed analysis was provided to support it.[10]

Bush's report received crucial support with the timely publication in 1947 of *Science and Public Policy: A Program for the Nation*, by the President's Scientific Research Board under the direction of John Steelman, an assistant to the president. The Steelman report argued that the government should allocate 1% of gross domestic product (GDP) to R&D,[11] while reaffirming the centrality of basic research for economic prosperity and growth, the belief that the private sector cannot reliably sustain such research, and the claim that R&D should be conducted principally by universities and industry with government funding.[12] The Steelman report also called for creation of a national science foundation to dispense government research funds. Congress did create the proposed agency in 1950 under the National Science Foundation Act. Since the 1950s, the essential contours of government and science interaction in the United States have taken the forms proposed in the Bush and Steelman reports.[13] The principal divergence has been in the magnitude of the funds the government has dispensed.

Thus, the long-standing but largely piecemeal incursion of government into science since the 18th century gave way in the 20th century to the creation of formal government institutions and associated funding mechanisms during World War I and especially during World War II. Most of this was war-related. In the aftermath of World War II, however, initiatives were taken to promote government involvement in science on the grounds of economic development as well as national defense; the Bush and Steelman reports were pivotal in molding government science policy after World War II. Creation of the NSF in 1950 actually brought to an end a controversy over science policy within the government that had raged for several years among those such as Bush and Steelman who argued for an indirect government role in science (by means of government financing of university and industry science via a collection of mission-oriented agencies) and those who argued for a direct role (by means of governmental coordination and management of science). The latter position, most famously maintained by Democratic senator Harley Kilgore of West Virginia, envisioned a centralized government agency that, according to Kleinman (1995, p. 6, emphasis in original), would "*direct* and consciously *plan* the advance of scientific research and technology". For about five years, beginning in 1942, Kilgore introduced several legislative proposals for the creation of a centralized government science agency controlled and administered by representatives of a wide range of social interests, including both scientists and nonscientists – see Kleinman (1995, ch. 5).

The eventual defeat of Kilgore and his New Deal associates by Vannevar Bush, both in legislation and in the widespread acceptance of Bush's *Science – The Endless Frontier* (1945), is traditionally viewed as a victory for a decentralized approach – see Kleinman (1995) and Feldman *et al.* (2002). But if this outcome can be called a victory, it is certainly a shallow one. In the aftermath of World War II, government involvement in science followed the outlines of the Bush approach, but the scale of government funding swept away historical precedents and established funding norms that have persisted with little change into the present.

The precedent for increased government funding of science, established during the war years with an emphasis on military R&D, and the subsequent legitimizing of a broader justification for government in science, set the stage for substantial increases in government funding after 1949.[14] In 1949, total Federal R&D spending (measured in 2001 dollars) was approximately $5 billion; by 1964 it had increased to approximately $65 billion – a 13-fold increase, bolstered by the political considerations that attended the Cold War. The proportion of defense to non-defense R&D spending was approximately 5 to 1 in 1949 but decreased steadily to approximately 1.4 to 1 by 1963, a ratio that is typical for much of the period since then. From 1964 to 1969, nondefense spending – of which spending for the National Aeronautics and Space Administration (NASA) was a large component – increased dramatically, and total R&D spending hovered in the $60 billion to $70 billion range. In the 1970s, some retrenchment occurred, but thereafter defense spending increased sharply (whereas the nondefense component shrank modestly), so that total R&D spending edged higher. Declines in defense spending beginning in 1991 and continuing until 2001 were more than offset by nondefense increases that kept total Federal R&D spending approximately level.

As Figure 10.1 shows, R&D outlays (in 2020 dollars) for defense increased sharply until leveling out and then decreasing during the recession beginning in 2008. After a sharp (approximately $30 billion) dip in 2017, due to a narrower definition of "development" being adopted, the upward trend has resumed.

We also note that since the mid-1960s, the share of Federal R&D expenditures in discretionary budget outlays has declined and given way to a more-or-less stable

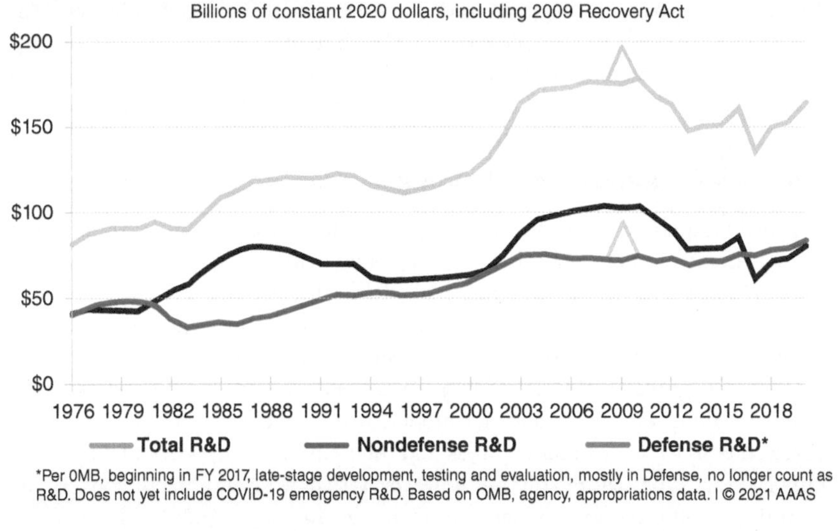

Figure 10.1 Federal R&D spending.

Source: Hourihan (2021).

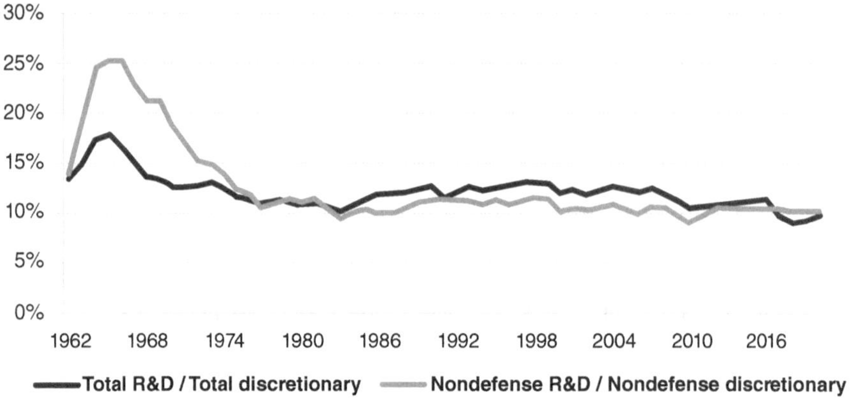

Figure 10.2 Federal R&D spending as a percentage of total discretionary spending.

Source: Hourihan (2021).

ratio. As Figure 10.2 shows, this ratio has averaged approximately 10% since the early 1970s. Of course, given the rise in the Federal budget during this period, the declining and now-stable ratio of Federal R&D to discretionary outlays still represents significant increases in Federal funding for R&D in absolute (and constant dollar) terms.

The empirical data presented here suggest that the explosion in government funding of science following World War II is significant and without precedent. This ratcheting in the magnitude of government funding reflects the effects of the interplay between the machinations of the political process and justifications stemming from threats to national security, the desire to attain top-shelf world ranking in (nondefense) basic research, and, more recently, post-9/11 antiterrorist R&D funding.[15] But whatever the perceived immediate need (real and otherwise) or political pressure used to justify government funding of science, a set of arguments exists behind the screen that claims to establish a general theoretical justification for such funding. We turn next to a critical examination of these arguments.

Rationales for government funding

The principal theoretical justification for government involvement in funding and directing the activities of scientists and the dissemination of scientific knowledge rests on a "market failure" argument which claims that the characteristics of scientific knowledge are such that it will be produced in suboptimal quantities without intervention.[16] Nelson (1959) and Arrow (1962) offer the classic statements of this argument; Dasgupta & David (1994) have restated and augmented it more recently.[17] Taking the classic and the modern treatments in turn, we show their theoretical basis to be surprisingly weak and their empirical support to be conspicuously lacking. Our major criticism, however, is that these authors, in concentrating on the "simple economics" (and on sociology, in Dasgupta & David's case) of scientific research, ignore the political economy of government funding arrangements and their effects on the system that generates scientific knowledge.

Nelson (1959, p. 306) suggests that in a regime of nonintervention, underinvestment in basic research would of necessity occur largely because of "the classic external-economy problem".[18] Firms other than the one conducting the research can benefit from the results, but the generating firm's ability to internalize that value by patenting is severely limited.[19] Further, the inability to appropriate their results effectively leaves the firms with the option of keeping the results secret, but this practice is inefficient from a societal perspective, owing to the public-good nature of knowledge. As Nelson (p. 306) puts it, the "marginal social cost of using knowledge that already exists is zero", and so whereas free access to all knowledge generated is optimal from a societal point of view, such is not the case from the generating firm's point of view. To mandate a common pool for all basic research generated by private firms would reduce the incentive for knowledge production in the first place. Nelson concludes, then, that publicly funded industry-independent research institutes and universities are the preferred organizations for conducting basic research because (p. 304) "were the field of basic research left exclusively to private firms operating independently of each other and selling in competitive markets, profit incentives would not draw so large a quantity of resources to basic research as is socially desirable". Moreover, because private firms (presumably operating at the point where expected marginal revenue is equal to marginal cost) do in fact conduct some basic research in the face of reduced incentives, this activity is an indication that the current funding of public research is less than optimal.

Arrow elaborates on Nelson's arguments, highlighting the inherent riskiness of research, the indivisibility of its product, and lack of appropriability of the product's value as sources of inefficiency in a free-market environment that government intervention can ameliorate. The problem of risk is straightforward (1962, p. 616): "Since [invention] is a risky process, there is bound to be [on the part of risk-averse individuals] some discrimination against investment in inventive and research activities". Arrangements for shifting the risk, including insurance, are incomplete or have optimality problems of their own. Therefore, as the solution to this problem, he posits (p. 619) that "government or some other agency not governed by profit-and-loss criteria" and capable of risk neutrality. The problems of indivisibility and lack of appropriability are simply aspects of the public-good issue raised by Nelson, and Arrow (p. 615), following Nelson, concludes that in "a free enterprise economy, inventive activity is supported by using the invention to create property rights; precisely to the extent that this is successful, there is an underutilization of the information".

Setting aside for the moment the political economy of government intervention in science, the economics of the Nelson and Arrow analysis has three fundamental problems:

1 Their underlying model of the processes of knowledge generation, appropriation, and utilization is institutionally inadequate. In fact, for the case of a private firm, no process is envisaged that differs in principle from that of making, selling, or using a commercially useful good. The good in question is simply problematic from the point of view of the profit-seeking firm because of uncertainty in production, difficulties in appropriation, and indivisibilities

in consumption.[20] No account is taken of the more complex arrangements in which firms can and do hire scientists, encouraging them to conduct basic research and to publish the results freely, expecting that this will enable them to learn about and make use of published research appropriate to the firm's narrower production goals.[21] And no account is taken of the fact that scientific knowledge is in general not like a simple "recipe" or "blueprint" that can be put to immediate use.[22] To understand it, let alone to utilize it profitably, requires both entrepreneurial insight and a considerable investment in acquiring and maintaining the requisite background knowledge. In short, scientific knowledge has a tacit component that cannot be conveyed easily and which renders published scientific information, though necessary, insufficient for garnering free-rider profits.[23]

Kealey's (1996, pp. 225–230) analysis is particularly instructive here. It is based, first, on identifying two kinds of advantages associated with basic research and, second, in recognizing some pertinent institutional detail about firms, scientists, and R&D. Basic science, says Kealey, confers "first-mover advantages" on a company when it discovers something first. This may position the company farther along the learning curve in developing the discovery's commercial applications. At the same time, though, if companies only derived first-mover advantages from basic research (as Nelson and Arrow assume), such research would be unlikely to enjoy widespread commercial support because basic science is commercially unpredictable. "Second-mover advantages", in contrast, derive from a company's ability to generate commercial applications of *existing* basic research; these second-mover advantages are less risky and more profitable than basic research.[24] As Kealey (1996, p. 229) observes, "first- and second-mover advantages are indissolubly linked, and one cannot be performed without the other … [Thus,] second-mover advantages enforce a vast expenditure on basic science".

2 Nelson's and Arrow's analyses of what set of institutional arrangements for managing the activity of basic science would be more efficient than the autistic "market" arrangements they model commits what Demsetz (1969, p. 1) calls "the nirvana fallacy". A model of a supposedly realistic institutional arrangement is analyzed and found to be suboptimal relative to an idealized arrangement whose possible shortcomings are not analyzed. As Demsetz (1969, p. 12) puts it:

> Arrow compares the workings of a capitalistic system with a Pareto norm that lends itself to static analysis of allocation but, nonetheless, that is poorly designed for analyzing dynamic problems of production. He finds the capitalistic system defective. The socialist ideal, however, resolves static allocation problems rather neatly. But this is only because all the dynamic problems of production are ignored. The comparison of a real capitalistic system with an ideal socialist system that ignores important problems is not a promising way to shed light on how to design institutional arrangements for the production and distribution of knowledge.

On the matter of the riskiness of basic research, for example, it is quite invalid to assume that the risk-averse actors populating the "free-market arrangements" model would be replaced by risk-neutral actors in the "ideal arrangements" model. And questions of "underutilization" presume an ability to determine, under the ideal arrangements, what quantity and direction of research to pursue for maximum utilization – a dubious assertion at best.[25]

3 Nelson and Arrow assume without analysis that the only adequate source of funding for basic research is the government.[26] The empirical record shows, however, that private sources consistently commit substantial sums to research, including basic research, as well as to overall R&D.[27] Figure 10.3 shows industry research overtaking Federal research at around 0.4% of GDP.

For total R&D expenditures by source, the data reveal that industry has allocated increasingly significant resources toward R&D. As seen in Figure 10.4, total industry-funded R&D since 1980 has exceeded Federal R&D expenditure and is now about three times greater as a percentage of GDP.

Whether the amounts of basic science and total R&D expenditures undertaken by the private sector are "optimal" survives only as a model-dependent question and lacks empirical content. Indeed, the standard neoclassical argument assesses optimality across only the quantity dimension. More is always better. Because the argument cannot rule out utterly perverse kinds of scientific research funding, it implicitly requires a second-order criterion for the allocation of research funds that must emanate from a political process.[28] Once account is taken of this political element, the presumed "optimality" argument is underdetermined. In short, all that can actually be said is that the private sector, of its own choice, does undertake the funding of significant amounts of both basic research and R&D.

In the standard market failure argument, no account is taken of the possibility, discussed by Martino (1992, ch. 27), that a side-effect of government funding of science has been the driving out of funding contributions from private foundations and endowments, rich private donors, and the general public. No evidence is presented to support the assumption that these sources of funding would simply remain at their current levels were government funding to be significantly reduced or eliminated. In addition to the opportunities for reputational enhancement (individual or institutional) and even for immortality that funding of a selected institution, research project, or individual scientist might present, science has popular appeal as a societal "good" and is unlikely to be left seriously impoverished by a retreat of government intervention.

Dasgupta & David (1994) restate the Nelson–Arrow economics of science while augmenting it significantly by taking into account the particulars of the different institutional arrangements through which scientific and technical knowledge is generated. They distinguish sharply between "open science" (the research arrangements characteristic of universities and nonprofit or government research institutes in which the reputation-based reward system works to hasten both discovery and its disclosure) and commercial R&D, or "technology", in which the reward system is oriented to

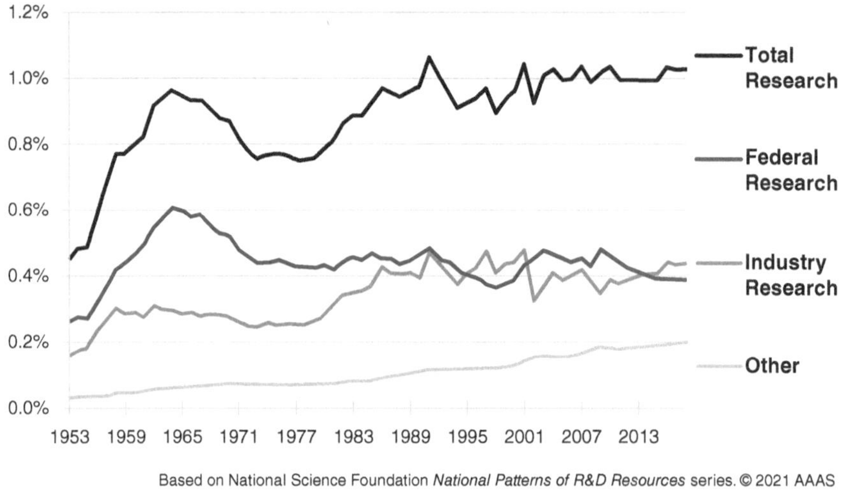

Figure 10.3 Research spending as a percentage of GDP.

Source: Hourihan (2021).

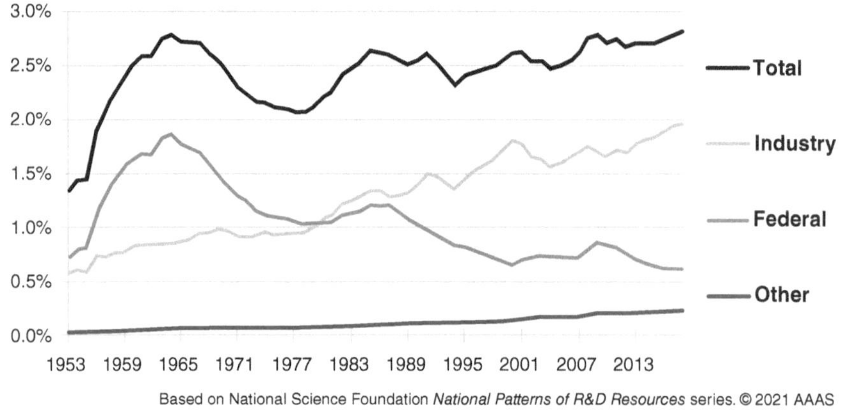

Figure 10.4 R&D spending as a percentage of GDP.

Source: Hourihan (2021).

material benefit and the desire for profit is not conducive to open disclosure. They do not advocate one of these arrangements over the other (p. 498):

> [Although] it is evident from the contradictory norms on which they are based that there is a tension between these two modes of economic and social organization, so that they do not 'mix' easily, the two are not mutually exclusive ways to successfully organize the pursuit of scientific knowledge within the same society.

In fact, given that both modes are operative in modern society, the relevant policy problem is to "attend to maintaining a synergetic equilibrium between them".

This is not to say that no "inefficiencies" exist in each of the two knowledge-production arrangements. Dasgupta & David (pp. 496–497) point to problems in technological knowledge markets, including thinness (and therefore lack of efficient pricing),[29] leakage (owing to the inevitable disclosures that must be made in a sales situation), and underutilization on a societal basis (echoing Nelson and Arrow). These problems can be offset in large part, but certainly not completely, by patenting, secrecy, and the incentive provided by the anticipation of monopoly profits.[30] Open science, they say (pp. 500–501 & 505–510), has problems of rivalry (which can weaken the incentive to prompt disclosure), resource allocation (in which the "all-or-nothing" aspect of the priority-based reward structure encourages the selection of research projects that are unduly risky or overly similar, and leads "to the possible neglect of other areas in which the entry of even a few competitors might be socially beneficial"), and timing (the difficulty of achieving optimal sequencing of projects in a decentralized arrangement). These problems, they allege, can be dealt with, at least partially, by the diligence of public funding agencies.[31]

The main conclusion emphasized by Dasgupta & David (p. 510) is the policy point, noted above, that these two modes of knowledge generation, each adequate (if not perfectly optimal) in its own environment, need to be maintained "in dynamic balance". Firms benefit from the results of open science (not necessarily immediately, but eventually) and from its training and certification of researchers, and this benefit redounds to society (p. 510): "the important economic payoffs to society from basic research come in the form of higher rates of return on expenditures allocated to applied research".[32] They assert that this "science–technology nexus" *must* be maintained by government funding and offer a stark warning (p. 515) of the consequences of doing otherwise:

> Under conditions approaching the state of 'universally privatized science' that such ideologues [that is, 'conservative' policy commentators] call for, an unbalanced research regime might continue to generate economic growth through the exploitation of the scientific and technological knowledge base, but sooner or later, economic progress almost certainly would lose the sustained character that has been taken by many scholars to distinguish ours from previous historical epochs.

No evidence is presented for this claim, however.[33]

Although the introduction of real-world institutional considerations into the economics of science by Dasgupta & David (1994) is a welcome advance, we find the following deficiencies in their argument for government involvement in the funding of science:

1 They add nothing to the basic Nelson–Arrow assertion, criticized previously, that private funding would turn out to be inadequate were government removed as a source of funding. In contrast to the scenario described in the passage just quoted, it is not credible that the advance of basic science, important in the long run to technological development, would slow to an extent that had a marked effect on economic wellbeing. Our skepticism does not

reflect a blind faith in the workings of the market – we have no truck with the pronouncements of policy pundits, conservative or otherwise – but rather an appraisal of the many possible motives, not limited to profit-seeking, for supporting open science in the absence of government intervention and for maintaining the operation of the productive "science–technology nexus".[34]

2 They assume that basic science performed in a private funding environment would not be published openly (at least not without a considerable delay), but rather would be conducted in secrecy to guard against exploitation by competitors. There is no reason for such secrecy to prevail with private nonprofit funding, however, and even for science funded internally by profit-seeking firms, secrecy is not necessarily the best strategy, as our previous discussion of "second-mover advantages" makes clear.

3 Their insistence on the importance of government funding to the continuing growth of basic science, together with the downstream importance of the application of earlier basic science for economic growth, suggests that the massive increase in government funding of science immediately after World War II would show up sooner or later as a discontinuity in the pattern of economic growth. Yet, more than 50 years later, no such discontinuity has occurred. No significant correlation can be seen between the level of Federal expenditure on basic science and the trend in GDP per capita, as documented by Kealey (1996, p. 162) for the 19th and 20th centuries.

4 They do not extend their real-world institutional analysis to encompass the government funding mechanisms themselves. Although they allude to the possibility of commonalities with some areas of public economics (1994, p. 510), they do not consider the particular incentives characteristic of government funding agencies, such as those documented by Martino (1992), which manifest themselves in favoritism, scientific conservatism, and pork-barrel spending. In the absence of any serious institutional analysis in this area, one is left with a "public interest" picture of government that, in the face of public choice skepticism, requires for credibility specific attention to any mechanisms that would turn the normal self-interest of politicians and funding agency bureaucrats to the service of some concept of public interest.

Our conclusion is thus that the economic justification for government funding of science is (1) theoretically unconvincing because it ignores institutional arrangements within firms that negate the force of the "market failure" arguments and because it does not account for the institutional realities of political and bureaucratic funding agencies, and (2) empirically suspect because it ignores the substantial evidence of the robustness of the private provision of scientific knowledge and because it predicts that increased government funding above trend would (with an unspecified lag) result in increased economic growth above trend, a putative link for which no solid evidence exists. Nevertheless, the extent of government engagement in science has trended upward for decades. This trend suggests that the forces driving the increase have more to do with a confluence of interest between politicians and scientists – a dynamic investigated in some detail by several scholars, including Martino (1992), Savage (1999), and Greenberg (1967, 2001).[35]

Funding-induced destabilization

Economists have long understood that the economy's cyclical activity or dynamic stability reflects the effects of central bankers' credit policies and perhaps representative democracies electoral cycles. In economics, we can think of fiscal policy's effect on the average level of economic activity as opposed to monetary policy's effect on the system's dynamic stability. In proposing a similar kind of distinction for analyzing government intervention in science, our discussion considers such intervention in the context of the dynamic stability of science.

Windfall funding for science is like artificially cheap credit for business: the immediate effect is a growth in investment (including employment) and, with a lag, in output. The general quality of the output is not necessarily compromised, although by making it possible for people who would otherwise work elsewhere to pursue a scientific career, the tendency may be to lower the average quality of the practitioners. What may be noticeable is an increase the irrelevance of the investigations pursued, in the sense that the resulting papers are of little or no interest to other researchers and generate few, if any, citations and follow-on publications.

In the distribution of government science funding, one would expect to see bursts of heavy funding in some areas, cutbacks or neglect in others, with the identities of these areas changing as the political winds change direction.[36] When the Russians threaten to lead the way into space, astronautics and space science is favored in the United States, building up an impressive edifice of research capability and trained scientists ready to push the discipline farther. When the Japanese threaten to develop a "fifth-generation" computer, attention in the United States switches to computer science, and space-related science funding becomes insufficient to maintain the talent already developed. When the Japanese are no longer seen as a danger to national prestige, political attention wanders away from computer science and employment for newer PhD holders in the area of research for which they have been trained is much harder to come by than they had expected it to be. The scenario is one of localized booms and busts – "science cycles" – accompanied by the disruption of individual lives and the waste of talent and resources similar to that characteristic of business cycles.

Thus, temporarily unconstrained funding fosters unstable growth. Lavish funding results in more scientists being trained because the recipients of funds require assistants to pursue the funded projects; in turn, these assistants, if they are to become researchers in their own right, will require funding of their own.[37] Private funding sources, in contrast, naturally limit the growth of the system of science in a way that has a relatively direct connection to the perceived usefulness of the science itself to other scientists, and this sort of stabilized growth is likely to be more durable and productive than spurts of growth and retrenchment based on factors external to science.

The risk to quality of output and integrity of behavior comes with the downturns in funding, when the rate of increase of funding ceases to keep pace with the structural growth fostered by prior funding. Then, scientists compete with each other not merely for scientific reputation, but for their very livelihood.[38]

Central planning in science

Concentration of funding in large government-financed organizations brings to bear the usual symptoms of bureaucracy: success measured by budget rather than by results, unwillingness to take risks that may subject the organization and its managers to criticism, and a concentration on areas of research likely to be politically popular. As Greenberg (2001) notes, bureaucratic control of the funding process has led to conservatism (he calls it "calcification"). Although this result may not affect the general quality of research work, it tends to channel scientists who are seeking funding into more conservative, more obviously "acceptable" lines of inquiry, and makes funding for mavericks more difficult.

As formulated by Hayek, a "knowledge problem" arises because centralized institutional arrangements make it impossible for planners to marshal adequately the relevant explicit and tacit knowledge dispersed among economic agents, leaving the planners largely limited to their own personal knowledge in determining the allocation of resources.[39] As Hayek (1937, 1945) reminds us, it is precisely the knowledge peculiar to time, place, and circumstance, possessed by individual market participants but generating, via market interaction, a unique byproduct – a constellation of market prices – that allows agents to engage in a process of rational calculation in implementing their plans.

Although science is not a market and does not produce market prices, it nonetheless shares several characteristics with a catallaxy. First, science is characterized by a division of knowledge in that any individual scientist knows only a portion of the existing knowledge in or germane to his own field. As scientific knowledge progresses overall, each individual scientist knows relatively less, even as his own increasingly specialized knowledge itself increases. Second, in the appropriate institutional setting, science has the capacity to function as an unplanned, complexly organized order. Thus, like the catallaxy, it functions as an emergent order capable of generating novel outcomes that arise as unintended byproducts of the interactions among scientists. If we think of science as generating warranted knowledge in the form of definitions, theories, and empirical findings about reality, that knowledge is a snapshot of a mutable structure resulting from an ongoing process of appraisement and absorption of the individual contributions of past and current scientists.[40] Although constrained by the procedures scientists deploy, what emerges as scientific knowledge from the crucible of scientists' individual work is unplanned. Even if we may find it comforting to describe "truth" as an abstract goal of scientific activity, the specific content of that goal is something that can be discovered only as a byproduct of the process itself. In this sense, science is end-independent.

Attempts to plan science centrally, whether overtly or indirectly by monopolization of its funding, foster an institutional framework incompatible with science as a self-ordering and self-correcting order.[41] Planning's implicit (and no doubt unintended) aim is to remake science into a constructed order having particular ends specified in advance and resources directed so as to achieve such ends or to serve special purposes. This objective entails that government science tends toward dominating scientific activity both in terms of the specific allocation of scientific manpower and capital and in terms of the specific objectives that scientists seek to achieve. Underlying this tendency are two incorrect presumptions: first, that the planning board can somehow overcome the inherent division of both explicit and tacitly held knowledge within the scientific community to organize and direct science rationally, and, second, that in establishing specified goals for science and directing scientific activity toward those purposes, the planning board will not subvert the inherent discovery process associated with free science by reorienting science toward the generation of preordained sorts of knowledge. Even if one were to concede that free science is subject to "market failure", it does not follow that interventionist (and centrally planned) science represents a coherent framework for correcting such putative failure.[42]

Another kind of knowledge problem also bears an equally and perhaps even more important connection with science. At the very foundation of what science is understood to be is the notion that it has the capacity to generate new knowledge. The circumstances and conditions that induce the creation of knowledge are bound up in the specific institutional arrangements that compose science and govern the sorts of interactions in which scientists engage. As noted earlier, science is a particular kind of order that generates as a byproduct of scientists' activities something we recognize as "scientific knowledge". The principal characteristics of social orders such as science are their dynamic stability and adaptability, which allow them to function successfully as knowledge-generating systems. Yet, as we have seen, the structure of government funding of science has adverse implications for long-term stability and adaptability and therefore for the generation and use of scientific knowledge.

Distortion in nutritional science

The relationship between health and diet has long been of interest to scientists, medical clinicians, policymakers, and the general public. Up until the early 1970s, medical researchers, dietary clinicians, a large body of empirical work, and long-standing reputable weight reduction programs stressed the connection between obesity and carbohydrates. Within a decade, however, a sea change within the medical establishment had occurred that recommended low-fat diets to reduce the risk of heart disease and for treating weight-control problems. As Taubes (2007, p. xv) notes: "This was one of the more remarkable conceptual shifts in the history of public health."

Our interest here is not, of course, to render a judgment about the merits of the science surrounding this shift. Clearly, doing so requires the kind of knowledge that only science can provide and it is this that finally is the essence of the question. Science will typically entail a spectrum of theories, data, and clinical approaches open for debate and critical assessment, and it is as a consequence of that process that we would expect to generate better understanding of the questions at hand. But scientific questions are not always analyzed through the standard filters of scientific discourse, and a closer look at this most interesting episode reveals that the emergence of what is now the consensus stance on diet and health involved a cast of players that included, perhaps decisively so, the US Congress and government agencies. It is an illustration of how science may be affected when political bodies and regulatory authorities insinuate themselves into science in order to make policy.

This saga of the scientific understanding of the relation between diet and heart disease highlights the overall impact of events that singularly seemed of minor significance, but which together had the effect of introducing the political process and policy initiatives into an already difficult scientific question.[43] In particular, this episode illustrates the interplay arising from a directional shift in government heart disease funding in 1948, the role of cardiologist Dr. Ancel Keys in the American Heart Association (AHA),[44] the subsequent adoption by a Congressional committee and other government bodies of Keys' position on the correlation between dietary fat and heart disease, and the subsequent and ongoing developments in public policy toward diet and health.[45] The overall point we wish to make here is that the marriage of science and the political process illustrates a *distorting* effect of government on science.

In 1957, the AHA claimed that the evidence did not support the correlation between dietary fat and heart disease. But three years later, and without any new evidence, the AHA published a report that completely reversed its prior position. This report, issued by an *ad hoc* AHA committee, was written by Dr. Keys and a close ally. Leading up to this report and during the ensuing years, Keys campaigned tirelessly for his position. Shortly after the report's release, *Time Magazine* brought Keys into the national spotlight by featuring him on its January 13, 1961 cover and related cover story. Despite the growing popular acceptance of Keys' and the AHA's increasingly trenchant low-fat dietary recommendations, the underlying science still remained subject to further research and would have been expected to produce over time further insights in the complex of questions pertaining to diet and health. Nonetheless, a tipping point was reached in 1977 when, according to Taubes (2007, p. 44), "the controversy was shifted irrevocably in favor of Keys' hypothesis". The occasion of this turning point was the publication of *Dietary Goals of the United States* by George McGovern's Senate Select Committee on Nutrition and Human Needs, SCNN (1977).[46] The report fully reflected Keys' views, arguing that various dietary guidelines as part of a "plan for the nation" be accepted.[47] It is interesting to note that important segments of the scientific community testifying before the Committee, including the AMA and the National Heart, Lung, and Blood Institute, disputed not only the Committee's dietary guidelines and the research used to arrive at those guidelines, but also the evidence regarding the underlying premise with respect to heart disease and fat.[48]

Although the McGovern report had turned a scientific question into a political one, it received further support when other government agencies joined in. In March of 1977, the US Department of Agriculture (USDA), under Carter appointee and consumer advocate Carol Foreman, decided to get involved in the McGovern Committee's controversial report. The job of drafting the dietary guidelines fell to the USDA and its successful solicitation of the Surgeon General's Office.[49] When the Food and Nutrition Board of the National Academy of Sciences released its own version of dietary "guidelines" as *Toward Healthful Diets*, FNB (1980), it aligned itself in opposition to the McGovern Committee, the

USDA, and AHA by suggesting that weight control was the only sort of reliable and safe dietary advice that could be scientifically recommended. This brought forth a firestorm of criticism from its aforementioned adversaries, and also from Henry Waxman's House Subcommittee on Health, and from the press, which impugned the professional ethics of Board members as being in "the pocket of the industries being hurt", as *New York Times* columnist Jane Brody, quoted in Taubes (2007, p. 50), claimed. In this political battle, the McGovern guidelines became the de facto position of the government.

Needless to say, what emerged from this episode was a quasi-official government stance and popularly accepted belief that legitimated the basic contention of a controversial scientific and clinical take on dietary issues. By the early 1980s, the policy debate effectively ended, despite the fact that a scientific consensus proved elusive. Taubes (p. 60) notes that when the NIH simply announced that such a consensus did exist, "the controversy over dietary fat appeared to be over".

This brief overview suggests that the McGovern Committee's insinuation into a controversial question of science turned that question into a political issue that was resolved by political means and not scientific ones. With the eventual marshaling of government resources and agencies, it is easy to recognize that the government was able to override and dominate all comers opposed to it and, as a result, able to impose its view on the public and "conventional wisdom". This episode reveals the potency of the government when it chooses to act as a Big Player.

But what does this episode have to say about the effect on the scientific order and its knowledge-generating processes? As noted above, government funding in medical research took a directional change in 1948 when Congress passed the National Heart & Lung Institute National Heart Act creating the National Heart Institute and the National Heart Council, ostensibly to increase public awareness of heart disease. Funding for heart research passed through the Institute; within a year it had allocated \$9 million, by 1960 \$54 million, and in 2008 \$2.5 billion.[50] The magnitude of these amounts gives credence to the assertion that government was the dominant funder for heart research during the period this episode covers. Of particular interest is the effect on the disbursement of these monies once the government's political process established its basic posture. Taubes' (2007, p. 52) discussion of conflicts between science and industry is worth quoting at length:

> Scientists were believed to be free of conflicts if their only source of funding was a Federal agency, but all nutritionists knew if their research failed to support the government position on a particular subject, the funding would go instead to someone whose research did. "To be a dissenter was to be unfunded because the peer-review system rewards conformity and excluded criticism," George Mann has written in *The New England Journal of Medicine* in 1977 … David Kritchevsky, a member of the Food and Nutrition Board when it released *Toward Healthful Diets*, put it this way: "The US government is as big of a pusher as industry. If you say what the government says, then it's okay. If you say something that isn't what the government says, or that be parallel to what industry says, that makes you suspect."

The admissions in the quote above actually go farther than simply highlighting questions about the objectivity of industry- versus government-funded research, as important as that might be. They also speak to the effect of government funding on nutrition science by virtue of its providing an implicit entitlement to those whose scientific reputations are enhanced because they agree with "correct" science as deemed by the government. If funding success helps to engender further funding, reputation-seeking scientists have an incentive to align research questions, if only marginally, to those of the funder, while providing additional incentive to those whose views are consistent with those of the funder to seek such funding.

In addition, the reputational costs of dissent can be significant. As the quote above suggests, dissenters have an incentive to seek funding from nongovernment sources in order to carry out their research. But what if privately supported research is routinely vilified, thereby inducing a reduction in dissent as scientists adapt to the prospect of incurring reputational costs? Such costs are not generated because the science is sloppy or incompetent; rather, they arise as a result of who the funder is. This constitutes a mechanism whereby reputation is conferred on scientists by criteria distinct from criteria irrelevant to science; it is "science" by other means. This is illustrated by the reaction to critics of the McGovern Committee's "Dietary Guidelines", several of whom served on the Food and Nutrition Board, whose criticisms were dismissed because they had received industry funding support earlier in their careers.[51]

Funders are able to nudge research in desired directions while attracting self-selected funding-seekers. And the larger the share of funds provided by a single funder, the more significant is the likely effect of that funder on the kind of work that gets published and hence on the reputation status of researchers. The political dimensions to science funding suggest, as a consequence, that government funding enjoys the possibility of imposing on the processes of science an additional and distorting element to science as a consequence of its Big Player status.

The boom in climate science: background

Climate science has grown from a scientific backwater to an active, well-funded, and important area of research over a period of about 30 years.[52] In the 1980s, after a decade of generally rising global temperature measurements (which followed about 30 years of generally falling temperatures and some speculation about an impending ice age[53]), the hypothesis that the rise was driven by a greenhouse effect caused predominately by carbon dioxide emitted as a result of human activity was debated and, although there was dissent, the hypothesis was widely seen by climate scientists to be plausible.[54] But an extreme inference from the hypothesis – a human-induced global catastrophe – was publicized by environmental pressure groups, including the Environmental Defense Fund[55] and the Union of Concerned Scientists,[56] and the tentative scientific hypothesis began to be transformed, without anything close to rigorous scientific confirmation, into almost-certain knowledge of an impending crisis of worldwide proportions in the face of which no reasonable person could remain unconcerned.[57] Funding in generous quantity began to be directed, initially by philanthropic organizations such as the MacArthur

Foundation[58] but increasingly by various government agencies both in the US and overseas, toward research projects in climate science, a significant part of which was explicitly aimed at documenting a real and present man-made danger.

The United Nations took up the issue in 1988, forming the Intergovernmental Panel on Climate Change (IPCC) as an independent body of scientists charged with assessing current climate science research (specifically emphasizing the effects of human activity on climate) and producing summary and detailed reports geared to public consumption[59] – on the face of it, a very useful service. But the way in which the IPCC is organized[60] and its methods for eliciting agreement on the conclusions given in its reports[61] have opened it up to be the conduit of pervasive bias. Scientists are appointed to the panel by government officials, the panel's summary reports are edited by politicians and environmental activists without further scientific review, lax oversight allows scientists to assess their own work, relevant peer-reviewed literature is often ignored, and the much-quoted percentage assessments of confidence in particular conclusions are arrived at by a process of discussion and compromise which is hardly a scientific method of characterizing uncertainty.

Nonetheless, the IPCC has emerged as the purveyor of definitive conclusions deduced from climate science research. And there are very good reasons why its pronouncements would be taken as authoritative. If one does not inquire closely as to the details of the process by which it produces its reports, it has the appearance of a thorough, competent, and disinterested body. It engages the unpaid services of hundreds of scientists and expert reviewers from all over the world in order to produce, every six years or so, an exhaustive summary of findings in many climate-related fields. Through a process of discussion and negotiation intended to resolve differences in interpretation, it purports to present, as one voice, a definitive assessment of the current state of the science. It enjoys the backing of governments around the world, and as a UN organization it has special status. Its receipt of the Nobel Peace Prize in 2007 has cemented its reputation generally as a climate science oracle.[62]

The IPCC qualifies as a Big Player in science in that it possesses all of the attributes characteristic of Big Players in markets: bigness in terms of influence, insensitivity to the usual constraints, and discretion in its ability to promote a favored direction of research. Its influence in climate science is pervasive, and the complex nature of the climate system and the lack of understanding of the feedbacks at play enable it to champion the most politically attractive of the several plausible hypotheses and to largely ignore uncertainties and potential disconfirmations which are the usual scientific constraints on the acceptance of hypotheses. Professional success in climate science has become more tied to the acceptance of the IPCC's pronouncements than with the exploration of contrary possibilities; in fact, scientists who profess competing hypotheses are routinely castigated as "deniers" and some have reported unusual difficulties in negotiating the publishing process.[63]

While a large majority of climate scientists are reported as being in general agreement with the anthropogenic global warming (AGW) hypothesis and with the IPCC's pronouncements, the accuracy and extent of this consensus has been questioned.[64] But, despite the objections to vaguely worded questionnaires, selectivity in sampling, subjectivity in the analysis of paper abstracts, and disputes as to who actually qualifies as a "climate scientist", the results of several surveys are consistent in depicting an overwhelming acceptance, by scientists associated in some way with climate science, of the IPCC line.[65] The oft-quoted 97 percent number may be unrealistic and unsupportable, but the general acceptance by the majority of scientists having any connection to climate science seems real enough. This herding is a predictable result of the IPCC's Big Player presence.

There is, of course, the understandable concern that if in fact the climate is warming significantly as a result of human action there might be adverse effects that may be possible to mitigate through concerted action. Although this concern rests on three assumptions that are far from certain (that human activity is the overwhelmingly major cause of the observed warming, that the climate is warming at a rate that will make adaptation difficult and costly for some, and that the effects of warming will be a net negative), it is widely held, and it finds powerful (if usually unarticulated) support in the ideological bent which sees humanity as the despoiler of nature.

In science, when the "common wisdom" favors a particular hypothesis, there is an incentive, particularly for younger, not-yet-established researchers, to follow it. If the hypothesis turns out to be correct, you are seen to have the good sense to have espoused it; if it turns out to be incorrect, you have plenty of company. Either way, your scientific reputation will not be materially damaged. But if you flout the common wisdom but it turns out to be correct, your reputation will suffer greatly. This raises the following question: is the contrarian stance, with a potentially large reputational gain if the hypothesis turns out to be false, worth the risk? As Koppl (2002, pp. 129–130) points out, in the context of markets, that depends on the reliability of the evidence.[66]

Incentives influence the choice between idiosyncrasy and herding. If the penalty for a bad idiosyncratic decision is high compared with the penalty for the same bad decision made along with everyone else, then one has an incentive to concentrate less on evaluating reports about the empirical evidence and more on noting what other scientists believe. If the available reports about the empirical evidence are reliable, then they provide a powerful counterweight to this incentive, namely, the large gains to be expected from taking a correct but idiosyncratic position. When most of the available reports have been rendered unreliable by a Big Player's discretionary interventions, this counterweight no longer exists. The expected gain from taking a dissenting position then becomes too small to discourage herd behavior. Herd behavior is encouraged by discretionary interventions because of the role of reputation in the furtherance of scientific careers. The process is self-reinforcing – if herding begins, the fact that increasing numbers of scientists seem to espouse the common wisdom serves only to cement the appearance of consensus. The less reliable are the available empirical assessments, the longer such self-reinforcing movements can go unchecked.

The very nature of the IPCC's organization, from its politically motivated appointments of senior staff, to its process of producing allegedly scientific summaries by negotiated compromise, to its toleration of the intervention of political operatives into the production of the most publicized reports of the state of the science, has served to make it the purveyor of tainted science.[67] The introduction of political considerations has rendered the reported science unreliable and has obscured the uncertainties inherent in the studies of a very complex and poorly understood system. And as a herding-inducing Big Player in science, the IPCC has provided synergy for the interventions of Big Players of a different sort, the government entities who have seized on the IPCC-generated consensus to fund the climate science boom thereby justify increasing economic interventions citing the threat implied in the AGW hypothesis.

The boom in climate science: funding

The past three decades have seen a sustained program of funding, largely from government or quasi-government entities.[68] The funding efforts are spread across a bewildering array of sources and buried in a labyrinth of programs, agency initiatives, interagency activities, and Presidential Offices, but what they seem to have in common is an adherence to the assumption that human activity is primarily responsible for the warming observed in the latter part of the twentieth century. Funding appears to be driving the science rather than the other way around. The full extent of this funding is very difficult to fully document, but serious attempts have been made by Nova (2009) and Butos & McQuade (2015, pp. 174–181).[69]

Government-funded R&D, including those activities related to the development and financing of technologies and programs characterized as mitigation of and adaptation to the presumed effects of climate change, are embedded in scores of agencies and programs scattered throughout the Executive Branch of the US government. While such agency activities related to climate science have received funding for many years as components of their mission statements, the pursuit of an integrated national agenda to study climate change and implement policy initiatives took a critical step with passage of the Global Change Research Act of 1990. This Act established institutional structures operating out of the White House to develop and oversee the implementation of a National Global Change Research Plan and created the US Global Change Research Program (USGCRP) to coordinate the climate change research activities of Executive Departments and agencies.[70]

The USGCRP operates as a confederacy of the research components of thirteen participating government agencies, each of which independently designates funds in accordance with the objectives of the USGCRP; these monies comprise the program budget of the USGCRP to fund agency cross-cutting climate science R&D.[71] The departments and agencies whose activities comprise the bulk of such funding include independent agencies such as the National Aeronautics and Space Administration, National Science Foundation, Environmental Protection Agency, US Agency for International Development, the quasi-official Smithsonian Institute, and Executive Departments that include Agriculture, Commerce (National Oceanic and Atmospheric Administration, National Institute of Standards and Technology), Energy, Interior (the US Geological Survey and conservation initiatives), State, and Treasury.[72]

The coordination of climate change-related activities has resided largely in the President's Office of Science and Technology Policy, which houses several separate offices, including the offices of Environment and Energy, Polar Sciences, Ocean Sciences, Clean Energy and Materials R&D, Climate Adaptation and Ecosystems, National Climate Assessment, and others. The Office of the President also maintains the National Science and Technology Council, which oversees the Committee on Environment, Natural Resources, and Sustainability and its Subcommittee on Climate Change Research. The Subcommittee is charged with the responsibility of planning and coordinating with the interagency USGCRP. Also, the Office of Energy and Climate Change Policy is housed within the President's Domestic Policy Council. While Congress authorizes Executive branch budgets, the priorities these departments and agencies follow are set by the White House.

The US Government Accountability Office (GAO) provides, in GAO (2018), a recent account of climate change funding based on various (and not always compatible) data provided by the US White House Office of Management and Budget (OMB). It covers the period 1993 through 2017 and, as can be seen in Figure 10.5, shows Federal climate funding rising from about $2.4 billion in fiscal 1993 to about $13.2 billion in 2017.[73] The funding is reported (p. 58) in three main categories: technology "to reduce emissions", science "to better understand climate change", and international assistance "for adaptation, clean energy, and sustainable landscapes". The total funding over the period shown is over $154 billion. However, the graph does not show the additional $26.1 billion authorized by the American Recovery and Reinvestment Act of 2009, and it does not include the various tax provisions and subsidies related to reducing greenhouse gas emissions (which are treated as "tax expenditures").[74]

By any measure, the scale of climate science R&D has increased substantially since 1993. The largest funding increases have occurred in developing new technologies and tax subsidies. Funding to develop and implement "clean energy technologies" have increased from $0.8 billion in 1993 to $9.0 billion in 2017, and energy tax subsidies have increased from $0.6 billion in 2003 to $5.2 billion in 2017, with the largest increases happening since 2010.[75] This recent pattern of Federal climate science funding, moving toward emphasis on the development of

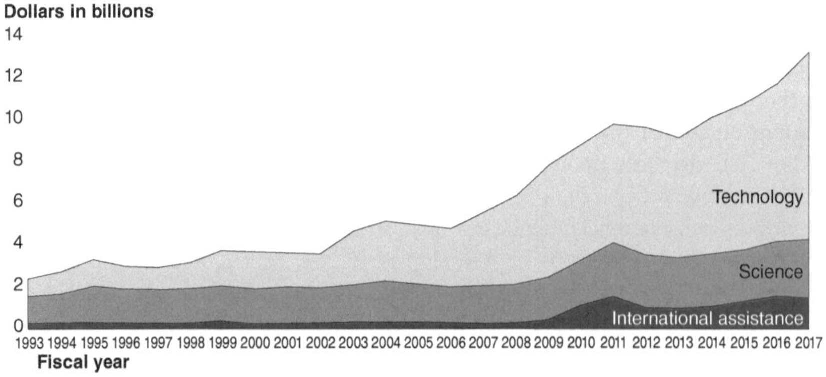

Figure 10.5 Federal climate funding categories.

Source: GAO 18-223, https://www.gao.gov/products/gao-18-223.

technologies and their subsidization through the tax system, suggests that climate change funding has become more tightly connected to agencies like the Department of Energy, NASA, the Department of Commerce (NOAA), EPA, and cross-cutting projects and programs involving multiple agencies under integrating and coordinating agencies, like the USGCRP, lodged within the Executive branch. The allocations of budgets within these agencies are more directly determined and implemented by administration priorities and policies. We note that the traditional role of the NSF in supporting basic science based on a system of merit awards provided (despite some clear imperfections) certain advantages with regard to generating impartial science. In contrast, even a casual perusal of current agency documents, such as The National Science and Technology Council's *The National Global Change Research Plan 2012–2021*, shows that those driving this movement make no pretense as to their premises and starting points.[76]

The impact on scientific research of government funding is not just a matter of the amounts but also of the concentration of research monies that arises from the focus a single source can bring to bear on particular kinds of scientific research. Government is that single source and has Big Player effects because it has access to a deep pool of taxpayer (and, indeed, borrowed and created) funds combined with regulatory and enforcement powers which necessarily place it on a different footing from other players and institutions. Notwithstanding the interplay of rival interests within the government and the separation of powers among the different branches, there is an important sense in which government's inherent need to act produces a particular set of decisions that fall within a relatively narrow corridor of ends to which it can concentrate substantial resources.

By any standard, what we have documented here is a massive funding drive, highlighting the patterns of climate science R&D as funded and directed only by the Executive Branch and the various agencies that fall within its purview.[77] It is more than enough to sustain a science boom. Its directional characteristic, concentrated as it has been on R&D premised on the controversial issue of the actual sensitivity of climate to human-caused emissions, has gone hand in hand with the IPCC's expressions of increasing confidence in the AGW hypothesis and increasingly shrill claims of impending disaster.

The boom in climate science: distortion

Scientists are no less likely than anyone else to be swayed by a fear of crisis, and this is especially the case for those who see that they, with their relevant expertise, may be able to contribute to doing something about it. It is surprisingly easy for scientists to overstate the certainty of their results and to ignore or attempt to explain away conflicting data, but this is not unusual and it does no lasting damage provided that the basic procedures of science (review, publication, criticism, citation, and the feedbacks to reputation) are functioning normally. But when a particular set of conclusions is widely held not only to fit one's preconceptions but also to have serious social implications, the harsh and critical judgments necessary for weeding out shaky science can be significantly toned down. The ideologically primed sense of impending global warming catastrophe, transformed into near-certainty by the influential publications of the IPCC, has endangered the integrity of the processes of science.

The scientific process for the generation of reliable knowledge relies heavily on general adherence to the norms of publication and citation, with feedback effects on the reputations and credibility of contributing scientists. Were these norms to be systematically violated within a scientific discipline, knowledge and reputations would still be generated, but the knowledge would be counterfeit and unreliable, and the reputations would be similarly tainted.[78] In climate science, the presence of Big Players – the IPCC in its ability to direct the science and the government in its supporting role of ensuring that IPCC-compatible science is funded – has engendered a growing politicization of the discipline, showing up in attempts to restrict publication of dissenting views and to attack the reputations of scientists who question the IPCC "consensus".

There have been a number of allegations of scientific misbehavior within climate science, ranging from extreme bias in the publishing process to removing so-called "deniers" from academic positions.[79] But these are anecdotal, subject to claim and counter-claim, and cannot be held up as definitive evidence. Lindzen (2012, sect. 4), however, does attempt to document some serious instances of violations of scientific norms. These include pressure placed on some editors and reviewers to reject papers even mildly criticizing the AGW hypothesis, collaboration between some editors and reviewers with a view to suppressing papers critical of AGW, pressures on authors during the review process to remove findings that could be construed as disputing AGW, and instances of ostracization and vilification of some researchers for their publication of papers criticizing AGW. In addition, Lindzen claims that journals have solicited "attack papers" (published as independent papers rather than, as is conventional, critical comments) in the wake of publication elsewhere of papers considered to question AGW. If rebuttals of the attack by the original authors do get published, it is with a delay, and as comments only. The result is to make the original papers appear to have been discredited.

These claims find some substantiation in the collection of emails and other data hacked from the Climate Research Center of the University of East Anglia in 2009.[80] In these emails, leading IPCC-affiliated scientists such as Michael Mann and colleagues in the US and Phil Jones and colleagues in the UK[81] vent their distaste for researchers who dispute aspects of the AGW hypothesis, discuss their frustrations with requests for supporting data and their strategies for not complying with such requests, attempt to influence the reviewing process for papers they consider "dangerous", berate journal editors and reviewers for allowing dissenting papers to be published, and discuss boycotting journals thought to be open to such papers. In one email[82] Jones, then an IPCC chapter lead author, referring to two papers not supportive of AGW published in a peer-reviewed journal, wrote: "I can't see either of these papers being in the next IPCC report. Kevin[83] and I will keep them out somehow – even if we have to redefine what the peer-review literature is!"

While this quote reflects poorly on the IPCC's process of summarizing the extant peer-reviewed literature and the steadfast refusal to provide data to researchers attempting to reproduce published results is a clear violation of scientific norms, the extent of successful scientific distortion involved is hard to assess. It is not clear that the emails reveal more than a fairly extreme version of the egoism, competitiveness, sensitivity to criticism, and disdain for those not in agreement that is not particularly uncommon in science circles. What does stand out rather clearly and consistently is a pervasive ideological bias in the scientists involved. As might be expected, there is a lot of discussion, expressed doubts, and disagreements among these scientists as to the reliability of their data, their assumptions, and the statistical methods being employed,[84] but none of this shows up in their public presentations.[85] Also, it is not prominent in the IPCC reports to which these scientists are major contributors and, to the extent it appears at all, it is buried in the jargon of the supporting scientific chapters but absent from the widely read summaries. There are excursions into political activism, with discussions about circulating alarmist statements for endorsement by other scientists (in furtherance of "the cause"), letters to the US Senate, and encouragement of environmental agendas.[86] The line between science and politics in climate science does appear to be rather blurred.

The boom in climate science: effects on markets

When a scientific discipline is subject to Big Player influences that circumvent normal scientific procedure to favor a particular hypothesis and to inject political considerations into the assessment of scientific achievement, the result can be termed "crony science" in analogy with the "crony capitalism" of an economy where particular industries and individual businesses are favored and the normal operation of profit and loss is blunted. And crony science can beget crony capitalism. When the result sought by crony science has obvious technological implications, then it is no surprise that businesses might see considerable profit opportunity in obtaining government support in pursuing such applications.

In the case of the climate boom, government resources are not only directed to sustaining the boom but also to enlisting a large number of client businesses who benefit from subsidies justified in terms of their advertised potential for mitigating the effects of human activity which have been designated as responsible for excessive global warming under the AGW hypothesis. The spillover into the wider economy is manifest in the pervasive emphasis on (and subsidy of) "green energy", including wind power, solar cells, automobile battery technology, and biofuels, and is accompanied by the demonization of more traditional and cheaper carbon-producing industries and technologies.

As noted above, the thrust of government climate change funding since 2009 has been directed at R&D expenditures for so-called "green technologies" via the Executive Branch. While the USGCRP under the White House Office of Science and Technology has become the principal agency orchestrating and coordinating climate science funding, various agencies, and especially DOE, have administered programs involving direct subsidies, loans, and tax preferences for green technologies.

Section 1705 of the American Recovery and Reinvestment Act of 2009 authorized the DOE to provide taxpayer loan guarantees and direct investment subsidies for the development of green technologies.[87] As the program wound down in 2014, $16 billion had been allocated to 27 firms. As reported in detail in Lakatos (2014), the majority of the firms had officers or investors with close ties to political insiders at the Federal and State levels, campaign bundlers, donors, and DOE agency officials. Of these firms, several have declared bankruptcy, accounting for $3 billion in taxpayer losses,[88] and several others listed by Nava and Morris (2013) as "troubled recipients" account for an another $3.5 billion.[89] Of the 18 firms who were not listed as "troubled", 14, representing $11.3 billion in loan guarantees, had not completed their projects as of the end of 2013, while 4 firms with loan guarantees of $352.6 million had completed projects. In summary, of the $16 billion in DOE loan guarantees, about $15.6 billion represent bankrupt, troubled, or incomplete taxpayer investments as of 2013.

Even if we assume that most of the loan guarantees in the "incomplete" category pan out, the taxpayer losses of perhaps $6.5 billion on a $16 billion "investment" are arguably unacceptable. What accounts for this flouting of conservative stewardship? The most obvious reason is that these investments cannot be ascribed to a market-driven process. Whatever the extent that cronyism played in the allocation of these loan guarantees, the entire process was driven by governmental objectives absent market-based constraints and mechanisms.

Beyond these considerations, Nava & Morris (2013) note that 83% and 11% of the loan guarantees went toward solar and wind technologies, respectively, violating basic precepts of investment portfolio diversification and *ex ante* exposing taxpayers to huge potential risks. In addition, at the outset of the loan guarantee program, 22 of the firms awarded loan guarantees were classified as "junk" grade investments or lower, and only the remainder classified above junk at BBB. As Nava & Morris (2013, p. 23) point out, "the entire portfolio of [Section] 1705 projects has an average rating of BB-, a junk grade rating".

The effects of Big Player activities in climate science have not been confined to the scientific arena, but are being felt in the wider economy. Taxpayer funds are being diverted on a large scale into government-favored businesses whose business plans are based on very uncertain science. This is hardly a recipe for economic success; indeed, the performance of such businesses to date would indicate that it is pure economic folly.

Scientific booms do burst, but in areas where the phenomena are complex and not well understood, the busts can be quiet and long-drawn-out. When and how the bust will occur cannot be predicted in advance. It is unlikely (except perhaps in the event of a financial catastrophe) that funding will be cut off. It is more likely that, slowly but surely, the scientific method will do its work and the disparity between the predictions of the theory and the observations of a recalcitrant world will become too obvious to ignore. It is also possible that, like eugenics, the political applications of the theory will have effects that will be seen as undesirable or even callously destructive – and there are indications already that, especially in Europe, "green" legislation and regulation is stifling growth and creating unnecessary hardship.[90]

Nonetheless, the science of genetics has survived eugenics, and climate science will probably survive the excesses surrounding the AGW hypothesis. The downside is that, possibly, little will be learned – there appear to be almost no scientists today who identify themselves as eugenicists and, to judge by the biographies of many of the important thinkers of the first half of the 20th century (when eugenics was considered reasonable science), there were very few serious eugenicists then! But if anything can be learned it is that in science, as in the economy, Big Players of any sort distort the normal systemic activity and render the emergent outcomes unstable and unreliable and create an ideal breeding ground for incentives that motivate ideologically biased people to circumvent normal constraints in the name of pursuing a "greater good".

Notes

1 This chapter contains text previously published in Butos & McQuade (2006, 2015) with permission from The Independent Institute, and in Butos & McQuade (2012) with permission from De Gruyter. Figures 10.1–10.4 are reproduced from Hourihan (2021) with permission from the American Association for the Advancement of Science.
2 The US Office of Management and Budget defines R&D as consisting of three categories: basic research, which is "experimental or theoretical work undertaken primarily to acquire new knowledge of the underlying foundations of phenomena and observable facts"; applied research, which is "original investigation undertaken to acquire new knowledge … directed primarily towards a specific, practical aim or objective"; and development, which is "systematic work, drawing on knowledge gained from research and practical experience, which is directed at producing new products or processes or improving existing products or processes". See Hourihan (2021).
3 Based on historical tables in the Budget of the US Government, 2021, cited in Hourihan (2021).
4 See Dupre & Lakoff (1962) and Rahm *et al.* (2000, ch. 2).
5 The idea that science should serve social and political objectives, as opposed to seeking "scientific truth", was not confined to America. Indeed, such enthusiasms were especially pronounced in England during the 1930s. Fueled by beliefs of the presumed success of Soviet central planning, the British government came under increasing pressure to organize scientific institutions so as to establish central planning for science. This movement was countered, almost single-handedly, by John Baker, Michael Polanyi, and their Society of Freedom in Science. This episode is analyzed in detail in McGucken (1984).
6 The University of California's Los Alamos Laboratory in New Mexico is an example of the OSRD's efforts. The laboratories built for the Manhattan Project came under the aegis of the OSRD and would later begin the US national laboratory system.
7 Letter from Roosevelt to Bush, November 17, 1944, quoted in Feldman *et al.* (2002, p. 15).
8 Of the fifty individuals who served on committees that reported to Bush, a majority listed academic affiliations (generally at the higher administrative levels); the next-largest group comprised personnel from government agencies. The so-called Medical Committee was composed entirely of nine university-affiliated physicians.
9 See Feldman *et al.* (2002, p. 16). Bush's claim that basic research necessarily precedes applied R&D and its eventual effects on material progress is often referred to as the "linear model", a paradigm that dominated policymakers' and academic researchers' views for decades, as we discuss later in more detail.
10 The Bush report's argument for government funding of science does not rest on claims about market failure, but on a vague sense that "more scientific knowledge is desirable". The report in Appendix 3 by The Committee on Science and Public Welfare, the one committee most closely associated with economics, provides data on scientific research

expenditures by industry, colleges and universities, and government. However, only two economists, Rupert MacLaurin of MIT and Harold Moulton of The Brookings Institute, sat on this committee and neither of them ever advanced market-failure arguments for science in their own academic work. Moulton, who came into prominence in the 1920s, was a leading authority on money, banking, and business cycles. MacLaurin did write on R&D issues; see, for example, his *Invention and Innovation in the Radio Industry* (1949).

11 *The Endless Frontier* urged that Federal funding attain an annual level of $122 million.

12 PSRB (1947, 1, pp. 3–7). The President's Scientific Research Board was composed entirely of Cabinet secretaries and other government officials, including Vannevar Bush.

13 See Feldman *et al.* (2002, p. 19) for an overview.

14 As defined by the NSF (2005, p. 1), research is "systematic study directed toward fuller scientific knowledge or understanding of the subject studied," and comprises *basic research* ("systematic study directed toward fuller knowledge or understanding of the fundamental aspects of phenomena and of observable facts without specific applications toward processes or products in mind") and *applied research* ("systematic study to gain knowledge or understanding necessary to determine the means by which a recognized and specific need may be met"). *Development* is "systematic application of knowledge or understanding, directed toward the production of useful materials, devices, and systems or methods, including design, development, and improvement of prototypes and new processes to meet specific requirements".

15 Budget appropriations to combat terrorism have been one of the fastest-growing aspects of Federal R&D funding. For example, from fiscal year 2002 to 2003, according to the NSB (2004, pars. 4.28 & 4.29), appropriations for counterterrorism activities by various agencies, including Defense, Health and Human Services, National Institutes of Health, Environmental Protection, and Justice increased from $1.2 billion to $2.9 billion. Subsequent budgets (since the creation of the Department of Homeland Security in January 2003) have not separated counterterrorism R&D from other R&D programs.

16 Of course, within the context of neoclassical economic analysis, as Buchanan & Stubblebine (1962, p. 381) point out, "the observation of external effects, taken alone, cannot provide a basis for judgment concerning the desirability of some modification in an existing state of affairs. There is not a *prima facie* case for intervention in all cases where an externality is presumed to exist. The internal benefits from carrying out the activity, net of costs, may be greater than the external damage that is imposed on other parties."

17 Many commentators on the economics of scientific research, in addition to Dasgupta & David (1994), are indebted to Nelson and Arrow for various aspects of their analysis. See, for example, Radnitzky (1986), Diamond (1988), Brock & Durlauf (1999), many of the papers republished in Mirowski & Sent (2002), and a series of papers summed up in Ziman (2002). We do not deal here with treatments of science that explicitly represent science as a type of market. The most thoughtful of these treatments is Walstad (2002); for an analysis and criticism of the analogy see McQuade (2007).

18 Nelson (1959, p. 305) allows that "the profit motive may stimulate private industry to spend an amount on applied research reasonably close to the amount that is socially desirable". His characterization of applied research, in contrast to basic research, is one of a matter of degree (p. 300): research is more basic to the extent that "the degree of uncertainty about the results … increases, and the goals become less clearly defined and less closely tied to the solution of a specific practical problem or the creation of a practical object".

19 Nelson (1959, p. 304) also suggests two other factors that reduce the incentive for private firms to pursue basic research: "the long lag that very often occurs between the initiation of a basic research project and the creation of something of marketable value" and "the very large variance of the profit probability distribution from a basic research project".

20 Even if these characterizations of knowledge are taken at face value, the presumed incentive effects do not necessarily follow. As Rosenberg (1990, p. 167, emphasis in original) argues, the "mere *existence*" of uncaptured benefits "is never an adequate explanation for the reluctance to perform basic research", provided the firm can capture sufficient benefits from its research. Even though the research may generate spillovers, it is not their magnitude that matters, but the return on investment the firm is likely to realize from derivative commercial applications.

21 Rosenberg (1990) reports that firms fund basic research because it generates cross-fertilization of ideas, problem-solving, and creativity among scientists and other company employees. Hicks (1995) observes that firms find it in their interest to hire freely publishing research scientists for a variety of reasons: such an employment practice provides access to research networks, keeps their scientists engaged and up-to-date, and presents an image in the academic and scientific community conducive to recruitment.

22 On this point, see Pavitt (1987) and Rosenberg (1990).

23 Dasgupta & David (1994, p. 494) appear to disagree, saying that they "find no compelling grounds for associating the tacit knowledge of either technologists or scientists necessarily with skills that are specific rather than 'generic' in their applicability". But simply to say (p. 495) that "the boundary between the codified information and tacit knowledge in a specific field of scientific research may be shifted endogenously by economic considerations" does not do away with the disincentive of the cost of actually acquiring the skills, especially given that the particular skills needed may not be predictable in advance.

24 Kealey (1996, pp. 227–228) reports on a study of Japanese pharmaceutical firms by Odagiri & Murakimi (1992) that found rates of return from basic research and "second-mover" research to be 19% and 33%, respectively.

25 These issues are discussed in detail in Demsetz (1969). Although we endorse Demsetz's criticisms of Arrow (1962), we have reservations about some of his suggested solutions. For example, we do not see that the creation of property rights in basic scientific results is a reasonable or viable arrangement. (We should be clear here that we *do* see the viability and desirability of the appropriation of services that enable the dissemination and use of basic scientific discoveries. For example, the base sequence of the human genetic code is a scientific discovery published openly and owned by nobody, but the database containing this code and allowing access to tools for gene search and identification is the property of its developer.) Also, see Walstad (2002, p. 25) for a sensible critique of treating research contributions as "intellectual property".

26 No indication is given as to how one would actually determine the marginal social return for a research project in order to contrast this return with the (equally indeterminate) social opportunity costs of activities forgone owing to the government's extraction of the funds from the public.

27 They do this because they expect the action to be profitable. Mansfield (1980) estimates an implicit rate of return of 27% on total R&D between 1960 and 1976 for chemical and petroleum firms. He finds a strong independent relationship between basic research and productivity; however, that finding (p. 871) may "reflect a tendency for basic research findings to be exploited more fully by industries and firms for responsible for them". He suggests (p. 866) that basic research may be a proxy for long-term applied R&D. Griliches (1986, p. 149) finds that R&D, especially basic research, and the fraction of research financed privately (versus Federally) contribute positively to productivity growth. According to his estimates, "raising the stock of R&D by 20 percent but shifting it all into the private component doubles the effect of such dollars". Interestingly, he acknowledges that such results may be flawed because R&D often aims at creating new products as opposed to increasing productivity. He finds that firms tend to capture high returns from basic research, even if it is assumed that 50 percent of the positive effects of basic research are diffused throughout the industry. Working with data for the years 1967 to 1977, Griliches (1987) also shows that dollar for dollar, industry-financed basic research contributes far more to economic growth than did government-financed

basic research. Kealey (1996, p. 225) claims that these findings support the notion that private companies "fund basic science comprehensively" and that it is "highly profitable".

28 For example, scientific tests of radiation exposure on US servicemen and prison inmates during the 1950s.

29 Also see Arrow (1971).

30 The existence of monopoly profits would indicate an inefficiency, however, at least relative to a Pareto ideal.

31 In this context, peer review is widely regarded as a vital mechanism for ensuring a rational allocation of public funding. But see Martino (1992, ch. 5) for a discussion of its strengths, limitations, and inherent problems. However, given that there is to be public funding, with its inevitable conflict between expert judgment and public accountability, then peer review seems as good a mechanism as any relative to the alternatives (bureaucratic selection, selection by political influence, and formulaic selection such as seniority – all of which have that conflict).

32 Dasgupta & David (1994) do not make the mistake of subscribing to the simplistic and unidirectional "linear model" in which investments in basic science lead directly to economic growth via technological change. This model of economic development through science was recognized as defunct on scientific grounds in the 1960s, although it lives on for political purposes. Its proponents argue that without the appropriate amount of basic research, technological innovations and material progress will lag, and the government must provide the funding necessary to sustain an adequate amount of basic research and thus to promote economic growth. The basic error in the model (apart from the assumption of the necessity of government provision of funding) is the claim that new basic science drives technological change. Existing science and existing technology, however, have been found to cause technological change. For more discussion on this topic see Kealey (1996, pp. 204–205), Greenberg (1967, pp. 29–30), Martin & Nightingale (2000) and Feldman *et al.* (2002, p. 17).

33 David (1997), in a very critical review of Kealey (1996), maintains that private R&D funding is no substitute for public funding, and he disputes Kealey's finding that government funding crowds out private funding. Suffice to say that the statistical evidence that can be gleaned in an environment of heavy government funding is inconclusive and probably subject to a variety of interpretations. Our appraisal of the institutional structures at play and the incentives they embody, however, leads us to expect that Kealey is closer to the truth.

34 Such motives include, in addition to profit-seeking, the usual motives of private donors (which range from a sense of civic duty to a desire for immortality by association) and the institutionalized motives of foundations and trusts.

35 Greenberg's (2001) work is particularly enlightening. He describes in detail the history of the increasing entanglement of science and politics in the United States from World War II to the present: the enormous growth in government funding of the physical and biological sciences; the ways in which scientists and their universities have operated to claim and foster the increase of that largesse; the surprisingly unscientific, but politically effective propositions they have promoted to justify their right to public funding on a large scale; and the practical political reasons why legislators are likely to have the incentive to go along with the arrangement. He sees scientists as having succeeded beyond their wildest dreams in extracting public funds for their own use, but cautions that this activity has come at the expense of "the ethics of science". According to Greenberg, access to funding is surpassing reputation as a motivating force in science, a change that has led to an undermining of collegiality and, in some cases, honesty within science. As he sees the situation, the traditional standards of science have been corrupted by decades of misleading representations to the public and the government in pursuit of public money.

36 Such effects may be observable in changes in the spectrum of paper citations. A trend toward more published papers that receive very low numbers (particularly zero) of

citations might be correlated with changes in funding amounts (specifically a lag). Zero-citation papers are the scientific analog of goods produced in excess of consumer desires. One would expect a period of lavish funding to be followed by an increase in the number of "useless" papers published and the reverse trend after funding downturns. Similar trends might be observed in journal start-ups and closings.

37 Changes in the number of trained scientists who are unable to find employment *as scientists* might be able to be correlated with changes in the amount of funding. One would expect to find unemployment trends in particular areas within science characteristic of economic boom and bust. Even if science funding levels never decreased absolutely, unemployment increases should be observed after a slowing of the rate of increase below that required to fund adequately the new scientists who are minted in times of plenty. Because politically motivated funding tends to concentrate on particular areas of current political attraction, the analysis would have to be at the level of the discipline or subdiscipline.

38 Although this outcome may be exceedingly difficult to document, reports of erosion of "scientific ethics" should increase during scientific funding recession and should decrease during scientific boom. Increases in "unethical" behavior driven by competition for funds would be the science analog of a scramble for loans at the height of a boom as businesses strive to complete production projects in the face of resource scarcity or credit hardening. For a more standard economic discussion of fraud in science, see Wible (1998).

39 See the essays on the socialist calculation debate by Mises and Hayek in Hayek (1935). See Lavoie (1985) for a more recent treatment.

40 We have previously described this process in Hayekian terms as science generating a particular kind of *classification* over some specified domain of inputs in order to capture the adaptive characteristics of various knowledge-generating orders. See McQuade & Butos (2005) and McQuade (2007).

41 See Polanyi (1945, 1962), Hayek (1973, ch. 2), and Butos & Koppl (2003).

42 Machan (2002, pp. xiii–xx) also associates government science with the problem of rational allocation under central planning.

43 For a more detailed history and analysis of this long-running episode, see Scheall *et al.* (2018).

44 The AHA was established in 1924 as a private charitable organization of doctors and is not supported by government funds. In 2007 the AHA had revenues of nearly $800 million and expenses of $690 million, of which nearly 22% was used to support research and nearly 40% for public health education. Among its corporate sponsors, donations by 34 pharmaceutical and device manufacturing firms account for about 6% of its income. See AHA (2007).

45 In one of many similar instances, in July 2008 the New York City Council implemented its ban on the use of non-naturally occurring trans fats in commercial food establishments. Earlier that June, the *New York Times* reported that other cities were studying New York's approach with an eye to installing similar bans in their own locales, with probably the most significant instance being California's adoption on July 26, 2007, of a state-wide ban on the use of trans fats by restaurants. See Hartocollis (2008) and Steinhauer (2008).

46 The motives for the Committee's work in this area have been the subject of speculation; its work on dietary issues was not closely connected to its original 1968 charge to address malnutrition. Taubes (2007, p. 45) suggests that the real driving force was "the committee staff, composed of lawyers and ex-journalists". He quotes staff director Marshall Matz: "we were totally naïve" and believed we "should do something on this subject before we go out of business". However, Taubes (p. 45) notes that the McGovern Committee believed it was about to be downgraded to a subcommittee (*i.e.*, effectively put out of existence) and that *Dietary Goals* was "a last-ditch effort to save the Committee".

47 These guidelines referred to the recommended dietary percentages of carbohydrate calories (55-60%) and fat calories (30%). See SCNN (1977).
48 Taubes (2007, p. 47) notes that reputable scientists were sandwiched between speakers representing the dairy, cattle, and egg industries, thereby tainting the testimony of scientists.
49 The USDA failed to solicit the assistance of other government agencies in generating the dietary guidelines: first, the National Academy of Sciences, whose President, Philip Handler, quoted in Taubes (p. 49), told Foreman that *Dietary Goals* was "nonsense". In turn, entreaties to the National Institutes of Health and the Food and Drug Administration were rebuffed.
50 The National Heart Institute was redesignated as the National Heart & Lung Institute in 1969 and as the National Heart, Lung, and Blood Institute in 1976.
51 Taubes (2007, ch. 3) provides a detailed treatment of this episode and rightly points out the obvious inconsistency of the underlying "guilt by association" premise, which typically is invoked because the accuser disagrees with the accused. Despite their logical incoherence, such arguments are often seen in the political and policy arenas.
52 For a comprehensive history of developments in climate science, see Weart (2008).
53 While there was no consensus (of any sort) in the scientific community regarding an imminent ice age, some peer-reviewed work did in fact raise the possibility of such a scenario – for example, Rasool and Schneider (1971). For some interesting documentation of the change in scientific opinion from likely cooling to likely warming, see Holcombe (2006).
54 While the hypothesis was certainly not original with them, a seminal paper was Hansen *et al.* (1981). For a prominent example of dissent, see Idso (1980).
55 See Oppenheimer & Boyle (1990).
56 See UCS (1997).
57 The rush to scientific judgment has been helped along by the active endorsement of the anthropogenic global warming (AGW) hypothesis by some very prestigious scientific organizations, including the Royal Society in the UK – see Montford (2012) – and the National Academy of Science in the US – see Lindzen (2012). The fact that scientific societies would take a strong public position on a matter of scientific controversy is unusual in itself, and not in keeping with the charters of such societies.
58 See MacArthur Foundation (2008).
59 For an insightful exposition of the political and cultural currents surrounding the formation of the IPCC, see Gilland (2007).
60 The IPCC operates under protocols formalized at the 1992 framework convention on climate change, in Article 1.2 of which "climate change" is defined as "a change of climate which is attributed directly or indirectly to human activity that alters the composition of the global atmosphere and which is in addition to natural climate variability observed over comparable time periods". This definition builds in a bias toward looking for the effects of human contributions to greenhouse gas concentrations and downplaying natural causes. See United Nations (1994).
61 For a general critique of the IPCC's "consensus-building" process, see Curry & Webster (2013).
62 This is despite the fact that the Nobel Peace Prize is political and not scientific in nature.
63 It has been noted that many climate science papers whose findings do not provide obvious support for IPCC-endorsed conclusions and may indeed contradict them still include gratuitous endorsements of those conclusions. Lindzen (2012) gives specific examples of papers which feature "the inclusion of an irrelevant comment supporting global warming accepted wisdom". This phenomenon may be indicative of extra-scientific pressures faced by authors in getting work published that does not endorse the AGW hypothesis.
64 For a comprehensive survey and assessment of peer-reviewed papers which documents a strong AGW consensus, see Cook *et al.* (2013). Note, however, that Cook *et al.*'s

assessment criteria have been contested by some authors of papers assessed – see Popular Technology (2013). For a detailed critique of studies claiming to document consensus, see Guenier (2013). For a critique of "consensus polls", see Singer (2014).

65 See Doran & Zimmerman (2009), Anderegg *et al.* (2010), Cook (2010), and Cook *et al.* (2013). But see also comment #12 in Cook (2010) by Spencer Weart, a respected physicist and historian of climate science, who says of the Anderegg paper: "this paper should not have been published in the present form ... the defects are obvious on a quick reading". For a comprehensive rebuttal of Cook *et al.* (2013), see Montford (2014).

66 In the following paragraph, we paraphrase Koppl directly, only substituting science terminology for his market terminology.

67 See Curry (2013). Her assessment of the IPCC's process is worth quoting: "Diagnosis: paradigm paralysis, caused by motivated reasoning, oversimplification, and consensus seeking; worsened and made permanent by a vicious positive feedback effect at the climate science-policy interface".

68 Here we concentrate exclusively on funding from US government sources. Other governments, particularly in Europe, have also provided significant funding for climate science research.

69 Compared to the Butos & McQuade results, Nova's numbers are uniformly low, but more detailed analyses of government spending had emerged between 2009 and 2015, especially Leggett *et al.* (2013). In addition, Nova does not include climate-science-related funding that does not go through the Global Change Research Program, the climate technology programs, and tax subsidies — i.e., additional monies that Congress authorizes to various agencies.

70 The motto of the USGCRP is "Thirteen Agencies, One Vision: Empower the Nation with Global Change Science". For a full setting out of the 1990 Act, see USGCRP (2014).

71 It is important to note that the USGCRP coordinates *interagency* climate science programs. This carries the implication that USGCRP funding does not capture the entirety of climate science R&D funding of the government. This point is relevant later in estimating the total funding by government of climate science R&D.

72 International climate change assistance is channeled through the Departments of State and Treasury and the US Agency for International Development (USAID) and totals approximately $2.5 billion from 2012 to 2014.

73 These are nominal amounts. By the GAO's (p. 58) calculation, the inflation-adjusted numbers are $3.6 billion in 1993 and $12.9 billion in 2017. The yearly funding numbers reflect actual budget authority except for fiscal years 2011 and 2017, for which they reflect proposed funding, and for 2013 they reflect final operating level funding.

74 Based on a comparison of the OMB numbers for 2010 to 2013 as reported in GAO (2018, p. 60) with those found by Butos & McQuade (2015, p. 180) for the same period, it would appear that the OMB reports only approximately a third of actual climate-related expenditure.

75 For tables of funding by year for each funding category, see GAO (2018, p. 60). For tax expenditures by year, see (p. 87).

76 See USGCRP (2012). While it is no surprise that the plan is a masterpiece of "man of system" prose, its certainty as to the deleterious effects of human-induced climate change is quite notable. It begins (p. 1) with: "The rate of global change today ... far exceeds anything observed and documented in human history". It appears to be completely oblivious to the controversies which surround such a conclusion. The new phrase "global change", if it means anything, is a more accommodating substitute for "global warming" and its postulated effects, and is uniformly used in the sense of "change for the worse".

77 It would be remiss not to mention the increasing opaqueness of climate science funding as the scope and magnitude of government funding and the implementing funding structures and programs increases.

78 For a full discussion, see Butos & McQuade (2012).

79 See, for example, Henderson (2014), Morano (2014), Readfearn (2012), and Douglass & Christy (2009). A useful way of understanding the behavior of individual scientists who depart from scientific norms is contained in Tullock (1966), whose insights are revived and elaborated by Peart & Levy (2012). In particular, bias can arise from either (or both) a quid pro quo (in funding, for example) or from ideological sympathy with a preferred result. The sympathy motive can easily foster the formation of factions within the scientific discipline. We thank a referee for directing us to this material.

80 The hacked batch of emails and data, the so-called "Climategate" materials, are available on Wikileaks (2009).

81 The tight coauthoring relationships between these groups of climate scientists is documented in Wegman *et al.* (2006).

82 Email 1089318616 in the Climategate collection.

83 Kevin Trenberth of the US National Center for Atmospheric Research, a fellow lead IPCC author.

84 See, for example, emails 0969618170, 0990119702, 1062592331, 1141398437, and 1255523796.

85 In fact, there appears to be a lot of concentration on maintaining a public appearance of settled science. See, for example, emails 0843161829, 0933255789, 1105019698, and 1225026120.

86 See, for example, emails 0876437553 and 1058906971. In email 0994083845, the writer expresses the opinion that, even if the science which seems to support alarmism turns out to be wrong, "we should be trying to wean ourselves off of unsustainable energy generation and use anyway".

87 Section 1703 of Title XVII of The Energy Policy Act of 2005 (Public Law 109-58) established a Loan Guarantee Program to provide incentives for innovative energy technologies to "avoid, reduce, or sequester air pollutants or anthropogenic emissions of greenhouse gases" and "employ new or significantly improved technologies". Among the categories of "eligible projects" the Act lists renewable energy, fossil fuels, and nuclear energy (119 STAT. 1120). See US Congress (2005). ARRA's Section 1703 broadened this program to include existing technologies while narrowing the scope of energy sources to renewable and biofuel projects and substantially loosening the eligibility criteria and financing arrangements. See Nava and Morris (2013) for further details.

88 Lakatos (2014) calculates the largest amounts of losses (in millions) thus far to have been: Solyndra ($570.4), Abound Solar ($494.3), A123 Systems ($390.1), Babcock and Brown ($178), Range Fuels ($162.3), ECOtotality ($135), and Energy Conservation Devices ($110.3).

89 According to Nava and Morris (2013), these firms (with loan guarantee amounts) are: Abengoa ($2.8 billion), Kahuku ($117 million), Nevada Geothermal Power ($98.5 million), and LS Power Associates ($343 million).

90 According to *The Economist* (2014), energy policies in Germany were by then costing the average an extra $355 a year to subsidize renewable energy generation while, ironically, having the unintended consequence of increasing greenhouse gas emissions. This trend of increased energy prices accompanied by presumably unintended environmental effects has continued with the closure of nuclear power plants, as McDonnell (2022) describes. See also, for example, Calzada Álvarez *et al.* (2010) for an analysis of job destruction by "green jobs" policies in Spain, Hughes (2011) for a similar assessment of UK policies, and Kelly (2014) for a demonstration of how carbon mitigation policies directly harm the poor. Averaged over the EU, the weight of energy taxes on medium-sized consumers has increased from 31.2% in 2008 to 39.4% in 2021 – see "Electricity price statistics" at ec.europa.eu/eurostat/statistics-explained. Although the rate of increase has moderated, consumer electricity prices in Germany have risen from €297.70 per MWh in 2016 to €319.30 in 2021 – see the comprehensive data on recent EU energy prices at ec.europa.eu/eurostat/databrowser/view/NRG_PC_204__custom_1842108.

Bibliography

AHA (American Heart Association) 2007. *2007 Annual Report*. http://www.americanheart.org/downloadable/heart/1197300581631AHA%202007%20AR-SPREAD.pdf.

Anderegg, W.R.L., J.W. Prall, J. Harold, & S.H. Schneider 2010. Expert credibility in climate change. *PNAS* 107 #27, pp. 12107–12109. http://www.pnas.org/content/107/27/12107.full.pdf+html.

Arrow, K.J. 1962. Economic welfare and the allocation of resources for inventions. In R.R. Nelson (ed.), *The rate and direction of inventive activity: economic and social factors*, pp. 609–625. Princeton University Press.

——— 1971. Political and economic evaluation of social effects and externalities. In M. Intriligator (ed.), *Frontiers of quantitative economics*, pp. 3–23. North-Holland.

Brock, W.A. & S.N. Durlauf 1999. A formal model of theory choice in science, *Economic Theory* 14, pp. 113–130.

Buchanan, J.M. & W.C. Stubblebine 1962. Externality. *Economica* (n.s.) 29 #116, pp. 371–384.

Bush, V. 1945. *Science: the endless frontier – a report to the President*. US Government Printing Office.

Butos, W.N. & R.G. Koppl 2003. Science as a spontaneous order: an essay in the economics of science. In H.S. Jensen, L.M. Richter, & M.T. Vendelø (eds.), *The evolution of scientific knowledge*, pp. 164–188. Edward Elgar.

Butos, W.N. & T.J. McQuade 2006. Government and science: a dangerous liaison? *The Independent Review* 11 #2, pp. 177–208.

——— 2012. Nonneutralities in science funding: direction, destabilization, and distortion. *Journal des Economistes et des Etudes Humaines* 18 #1, article 4. DOI: 10.1515/1145-6396.1262.

——— 2015. Causes and consequences of the climate science boom. *The Independent Review*, 20 #2, pp. 165–196.

Calzada Álvarez, G., R. Merino Jara, J.R. Rallo Julián, & J.I. García Bielsa 2010. Study of the effects on employment of public aid to renewable energy sources. *Procesos de Mercado* 7 #1. http://www.juandemariana.org/pdf/090327-employment-public-aid-renewable.pdf.

Cook, J. 2010. How many climate scientists are climate skeptics? http://www.skepticalscience.com/How-many-climate-scientists-are-climate-skeptics.html#16811.

Cook, J., D. Nuccitelli, S.A. Green, M. Richardson, B. Winkler, R. Painting, R. Way, P. Jacobs, & A. Skuce 2013. Quantifying the consensus on anthropogenic global warming in the scientific literature. *Environmental Research Letters* 8 #2, article 024024.

Curry, J.A. 2013. IPCC diagnosis – permanent paradigm paralysis. http://judithcurry.com/2013/09/28/ipcc-diagnosis-permanent-paradigm-paralysis.

Curry, J.A. & P.J. Webster 2013. Climate change: no consensus on consensus. *CAB Reviews* 8 #1, pp. 1–9. http://judithcurry.com/2012/10/28/climate-change-no-consensus-on-consensus.

Dasgupta, P. & P.A. David 1994. Toward a new economics of science. *Research Policy* 23, pp. 487–521.

David, P.A. 1997. From market magic to calypso science policy. *Research Policy* 26, pp. 229–255.

Demsetz, H. 1969. Information and efficiency: another viewpoint. *Journal of Law and Economics* 12, pp. 1–22.

Diamond, A.M. 1988. Science as a rational enterprise. *Theory and decision* 24, pp. 147–167.

Doran, P.T. & M.K. Zimmerman 2009. Examining the scientific consensus on climate change. *Climate Change* 90 #3, pp. 21–22. http://tigger.uic.edu/~pdoran/012009_Doran_final.pdf.

Douglass, D.H. & J.R. Christy 2009. A climatology conspiracy? http://www.americanthinker.com/2009/12/a_climatology_conspiracy.html.

Dupre, J.S. & S. Lakoff 1962. *Science and the nation: policy and politics*. Prentice-Hall.

Economist, The 2014. Germany's energy transition: sunny, windy, costly, and dirty. January 18. http://www.economist.com/news/europe/21594336-germanys-new-super-minister-energy-and-economy-has-his-work-cut-out-sunny-windy-costly.

Feldman, M.P., A.N. Link, & D. Siegel 2002. *The economics of science and technology*. Kluwer.

FNB (Food and Nutrition Board) 1980. *Toward healthful diets*. National Academy of Sciences. https://web.archive.org/web/20021215084513/http://www.ulib.org/webRoot/Books/National_Academy_Press_Books/healthful_diets/index.html

GAO (US Government Accountability Office) 2018. Climate change: analysis of reported Federal funding. GAO-18-223.

Gilland, T. 2007. Digging up the roots of the IPCC. *Spiked*, June 28. http://www.spiked-online.com/newsite/article/3540#.U8f_Ae9OUuT.

Greenberg, D.S. 1967. *The politics of pure science*. University of Chicago Press, 2/e, 1999.

——— 2001. *Science, money, and politics*. University of Chicago Press.

Griliches, Z. 1960. Hybrid corn and the economics of innovation. *Science* 132, pp. 275–280.

——— 1986. Productivity, R&D, and basic research at the firm level in the 1970s. *American Economic Review* 76, pp. 141–154.

——— 1987. R&D and productivity: measurement issues and econometric results. *Science* 237 #4810, pp. 31–35.

Guenier, R. 2013. Written evidence submitted by Robin Guenier (IPC0024). *House of Commons Select Committee: IPCC 5th Assessment Review*. http://data.parliament.uk/writtenevidence/WrittenEvidence.svc/EvidencePdf/4191.

Hansen, J., D. Johnson, A. Lacis, S. Lebedeff, P. Lee, D. Rind, & G. Russell 1981. Climate impact of increasing atmospheric carbon dioxide. *Science* 213, pp. 957–966. http://pubs.giss.nasa.gov/docs/1981/1981_Hansen_etal_1.pdf.

Hartocollis, A. 2008. Restaurants prepare for the big switch: no trans fats. *New York Times*, June 21, 2008. http://www.nytimes.com/2008/06/21/nyregion/21trans.html.

Hayek, F.A. 1937. Economics and knowledge. *Economica* 4 (n.s.), pp. 33–54.

——— 1945. The use of knowledge in society. *American Economic Review* 35 #4, pp. 519–530.

——— 1973. *Law, legislation, and liberty* 1: *Rules and order*. University of Chicago Press.

Hayek, F.A. (ed.) 1935. *Collectivist economic planning: critical studies on the possibilities of socialism*. Routledge.

Henderson, D. 2014. The Bengtsson Affair and the Global Warming Policy Foundation. http://www.thegwpf.org/the-bengtsson-affair-and-the-global-warming-policy-foundation.

Hicks, D.M. 1995. Published papers, tacit competencies, and corporate management of the public/private character of knowledge. *Industrial and Corporate Change* 4 # 2, pp. 401–421.

Holcombe, R.G. 2006. Should we have acted thirty years ago to prevent global climate change? *The Independent Review* 11 #2, pp. 283–288.

Hourihan, M. 2021. A primer on Federal R&D budget trends: breaking down the basics of Federal investment. https://www.aaas.org/news/primer-federal-rd-budget-trends (full report).

Hughes, G. 2011. The myth of green jobs. *GWPF Reports* 3. http://www.thegwpf.org/images/stories/gwpf-reports/hughes-green_jobs.pdf.

Idso, S.B. 1980. The climatological significance of a doubling of Earth's atmospheric carbon dioxide concentration. *Science* 207 #4438, pp. 1462–1463.

Kealey, T. 1996. *The economic laws of scientific research*. St. Martin's Press.

Kelly, A. 2014. Climate policy and the poor. *GWPF Notes* 9. http://www.thegwpf.org/content/uploads/2014/06/Kelly-climate-and-poor.pdf.

Kleinman, D.L. 1995. *Politics on the endless frontier: postwar research policy in the United States*. Duke University Press.

Koppl, R.G. 2002. *Big Players and the theory of economic expectations*. Macmillan.

Lakatos, C. 2014. Cleantech crash. *The Green Corruption Files*. http://greencorruption.blogspot.com/2014/01/cleantech-crash-cbs-lesley-stahl.html#.U7s0BO9OUuR.

Lavoie, D. 1985. *Rivalry and central planning: the calculation debate revisited*. Cambridge University Press.

Leggett, J.A., R.K. Lattanzio, & E. Bruner 2013. Federal climate change funding from FY2008 to FY2014. http://www.hsdl.org/?view&did=745487.

Lindzen, R.S. 2012. "Climate science: is it currently designed to answer questions?" *Euresis Journal* 2, 161–193. http://arxiv.org/ftp/arxiv/papers/0809/0809.3762.pdf.

MacArthur Foundation 2008. Climate change and conservation. http://www.macfound.org/media/article_pdfs/CLIMATECHANGE_INFO_3.PDF.

Machan, T. 2002. Introduction: some skeptical reflections on research and development. In T. Machan (ed.), *Liberty and research and development: science funding in a free society*, pp. xi–xx. Hoover Institution Press.

MacLaurin, W.R. 1949. *Invention and innovation in the radio industry*. Macmillan.

Mansfield, E. 1980. Basic research and productivity increase in manufacturing. *American Economic Review* 70, pp. 863–873.

Martin, B. & P. Nightingale 2000. Introduction. In B. Martin & P. Nightingale (ed.), *The political economy of science, technology and innovation*, pp. xiii–xlii. Edward Elgar.

Martino, J.P. 1992. *Science funding: politics and porkbarrel*. Transaction.

McDonnell, T. 2022. Germany's exit from nuclear energy will make its power dirtier and moreexpensive.Quartz,https://qz.com/2108729/germany-just-closed-half-of-its-nuclear-power-plants/.

McGucken, W. 1984. *Scientists, society, and State: the social relations of the science movement in Great Britain, 1931–1947*. Ohio State University Press.

McQuade, T.J. 2007. Science and market as adaptive classifying systems. In E. Krecké, C. Krecké, & R. Koppl (eds.). *Advances in Austrian Economics* 9: *Cognition and Economics*, pp. 51–86. Elsevier.

McQuade, T.J. & W.N. Butos 2005. The sensory order and other adaptive classifying systems. *Journal of Bioeconomics* 7 #3, pp. 335–358.

Mirowski, P. & E.-M. Sent (eds.) 2002. *Science bought and sold*. University of Chicago Press.

Montford, A. 2012. *Nullius in Verba*: The Royal Society and climate change. *GWPF Reports* 6. http://thegwpf.org/images/stories/gwpf-reports/montford-royal_society.pdf.

——— 2014. Fraud, bias and public relations: the 97% "consensus" and its critics. *GWPF Notes* 11. http://www.thegwpf.org/content/uploads/2014/09/Warming-consensus-and-it-critics1.pdf.

Morano, M. 2014. Fired for "diverging" on climate: progressive professor's fellowship "terminated" after WSJ OpEd calling global warming "unproved science". http://www.climatedepot.com/2014/06/12/fired-for-diverging-on-climate-progressive-professors-fellowship-terminated-after-wsj-oped-calling-global-warming-unproved-science.

Nava, V. & J. Morris 2013. Stimulating green electric dreams: lobbying, cronyism, and Section 1705 loan guarantees. *Policy Brief* 111 (December). Reason Foundation. http://reason.org/files/green_electric_dreams.pdf.

Nelson, R.R. 1959. The simple economics of basic scientific research. *Journal of Political Economy* 67, pp. 297–306.

Nova, J. 2009. Climate money. *Science and Public Policy Institute*. http://joannenova.com.au/tag/climate-money. http://scienceandpublicpolicy.org/images/stories/papers/originals/climate_money.pdf.

NRB (National Resources Board) 1938. *Research – a national treasure.*

NSB (National Science Board) 2004. *Science and engineering Indicators, 2004* 1. NSF.

NSF (National Science Foundation) 2005. Federal R&D funding by budget function: fiscal years 2003-05.

Odagiri, H & N. Murakimi 1992. Private and quasi-social rates of return on pharmaceutical R&D in Japan. *Research Policy* 21, pp. 335–345.

Oppenheimer, M. & R.H. Boyle 1990. *Dead heat: the race against the greenhouse effect.* I.B. Tauris.

Pavitt, K. 1987. The objectives of technology policy. *Science and Public Policy* 14, pp. 182–188.

Peart, S.J. & D.M. Levy 2012. If germs could sponsor research: reflections on sympathetic connections among subjects and researchers. *Advances in Austrian Economics* 17, pp. 19–25.

Polanyi, M. 1945. The autonomy of science. *The Scientific Monthly* 60 #2, pp. 141–150.

——— 1962. The republic of science: its political and economic theory. *Minerva* 1, pp. 54–73. Reprinted in M. Grene (ed.), *Knowing and being: essays by Michael Polanyi*, pp. 49–72. University of Chicago Press, 1969.

Popular Technology 2013. 97% study falsely classifies scientists' papers, according to the scientists that published them. http://www.populartechnology.net/2013/05/97-study-falsely-classifies-scientists.html.

PSRB (President's Scientific Research Board) 1947. *Science and public policy: a program for the nation* 1–5. US Government Printing Office.

Radnitzky, G. 1986. Towards an "economic" theory of methodology. *Methodology and Science* 19, pp. 124–147.

Rahm, D., J. Kirkland, & B. Bozeman 2000. *University–industry R&D in the United States, the United Kingdom, and Japan.* Kluwer.

Rasool, S.I. & S.H. Schneider 1971. Atmospheric carbon dioxide and aerosols: effects of large increases on global climate. *Science* 173 #3992, pp. 138–141.

Readfearn, G. 2012. Climate sceptic professor sacked from Australian university was banned by National Science Foundation for "deceptive conduct". http://www.desmogblog.com/2013/07/12/murry-salby-sacked-australian-university--banned-national-science-foundation.

Rosenberg, N. 1990. Why do firms do basic research (with their own money)? *Research Policy* 19, pp. 165–174.

Savage, J.D. 1999. *Funding science in America: Congress, universities, and the politics of the academic pork barrel.* Cambridge University Press.

Scheall, S., W.N. Butos, & T.J. McQuade 2018. Social and scientific disorder as epistemic phenomena, or the consequences of government dietary guidelines. *Journal of Institutional Economics* 15 #3, pp. 1–17.

SCNN (US Senate Select Committee on Nutrition and Human Needs) 1977. *Dietary goals for the United States.* US Government Printing Office. https://naldc.nal.usda.gov/download/1759572/PDF.

Singer, S.F. 2014. Climate Consensus Con Game. *American Thinker*. http://www.americanthinker.com/2014/02/climate_consensus_con_game.html.

Steinhauer, J. 2008. California bars restaurant use of trans fats. *New York Times*, July 26, 2008. http://www.nytimes.com/2008/07/26/us/26fats.html.

Taubes, G. 2007. *Good calories, bad calories: challenging the conventional wisdom on diet, weight control, and disease*. Knopf.

Tullock, G. 1966. *The organization of inquiry*. Duke University Press.

UCS (Union of Concerned Scientists) 1997. World scientists' call for action. http://web.archive.org/web/20071012163018/http://ucsusa.org/ucs/about/1997-world-scientists-call-for-action.html.

United Nations 1994. Framework convention on climate change. http://unfccc.int/resource/docs/convkp/conveng.pdf.

US Congress 2005. Public Law 109-58: The Energy Policy Act of 2005. US Government Printing Office. http://www.gpo.gov/fdsys/pkg/PLAW-109publ58/pdf/PLAW-109publ58.pdf.

USGCRP (US Global Change Research Program) 2012. The national global change research plan 2012–2021: a strategic plan for the US Global Change Research Program, chapter III, pp. 17–91. http://library.globalchange.gov/u-s-global-change-research-program-strategic-plan-2012-2021; http://downloads.globalchange.gov/strategic-plan/2012/usgcrp-strategic-plan-2012.pdf.

——— 2014. Global Change Research Act of 1990. http://www.globalchange.gov/about/global-change-research-act.html.

Walstad, A. 2002. Science as a market process. *Independent Review* 7 #1, pp. 5–45.

Weart, S.R. 2008. *The Discovery of Global Warming*. Harvard University Press. Reprinted and updated at http://www.aip.org/history/climate/index.htm.

Wegman, E.J., Y.H. Said, & D.W. Scott 2006. Ad hoc committee report on the "hockey stick" global climate reconstruction. *Congressional Report*. US House Committee on Energy and Commerce. http://web.archive.org/web/20060716210311/http://energycommerce.house.gov/108/home/07142006_Wegman_Report.pdf.

Wible, J.R. 1998. *The economics of science: methodology and epistemology as if economics really mattered*. Routledge.

Wikileaks 2009. Climatic Research Unit emails, data, models, 1996–2009". https://wikileaks.org/wiki/Climatic_Research_Unit_emails,_data,_models,_1996-2009.

Ziman, J. 2002. The microeconomics of academic science. In P. Mirowski & E.-M. Sent (eds.), *Science bought and sold*, pp. 318–340. University of Chicago Press.

11 Hayekian systems[1]

Hayek's overall research program is a coherent, innovative, and path-breaking body of work, underlying which is a basic concern with the problems and difficulties inherent in the generation and use of knowledge. It has provided deep insights into the nature and functioning of market activity, and it has been deployed by Hayek and others with the aim of better understanding nonmarket social processes. It is our contention, however, that this attempted extension of the application of the Hayekian insights to more complex social arrangements has not been an unambiguous success, and that attempts to use them to justify societal arrangements of a classical liberal sort introduce normative presuppositions outside the basic scientific thrust of Hayek's work.

But the inability of Hayek's promising program to give rise to a fully analytical theory of social order cannot be ascribed solely to an inadvisable introduction of normative elements and certainly not to any obvious slips in the analysis itself. What is needed, as Coase so famously remarked (1960, p. 42), is a change of approach. And it is a change of approach that we think is fully consistent with the main thrust of Hayek's work – the furtherance of the understanding of the nature of knowledge and order. Hayek has left us with the basis for a social science research program that focuses on the investigation of the structure and function of a particular class of adaptive, anticipatory, knowledge-generating social systems. The scientific study of these systems, the types of system-dependent knowledge they generate in the process of adaptation, the structural requirements for the generation of this knowledge, and the ways in which the generation of knowledge can be hindered and thwarted, is the outline of the distinctively Hayekian approach to social science we have pursued. This is a fully positive and robust approach to the study of social order which advances the understanding of spontaneous order in general, allows for comparative systems analysis, and is grounded in generalizations from observable structures and characteristics of actual social systems.

We have paid particular attention to science as an anticipatory social system, with the obvious implication that science, as a system, is more than the simple sum of the endeavors of the participating scientists. Scientific knowledge is not just a selection from the best offerings of individual scientists; it is the outcome of an extended, institutionalized, social process of observation, hypothesis-forming, innovation, risk-taking, reputation-seeking, and publication, where individual contributions are subject to criticism, judgment, interpretation, citation,

DOI: 10.4324/9781003336150-11

argumentation, promotion, rejection, reinterpretation, assimilation, and even (from some participants' points of view) misinterpretation. Knowledge generation in science cannot be separated from the procedures through which scientists interact and through which individual efforts are transmuted to become accepted as scientific knowledge, and to attempt to characterize "scientific knowledge" apart from "scientific process and institutions" is a dualism on par with separating mind from matter. Individuals and their scientific interactions together form an adaptive system, and scientific knowledge is an emergent side-effect of the activity within that system. Scientific knowledge is a classification by the system of science of the environment to which that system is sensitive and to which it adapts – indeed, "knowledge" in general should refer to the classification produced as a side-effect of the adaptation to its environment by any adaptive system.

Government funding (and, by implication, at least partial control) of science is widely claimed to be an appropriate function of government. We have presented arguments that dispute this claim. Valid analysis of science funding requires a perspective rooted in the actual characteristics of scientific activity and its institutional arrangements and, most important, in the characteristics of government funding activity and its institutional arrangements and their consequences. Our approach is geared to distinctions that we believe are crucial for understanding the real world. The standard "science as a public good" argument turns out on closer inspection to carry less significance than the early work of Nelson, Arrow, and others suggests. As Martin & Nightingale (2000, p. xxii) point out, work during the 1990s

> has called into question many of the assumptions of the old economics of science, especially that science is a public good … What is now generally accepted is that the conventional 'market failure' justification for the public subsidy is weak.[2]

We find that the "new economics of science", although properly directing attention to the unique institutions of science, still falls back on the public-goods argument and the uncritical acceptance of government funding mechanisms as the only viable means of science funding. The current system of large-scale funding administered by a small number of government bureaucracies makes scientists' wellbeing dependent on the whims of political expediency. It creates winners and losers in the scientific community, where the winning is not necessarily based on scientific achievement, but on the ability to secure and maintain a flow of politically motivated funding. It affects science in a way analogous to the ways price controls, subsidies, credit expansion, and central planning affect markets. The only solution is for the political connections to be bypassed. Such circumvention is unlikely to happen as a result of initiatives from within science because the scientists most favored with government funding (those held up as the pillars of the scientific community) will naturally not want to forgo their political arrangements. A significant hope for such bypassing is that the trend in industrial support of science, in the form of the employment and funding of scientists in laboratories that are integral parts of profit-making firms, will continue to increase. Those in business have realized that scientific freedom and monetary profit are not necessarily incompatible in that scientists, free to pursue their research into whatever interests them and free to publish the results of such research openly in normal academic outlets, can still, through their expertise and specialized knowledge of the current publications in their field, contribute to in-house projects geared to producing revenue-generating products. Moreover, in certain areas, particularly in the biological sciences, access to findings prior to formal publication gives the firm a jump on the competition that can be profitable in itself.[3]

There is a major need for future research in extending the economic way of thinking, with its emphasis on incentives, the subjective pursuit of happiness, the inevitability of scarcity, and the unexpected consequences in reaction to imposed constraints, to social domains other than markets. It has not worked well to simply assume that other loci of human interaction can be regarded as market exchange institutions with various levels of imperfection, and much can be learned from the empirical observations of Nobel Laureate Elinor Ostrom, Vincent Ostrom, and their collaborators – see Ostrom (1990) for a good overview – about the characteristics of what are clearly nonmarket systems which nonetheless serve to further cooperation in areas where common-pool considerations would seem to preclude it. The anticipatory systems theory described above and, more generally, the ongoing multidisciplinary research into complex adaptive systems can provide a solid theoretical base for such an enlarged science of society. And there is real hope in finding common ground with sociologists such as Elder-Vass (2010) who are developing very compatible ideas on social structures and their emergent characteristics. One major lacuna seems to be the lack of a treatment of government and political systems as adaptive systems, and even authors such as Beinhocker (2006), who promote the wide applicability of a complex systems approach, tend to treat government simply as a device for making and applying (hopefully enlightened) rules. What is not taken into account is that the political system is itself complex and adaptive, with its own characteristic internal transaction repertoire and feedback mechanisms. The incentives inherent in the institutions of government have little to do with "the public good" and, despite the undoubted good intentions on the parts of some individual politicians and bureaucrats, the emergent products of the systemic interactions arise from the interplay of many more locally pressing considerations. Much is already known about the characteristic incentives and feedback mechanisms at play in the political environment, and Wagner's (2007) and Martin's (2010) treatments of polities as orders with feedback effects different from markets represents a significant change in perspective from an idealized to a more realistic view of government as a system with emergent characteristics. But fully integrating this into an anticipatory systems framework is a task that would seem to be necessary to finally erase the often-unstated, but nonetheless pervasive, conception of government as a potentially well-intentioned, if flawed, rule-maker.

One of the distinctive characteristics of Austrian economics is the emphasis on the issues of knowledge. Much of this is due to Hayek who, building on Mises' penetrating exposure of the systemic limitations of socialist planning, refocused the argument in terms of the inherent limits of individual knowledge, and the possibilities for certain systemic arrangements to generate knowledge which feeds back to individuals. Hayek's interest in the economic significance of dispersed and tacit knowledge continued to be a central element in the development of his social theory. It is perhaps not surprising, then, that this same Hayek also proposed a theory of mind that describes how an individual's knowledge of its environment can be instantiated in a neuronal network and which gives a firm basis for the concept of limited individual knowledge enhanced by systemic feedback. This confluence of theoretical interest in questions of knowledge and psychology with investigations in social theory has, we claim, profound consequences for future economic and social research.[4] It strongly suggests the need to move beyond models of economic behavior which assume unrealistic individual capability, which underplay the mutual feedback between the individual and the social environment, which focus on end states rather than on the understanding of the processes whose continuous interplay makes the very idea of "end state" suspect, and which have had an extremely disappointing track record for explaining macroeconomic phenomena. But better understanding of the nature and behavior of economic agents is one thing; integrating this into a real science of society is another. And here, the rich tradition of Austrian work on economic institutions and spontaneous order comes into play, and the combination of attention to individual characteristics and to the characteristics of the social environment in which they interact, and which is built and continuously modified by their interactions, offers real hope for scientific progress.

Complementing Hayek's work in social theory is that of the systems biologists, particularly Rosen. Rosen's (1991, pp. 119–120) epigram for encapsulating his approach to understanding biological systems was "throw away the matter and keep the underlying organization". While this is obviously a radical departure from the usual way in which systems are conceptualized, it is not an unscientific move for, as he put it:

> The organization of a natural system … is at least as much a part of its material reality as the specific particles that constitute it at a given time, perhaps indeed more so. As such, it can be modeled or described in full accord with Natural Law [*i.e.*, scientifically]; the resulting formalisms have at least as much right to be called images of material reality as any reductionistic model based on states and dynamical laws.

If understanding process organization is a path to understanding biological systems – in fact, the key to understanding how they work – then there is a reasonable chance that this insight can be useful in the quest to expand the understanding of social systems. We hope that the work here can bring that possibility to notice.

Notes

1 This chapter contains text previously published in Butos & McQuade (2002) with permission from Informa, in Butos & McQuade (2006) with permission from The Independent Institute, in McQuade (2010) with permission from Emerald, in Butos & McQuade (2015) with permission from Oxford University Press, and in McQuade (2019).

2 Martin & Nightingale (2000) is the editors' introductory essay to *The political economy of science, technology, and innovation* in the Elgar series *International library of critical writings in economics*.

3 The history of the Human Genome Project, described in Shreeve (2004), is particularly instructive in this respect.

4 See Camplin (2011) for a wide-ranging discussion of ongoing work linking evolutionary and cognitive psychology with spontaneous orders and self-organization and network theory.

Bibliography

Beinhocker, E.D. 2006. *The origins of wealth: evolution, complexity, and the radical remaking of economics*. Harvard Business School Press.

Butos, W.N. & T.J. McQuade 2002. Mind, market, and institutions: the knowledge problem in Hayek's thought. In J. Birner, P. Garrouste, & T. Aimar (eds.), *F.A. Hayek as a political economist*, pp. 113–133. Routledge.

——— 2006. Government and science: a dangerous liaison? *The Independent Review* 11 #2, pp. 177–208.

——— 2015. *The Sensory Order*, neuroeconomics, and Austrian economics. In P.J. Boettke & C.J. Coyne (eds.), *The Oxford handbook of Austrian economics*, pp. 612–639. Oxford University Press.

Camplin, T.E. 2011. Getting to the Hayekian network. In L. Marsh (ed.), *Advances in Austrian Economics*, vol. 15, *Hayek in mind: Hayek's philosophical psychology*, pp. 259–283. Elsevier,

Coase, R.H. 1960. The problem of social cost. *Journal of Law and Economics* 3, pp. 1–44.

Elder-Vass, D. 2010. *The causal power of social structures*. Cambridge University Press.

Martin, A. 2010. Emergent politics and the power of ideas. *Studies in Emergent Order* 3, pp. 212–245.

Martin, B. & P. Nightingale 2000. Introduction. In B. Martin & P. Nightingale (ed.), *The political economy of science, technology and innovation*, pp. xiii-xlii. Edward Elgar.

McQuade, T.J. 2010. Science and *The Sensory Order*. In W.N. Butos (ed.), *Advances in Austrian Economics* 13: *The social science of Hayek's "The Sensory Order"*, pp. 23–56. Emerald.

——— 2019. Organization, anticipation, and closure in markets and science. *Cosmos + Taxis* 6 #6&7, pp. 1–18.

Ostrom, E. 1990. *Governing the commons: the evolution of institutions for collective action*. Cambridge University Press.

Rosen, R. 1991. *Life itself: a comprehensive inquiry into the nature, origin, and fabrication of life*. Columbia University Press.

Shreeve, J. 2004. *The genome war: how Craig Venter tried to capture the code of life and save the world*. Random House.

Wagner, R.E. 2007. *Fiscal sociology and the theory of public finance*. Edward Elgar.

Index

Note: Pages in *italics* refer figures; Pages followed by n refer notes.